Question&Answer

# ENGLISH
# LEGAL SYSTEM

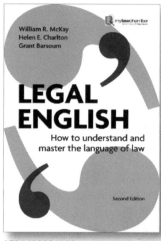

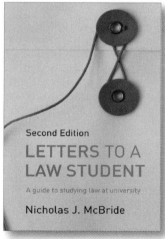

**Question&Answer**

# ENGLISH
# LEGAL SYSTEM

2nd edition

**Gary Wilson**
Liverpool John Moores University

Harlow, England • London • New York • Boston • San Francisco • Toronto • Sydney • Auckland • Singapore • Hong Kong
Tokyo • Seoul • Taipei • New Delhi • Cape Town • São Paulo • Mexico City • Madrid • Amsterdam • Munich • Paris • Milan

**Pearson Education Limited**
Edinburgh Gate
Harlow CM20 2JE
United Kingdom
Tel: +44 (0)1279 623623
Web: www.pearson.com/uk

First published 2012 (print)
**Second edition published 2014** (print and electronic)

ISBN: 978-0-273-78343-5 (print)
978-0-273-78346-6 (PDF)
978-0-273-78344-2 (eText)

**British Library Cataloguing-in-Publication Data**
A catalogue record for the print edition is available from the British Library

10 9 8 7 6 5 4 3 2 1
17 16 15 14 13

Print edition typeset in 10/13pt Helvetica Neue LT Pro by 35
Print edition printed and bound in Malaysia (CTP-PPSB)

NOTE THAT ANY PAGE CROSS REFERENCES REFER TO THE PRINT EDITION

# Contents

# Supporting resources

Visit the **Law Express Question&Answer** series companion website at
**www.pearsoned.co.uk/lawexpressqa** to find valuable learning material
including:

- **Additional essay and problem questions** arranged by topic for each chapter
  give you more opportunity to practise and hone your exam skills.
- **Diagram plans** for all additional questions assist you in structuring and writing
  your answers.
- **You be the marker** questions allow you to see through the eyes of the
  examiner by marking essay and problem questions on every topic covered in
  the book.
- Download and print all **Attack the question** diagrams and **Diagram plans**
  from the book.

**Also:** The companion website provides the following features:

- Search tool to help locate specific items of content.
- Online help and support to assist with website usage and troubleshooting.

For more information please contact your local Pearson sales representative or
visit **www.pearsoned.co.uk/lawexpressqa**

# Acknowledgements

I would like to thank Pearson for commissioning a second edition of this book. As always, I am particularly grateful to Jenny, Becky and Katie for their love and support. This book is dedicated to them.

Gary Wilson

## Publisher's acknowledgements

Our thanks go to all reviewers who contributed to the development of this text, including students who participated in research and focus groups which helped to shape the series format.

# English Legal System

## HOW TO USE THIS BOOK

Books in the *Question and Answer* series focus on the *why* of a good answer alongside the *what*, thereby helping you to build your question answering skills and technique.

This guide should not be used as a substitute for learning the material thoroughly, your lecture notes or your textbook. It *will* help you to make the most out of what you have already learned when answering an exam or coursework question. Remember that the answers given here are not the *only* correct way of answering the question but serve to show you some good examples of how you *could* approach the question set.

Make sure that you regularly refer to your course syllabus, check which issues are covered (as well as to what extent they are covered) and whether they are usually examined with other topics. Remember that what is required in a good answer could change significantly with only a slight change in the wording of a question. Therefore, do not try to memorise the answers given here, instead use the answers and the other features to understand what goes into a good answer and why.

English legal system (ELS) is a broad subject area which gives rise to possible questions are able to demonstrate a clear awareness of the functioning of the legal system in its wider setting.

While ELS is taught under a number of topic headings, it is important that you do not 'pigeon-hole' topics. Sometimes you will be able to draw upon a point or example learnt as part of one topic when answering a question on another. Occasionally, examination questions will span more than one topic. For example, a question on judicial law-making will benefit from the understanding you have from having studied judicial precedent, statutory interpretation and the composition of the judiciary. Weaker students often fail to make these wider connections and, consequently, produce narrow answers to questions which do not gain the highest marks.

ELS is invariably assessed through the use of essay-type questions and problem questions are relatively rare. Therefore, when preparing for examinations you need to ensure that you are not simply able to apply legal principles to given scenarios, but are actually able to subject key principles, features and processes of the legal system to scrutiny. More so than many other subjects, where problem questions are often at least as common as essay questions, your ability to critically analyse and discuss legal issues will be crucial if you are to score well in assessment.

When answering essay questions it is important that you understand what the question is asking you to do, and that you direct your answer towards doing exactly this. It is surprising how many students spot that a particular question relates to a specific topic and then proceed to simply write down everything they know about that topic, usually resulting in them failing to answer the question set. Good essays are always well structured, so take the time to think about what you need to cover in your answer and sketch out a brief plan before writing. This will ensure that your answer is logically structured and does not omit key information. Generalisation does not score well with examiners; make your arguments as clearly as possible and always provide supporting evidence from case law, statute, academic commentary or statistical evidence as and when appropriate.

By their nature, problem questions require a different approach to essay questions. Unless specifically directed otherwise, problem questions will usually only require you to identify the legal issues raised by a scenario and advise on the application of the relevant law to the facts. It will seldom be necessary to comment on the merits of substantive legal provisions. You should always identify the issues raised before beginning your answer. By making a quick plan of issues to consider, you minimize the danger of omitting consideration of key issues. For each issue raised you should identify the relevant law and its application to the scenario. Do not assume that there will always be a definitive answer. Sometimes you may need more information in order to be able to advise fully, or there may be a degree of ambiguity in the scenario's facts or the applicable law. Always indicate where this is the case, and if there are several possible outcomes indicate this with reference to the factors which may determine the exact outcome.

# Guided tour

**What to do for every question** – Identify the key things you should look for and do in any question and answer on the subject, ensuring you give every one of your answers a great chance from the start.

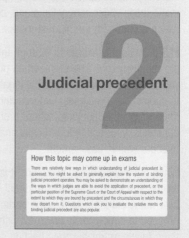

## Judicial precedent

### How this topic may come up in exams

There are relatively few ways in which understanding of judicial precedent is assessed. You might be asked to generally explain how the system of binding judicial precedent operates. You may be asked to demonstrate an understanding of the ways in which judges are able to avoid the application of precedent, or the particular position of the Supreme Court or the Court of Appeal with respect to the extent to which they are bound by precedent and the circumstances in which they may depart from it. Questions which ask you to evaluate the relative merits of binding judicial precedent are also popular.

**How this topic may come up in exams** – Understand how to tackle any question on this topic by using the handy tips and advice relevant to both essay and problem questions. In-text symbols clearly identify each question type as they occur.

 Essay question

 Problem question

**Attack the question** – Use these diagrams as a step-by-step guide to help you confidently identify the main points covered in any question asked. Download these from the companion website to use as a useful revision aid.

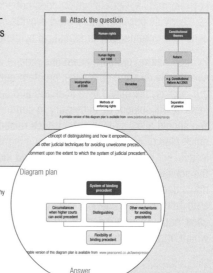

### Attack the question

| Human rights | | | Constitutional themes |
|---|---|---|---|

| Human Rights Act 1998 | | | Reform |

| Incorporation of ECHR | | Remedies | e.g. Constitutional Reform Act 2005 |

| | Methods of enforcing rights | | Separation of powers |

A printable version of this diagram plan is available from www.pearsoned.co.uk/lawexpressqa

**Answer plans and Diagram plans** – A clear and concise plan is the key to a good answer and these answer and diagram plans support the structuring of your answers, whatever your preferred learning style.

## Answer plan

→ Briefly explain the doctrine of judicial precedent and the importance of the court hierarchy to its operation.

→ Explain when the Supreme Court and the Court of Appeal may depart from their own previous decisions.

→ Explain the concept of distinguishing and how it empowers judges to avoid precedents.

→ Explain other judicial techniques for avoiding unwelcome precedents.

→ Comment upon the extent to which the system of judicial precedent operates flexibly.

### Diagram plan

| System of binding precedent | | |
|---|---|---|
| Circumstances when higher courts can avoid precedent | Distinguishing | Other mechanisms for avoiding precedents |

| | Flexibility of binding precedent | |

...table version of this diagram plan is available from www.pearsoned.co.uk/lawexpress...

Answer

**Answer with accompanying guidance –**
Make the most out of every question by using the guidance to recognize what makes a good answer and why. Answers are the length you could realistically hope to produce in an exam to show you how to gain marks quickly when under pressure.

[1] You should begin your answer by stating which government members have particular responsibility for the administration of justice.

**Answer**

The Attorney-General and Solicitor-General are generally referred to as the government's law officers.[1] They are government members drawn from either House of Parliament and appointed by the Prime Minister. In addition to these, although many government ministers have legal functions of some form, two have responsibilities that are particularly central to the administration of justice. These are the Lord Chancellor and the Home Secretary.

Historically, the Lord Chancellor's position compromised the principle of the separation of powers, him simultaneously sitting within the executive as a cabinet member, the legislature as speaker of the House of Lords, and the judiciary as its head capable of sitting on cases brought before the Judicial Committee of the House of Lords. However, the Constitutional Reform Act 2005 removed the latter two of these functions.[2] The Lord Chancellor may now be drawn from either House of Parliament, and in 2007 Jack Straw became the first MP appointed to the post. Today, the Lord Chancellor heads the

... in explaining the funct...

**Case names clearly highlighted –** Easy-to-spot bold text makes those all important case names stand out from the rest of the answer, ensuring they are much easier to remember in revision and an exam.

[3] This is a useful point to make as it illustrates the wide range of situations in which an action constituting a human rights violation will also give rise to liability, and thus a remedy, under the civil law.

[4] To illustrate the relevance of damages it is important that you are able to explain that they are not simply available as a matter of course, but

the form of the tort of trespass to the person. Section 8 of the Human Rights Act does provide that damages are only to be awarded where this is necessary to afford just satisfaction to the victim of the human rights violation,[4] and the courts have emphasised in a number of cases that damages should not be simply available as a matter of course. For example, damages were not considered just or appropriate in **R (IH) v Secretary of State for the Home Department** [2003] *The Times*, 14 November, where the violation in question had already been publicly acknowledged and put an end to. By contrast, in **R (Bernard) v Enfield LBC** [2003] HRLR 4, damages were awarded for a violation of Article 8 of the Convention when the claimants had been left in unsuitable accommodation for 20 years.

**Make your answer stand out –** Really impress your examiners by going the extra mile and including these additional points and further reading to illustrate your deeper knowledge of the subject, fully maximizing your marks.

✓ Make your answer stand out

- Explain clearly the different nature of *Hansard* and the Human Rights Act 1998 in terms of their influence upon the process of statutory interpretation.
- Illustrate the courts' approach to section 3 of the Human Rights Act through reference to case law examples.
- Illustrate the use of *Hansard* through reference to case law examples.
- Refer to academic commentary on the use of Hansard as an aid to interpretation, for example, Steyn (2001) 'Pepper v Hart: A Re-examination', *Oxford Journal of Legal Studies*, v.21, n.1, 59.

**Don't be tempted to –** Points out common mistakes ensuring you avoid losing easy marks by understanding where students most often trip up in exams.

! Don't be tempted to . . .

- Focus simply on *Pepper v Hart* without considering how later cases have contributed to the development of the debate over *Hansard's* utility.
- Discuss only the relative merits of *Hansard* as an aid to statutory interpretation in abstract form, without making reference to the relevant case law on the issue.

**Bibliography –** Use this list of further reading to really delve in and explore areas in more depth, enabling you to excel in exams.

# Bibliography

Abel, R.L. (1987) 'The Decline of Professionalism', *Arbitration*, v. 53, n. 3, 187
Abrahams, A. (2004) Council on Tribunals Conference Speech, www.ombudsman.org.uk/about-us/media-centre/ombudsmans-speeches/archive/sp2004-02
Allan, T.R.S. (1985) 'The Limits of Parliamentary Sovereignty', *Public Law*, 614
Auld, R. (2001) *Review of the Criminal Courts in England and Wales*, webarchive.

# Guided tour of the companion website

 Book resources are available to download. Print your own **Attack the question** and **Diagram plans** to pin to your wall or add to your own revision notes.

 **Additional Essay and Problem questions** with **Diagram plans** arranged by topic for each chapter give you more opportunity to practise and hone your exam skills. Print and email your answers.

 **You be the marker** gives you a chance to evaluate sample exam answers for different question types for each topic and understand how and why an examiner awards marks. Use the accompanying guidance to get the most out of every question and recognise what makes a good answer.

All of this and more can be found when you visit **www.pearsoned.co.uk/lawexpressqa**

# Table of cases and statutes

## ■ Cases

## ▨ Statutes

# European Treaties

# International cases

# 1

# Sources of law

## How this topic may come up in exams

Examination questions on this topic may test understanding of any one or more of the various primary and secondary sources of law. You will need to be familiar with the operation specifically of common law, equity, statute, EU law, delegated legislation and custom. While examination questions may focus upon any one of these sources, requiring you to be able to demonstrate a critical understanding of that source, you may also be asked to contrast more than one source of law and/or explore the relationship between these sources. Thus, you should not 'pigeon-hole' the various sources of law as free-standing topics.

# ■ Attack the question

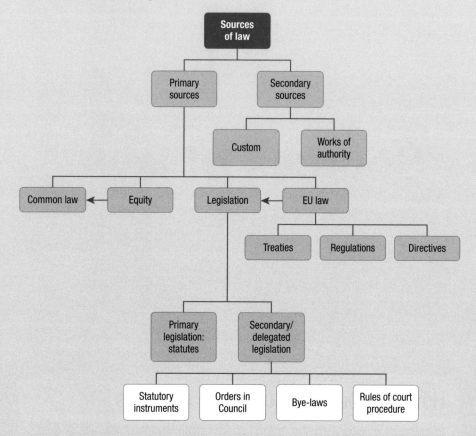

A printable version of this diagram plan is available from www.pearsoned.co.uk/lawexpressqa

#  Question 1

Explain the origins of the common law and how equity developed in response to its perceived shortcomings.

## Answer plan

→ Explain how common law originated within England.

→ Explain the problems which came to be associated with the common law by the thirteenth century.

→ Explain how equity originated in response to problems with the common law.

→ Explain how the same courts came to administer both common law and equitable remedies.

→ Comment upon the role of equity today.

## Diagram plan

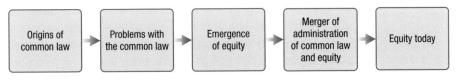

A printable version of this diagram plan is available from www.pearsoned.co.uk/lawexpressqa

## Answer

[1] It is important that you begin your answer by explaining what preceded the common law. You need to explain clearly that there was no system of law uniform to the country as a whole.

[2] Credit will be given for making a point like this. It shows a more detailed understanding of the system of law in force at the time and is likely to help make your answer stand out.

Prior to the Norman Conquest of 1066, there was no unified system of law[1] common to England as a whole. Instead, customary laws applied which varied from one area of the country to another in accordance with local customs. Often these would bear the influence of the invading forces prominent in those regions,[2] so, for example, Dane law was particularly influential in the north of England, whereas in the south and west of the country Wessex law was a more dominant force. Thus, there was no effective central government and the King had little legal control over the country as a whole. The Norman Conquest represented a landmark in the eventual emergence of English common law. William I initiated the process of standardising the laws applicable throughout the country. Representatives of the King, known as 'itinerant justices', were despatched throughout the

[3] By asking you to explain the origins of the common law, the question is asking for a historical narrative of the factors which resulted in its emergence. It is particularly important that you be clear about the role of the itinerant justices in this process.

[4] It is imperative that you connect the origins of the common law and the emergence of equity by explaining the problems which the common law came to give rise to. The key point to emphasise is the rigidity of the writ system and the range of remedies available at common law.

country to scrutinise local administration and adjudicate upon disputes in accordance with the customary law applicable in each region. As these itinerant justices returned to London and discussed their experiences from their visits to the regions, the principles of the common law began to emerge.[3] Over a period of time the justices would select the best local customs from which to develop uniform rules to be applied across the whole country. This process continued for about two centuries, and by the mid-thirteenth century there was an English common law. The principle of *stare decisis*, on which judicial precedent is founded, had been established, and common law courts of exchequer, common pleas and King's bench had been established.

Litigants soon came to experience difficulties in using the common law due to both rigidity in the system by which actions could be lodged, and the limited range of remedies available from the common law courts.[4] Civil actions had to be commenced by a writ which set out the cause of action. Initially, when an action could not be fit within existing writs, new writs could be used. However, by the thirteenth century the grounds on which writs could be based had become fixed. New writs were no longer possible and any actions had to be fit within existing writs. In short, the writ system had become rigid and deprived some litigants of the ability to commence an action within the common law courts. Furthermore, the only remedy granted by the common law was that of damages. In some disputes, for example those concerning the sale of land, this was hardly appropriate as monetary damages were often regarded as providing no substitute for a specific parcel of land.

As a result of these shortcomings in the common law, aggrieved individuals began to petition the King for a fair outcome to their case in those situations where the common law had proven inadequate to give them just satisfaction. In practice, the King would pass these petitions over to his Chancellor for adjudication. The Chancellor was known as the 'keeper of the King's conscience' and he would attempt to resolve such cases in accordance with what he perceived to be principles of fairness, or equity. Eventually, individuals would begin to petition the Chancellor himself and by 1474 he had begun to hear petitions and make decisions in respect of them under his own authority. This marked the origins of the Court of Chancery. The Chancellor was not restricted by the more rigid rules of the common law. He enjoyed the power to question the parties to a case themselves, a power not enjoyed by the common law courts. Nor were damages the only possible remedy which could be granted. Instead, the Chancellor could grant whatever remedy best suited the case at hand. For example, in cases concerning land transactions, the remedy of specific performance could usefully be granted so as to compel that a particular piece of land be sold in accordance with a prior agreement reached by the parties, as opposed to the mere grant of damages which is all that could have been awarded by the common law courts. The principles developed by the Chancellor and Court of Chancery became known as equity, reflecting their prime concern with achieving fairness in individual cases.[5]

For a considerable period of time equity and common law operated as two separate systems, administered by different courts, and there was tension between the two bodies of rules. This tension was resolved by the landmark ruling of James I in the *Earl of Oxford's Case* [1615] 1 Rep Ch 1,[6] that whenever there was a conflict between common law and equity, equity was to prevail. This case thus established the supremacy of equity over common law. The administration of the two systems was finally brought together by the Judicature Acts 1873–5,[7] which merged the common law and equity courts and finally gave all courts the power to administer both common law and equitable remedies.

Equity continues to be a very important and influential source of law within this country.[8] It is especially important in the context of trusts law, but also impacts upon other areas such as land and contract. Unlike common law, equitable remedies are discretionary. There is a series of equitable maxims which are of great importance in cases where equitable remedies are sought. An important one of these is the principle that 'he who comes to equity must come with clean hands', essentially preventing those who have acted inequitably from reaping the benefits which equity might otherwise afford them. In *D & C Builders* v *Rees* [1966] 2 QB 617, no equitable remedy was available to a party who had taken unfair advantage of another's financial difficulties. Another important maxim is 'he who seeks equity must do equity', meaning that strikers seeking an injunction to prevent their dismissal could not equitably continue to strike if the injunction were to be granted (*Chappell* v *Times Newspapers* [1975] 1 WLR 482). Another maxim is that equity cannot be invoked by those who delay their action. Thus, five years to eventually bring

[5] You need to explain the process by which equity came to emerge and the way in which it differed from the common law.

[6] It is essential for this case to be mentioned. It is a landmark case, asserting the superiority of equity over common law.

[7] This is another essential point. You must make clear that although equity and common law operated as rival systems, their administration was eventually brought together. However, ensure that you are clear that although their administration was merged, they continue to enjoy their own rules and principles.

[8] It is useful in your final paragraph to say something about the continuing important role of equity today. Relevant issues include its important role in particular areas of law, the discretionary nature of equitable remedies, important maxims equity lays down and the fact that most remedies are actually equitable in nature.

a case was held to be too long in *Leaf* v *International Galleries* [1950] 2 KB 86. Furthermore, it should also be noted that the most important remedies available from the courts today, apart from damages, are the product of equity. The remedies of injunction, specific performance, recission and rectification are all equitable in nature.

✓ Make your answer stand out

- Demonstrate that you have a clear understanding of the system of laws which preceded the emergence of the common law.
- Demonstrate that you are familiar with some of the key rules and remedies provided by equity, beyond simply being able to explain why it emerged.
- Make some comment upon the modern significance of equity.
- Read Burrows (2002) 'We Do This at Common Law but That in Equity', *Oxford Journal of Legal Studies*, v. 22, n. 1, 1–16, and cite his arguments to illustrate continuing inconsistencies between common law and equity today.

! Don't be tempted to . . .

- Simply explain what common law and equity are and the difference between them without any historical narrative of their origins.
- Explain the emergence of equity without first illustrating the problems in the common law which resulted in this.

# 📝 Question 2

Critically assess the relative importance of case law and statute as sources of law, and their relationship with one another.

## Answer plan

➡ Explain the difference between case law and statute.

➡ Illustrate the significance of statute as the supreme source of domestic law (subject to conflicting European law) with reference to the doctrine of parliamentary sovereignty.

→ Illustrate the continuing significance of case law with reference to the importance of judicial precedent and areas of law still covered predominantly by case law.

→ Explain the interaction that exists between case law and statute.

→ Conclude by commenting upon the relative significance of case law and statute as sources of law.

## Diagram plan

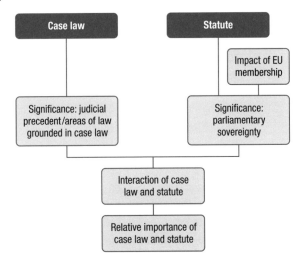

A printable version of this diagram plan is available from www.pearsoned.co.uk/lawexpressqa

## Answer

[1] The question asks you to consider the relative importance of these two sources of law. It will be helpful at the outset to explain that they are the two major domestic sources of law. You should also briefly explain what they are and how they differ from one another.

[2] In explaining the importance of statute, it is essential that you make reference to the doctrine of parliamentary sovereignty and explain its implications.

Case law and statute are the two major domestic sources of English law.[1] Case law (or common law) constitutes the body of law contained in judicial decisions. It is an uncodified source of law and operates through the system of judicial precedent, whereby in reaching decisions judges have regard to decisions from earlier cases sharing similar material facts. Statute law refers to legislation made by Parliament in the form of Acts of Parliament. It is a formalised source of law, a bill passing through several potentially time consuming stages before finally adopted as a statute.

Historically, statute has been regarded as the supreme source of law due to the doctrine of parliamentary sovereignty.[2] In the words of

# 1 SOURCES OF LAW

[3] You will receive credit for being able to cite relevant quotations to illustrate the doctrine of parliamentary sovereignty. Dicey is especially worthy of mention because of his considerable writings in this area.

[4] Relevant reference to case law to illustrate the doctrine shows an awareness of the doctrine in practice, for which you will also receive credit.

Dicey,[3] this holds that Parliament has 'the right to make or unmake any law whatsoever', there being 'no person or body having the right to override or set aside the legislation of Parliament'. Outrageous or immoral legislation is not precluded, as Lord Reid emphasised in **Madzimbamuto v Lardner-Burke & George** [1969] AC 645,[4] when he noted that although the moral reasons against a particular piece of legislation may be very strong, this would not prevent Parliament from enacting it or affect its legal validity before the courts. The doctrine of parliamentary sovereignty includes the rule that no parliament may bind its successors. This was forcefully set out by Herbert CJ in **Godden v Hales** (1686) 11 St Tr 1165 when he remarked that, 'if an Act of Parliament had a clause in it that it should never be repealed, yet without question, the same power that made it may repeal it'. It also embraces the doctrine of implied repeal, meaning that should a later statutory provision conflict with an earlier one, the later one will receive precedence and be said to implicitly repeal the earlier one.

[5] You cannot discuss the importance of statute without mentioning the restrictions placed upon parliamentary sovereignty by EU membership, as this goes directly to the heart of the question, reducing the relative significance of statute law when this clashes with European provisions.

[6] *Factortame* must be mentioned at this stage as it is the most significant case in terms of the impact of EU membership on parliamentary sovereignty.

[7] This is a relevant point, showing how statute has become more commonly used in law-making.

Parliament's sovereignty has been called into question by the impact of EU membership.[5] Section 2 of the European Communities Act 1972 implicitly provided that statute law would be overridden by contrary provisions of European law. The supremacy of EU law was finally firmly established in the case of **R v Secretary of State for Transport, ex parte Factortame** (No. 1) [1990] 2 AC 85,[6] where the European Court of Justice ruled that in any conflict between a provision of domestic law and a provision of European law, the latter would prevail. Parliamentary sovereignty is in practice therefore limited, European law being effectively the supreme source of law for the English legal system.

Nonetheless, statute remains the most important of the domestic sources of law. Statute overrides all conflicting common law provisions. The validity of statutes may not be questioned by judges, unless a question of compatibility with European law is raised. The twentieth century witnessed a surge in the significance of statute law,[7] as the growth of the welfare state and government activity was accompanied by a wave of unprecedented legislative action on the part of Parliament. The increased need for legislation is evident in the huge amount of law-making left to be done through delegated legislation. Statute law enjoys the advantage of being democratic in nature. It is made by elected representatives of the people, who are theoretically held accountable at election time. A major problem with statute law, however, is the time-consuming process through which it is made.[8] Any parliamentary bill is likely to take several months, if not years, before it has exhausted all of the procedures to enter the statute book, sometimes meaning law reform can be long overdue.

The supremacy of statute law should not detract from the continued significance of case law. Judicial precedent, through which it operates, is an important pillar of the English legal system and case law continues to fill many gaps and indeed still provides the main legal rules applicable in many important areas.[9] For example, the criminal law governing murder is still heavily based upon case law, as are many of the principles of tort law, perhaps most notably negligence, and the fundamental rules governing the making of contracts. Critics sometimes attack case law on the ground that it involves unaccountable judges effectively legislating on matters that are the proper province of Parliament, yet, at the same time an often extolled virtue of case law is its ability to be made instantaneously, responding to changing needs long before Parliament is able to do so.[10]

The relative importance of statute and case law cannot, however, be assessed simply by considering each as a separate source of law existing in isolation to the other.[11] The doctrine of the separation of powers emphasises the importance of the legislature and judiciary being separate and independent of one another, but they do not exist and work in isolation from one another. Parliament makes statutes and it is then the task of the judges to give effect to these. Through the tool of statutory interpretation[12] judges are given the means to shape the impact of legislation adopted by Parliament where its provisions are ambiguous, vague or not drafted with a particular scenario in mind. It is, thus, through case law that statute is given its practical meaning and effect. It has already been noted that statute law will be overridden by contrary provisions of European law. As a result of the **Factortame** decision, the courts are now empowered to set aside statutory provisions where there is such a conflict. Furthermore, in the human rights context the higher courts are able to declare statutory provisions to be incompatible with the Human Rights Act 1998,[13] although such declarations have no bearing on the legal validity or application of the relevant provisions. Clearly, there is a considerable degree of interaction between statute and case law. Regardless of the supremacy of the former, its application

[8] It is relevant to refer to some of the drawbacks of statute, as this will lead nicely into the discussion of the importance of case law.

[9] In showing the importance of common law, it is very useful to explain the extent to which some branches of law remain largely grounded in common law rules.

[10] Notwithstanding parliamentary sovereignty, you are showing here one of the key advantages of common law.

[11] This goes to the heart of the question. You must not just consider the relative importance of these two sources of law, but also their relationship with one another. There are several relevant points that you can make here.

[12] This is one obvious example where case law and statute law feed into one another.

[13] Credit should be given for pointing out this relatively recent development.

[14] Again, one of the virtues of case law vis-à-vis statute is illustrated with an example. Wherever appropriate, try to cite examples in support of your arguments.

[15] The conclusion drawn is reasoned, rational and flows naturally from the discussion that has taken place of these two sources of law and their relationship with one another.

is significantly affected by case law through judicial decisions in a variety of circumstances. Case law also contributes to the creation of statute law. The slow pace of statutory reform sometimes leads case law to step in to respond to social change, as occurred for example in *R v R* [1991] 3 WLR 767[14] where for the first time it was held that a man could be guilty of raping his wife. Sometimes developments in case law lead to statutory reform or case law is codified in statutory form, as occurred for example with the Sale of Goods Act 1979.

It is naïve to treat statute and case law as mutually exclusive sources of law.[15] While statute remains theoretically the more important due to the doctrine of parliamentary sovereignty, this should not detract from the obvious importance of case law, especially in light of its close relationship with statute law in practice.

 **Make your answer stand out**

- Pay particular attention to the relationship that exists between case law and statute.
- Use practical examples to illustrate the importance of case law and statute, and their interaction with one another.
- Provide a clear explanation of the doctrine of parliamentary sovereignty and the manner in which this has been limited by EU membership.
- In explaining the importance of parliamentary sovereignty, you might draw a distinction between legal and political concepts of parliamentary sovereignty, as exemplified by, for example, Allan (1985) 'The Limits of Parliamentary Sovereignty', *Public Law*, 614.

**! Don't be tempted to . . .**

- Discuss case law and statute as two separate sources of law without considering their relationship with one another.
- List the advantages and disadvantages of case law and statute and weigh up their relative importance in light of these, as this is not what the question asks for.
- Omit any reference to parliamentary sovereignty or the impact of EU membership upon this.

#  Question 3

Explain the process by which an Act of Parliament is made, and discuss the relative importance of the House of Commons, the House of Lords and the Sovereign within this process.

## Answer plan

➡ Explain how parliamentary bills originate and the different kinds of bills that can be introduced.

➡ Explain the different stages which a bill must go through in both Houses of Parliament.

➡ Explain the impact of the Parliament Acts 1911 and 1949 upon the relative importance of the House of Lords within the legislative process.

➡ Comment upon the extent to which royal assent is a mere formality within the legislative process.

## Diagram plan

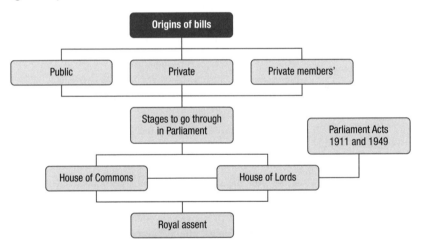

A printable version of this diagram plan is available from www.pearsoned.co.uk/lawexpressqa

## Answer

All Acts of Parliament begin life as bills.[1] The vast majority of bills are introduced by the government as part of its policy agenda. Government bills are usually preceded by white papers which set out the government's general proposals for new legislation. Sometimes green papers precede these, which set out more tentative policy

# 1 SOURCES OF LAW

[1] You should begin your answer by providing some explanation of the origins of bills before they begin the process of going through Parliament. It is useful to explain the different kinds of bills which exist, and also that the vast majority of Parliamentary legislation stems from government policy.

[2] It is worth mentioning private members' bills, although you should also point out that they are of very limited significance although some notable exceptions have been known.

[3] At this point your answer needs to focus upon explaining the various stages which a bill must go through in Parliament. This is explicitly asked of you by the question.

[4] This is an important point which can easily be overlooked. However, this provision clearly impacts upon the process by which a bill passes through parliament as it imposes a mandatory requirement upon the minister introducing a bill and so therefore, should, be mentioned.

options. Public bills apply to the country as a whole and affect everyone, for example by changing the criminal law. Private bills have limited application, for example to a specific corporation or local authority. Government bills are drafted by parliamentary counsel, skilled in the art of translating desired policy objectives into tight provisions that are understandable and enforceable.

Some bills, known as private members' bills,[2] are introduced by individual MPs. However, the lack of time set aside for these to be debated means that they rarely pass into law. There are some notable exceptions though, such as the Abortion Act 1967 sponsored by David Steel MP.

Bills must pass through several stages in both Houses of Parliament.[3] Ordinarily a bill will begin life in the House of Commons before moving to the House of Lords, but it may proceed the other way around. Indeed, private bills will usually proceed in the House of Lords first of all. At its first reading the title of the bill is simply read out. It is then printed and published. Before the bill receives its second reading, section 19 of the Human Rights Act 1998 requires that the responsible minister must make a statement to the effect that in his view the bill's provisions are compatible with the Convention rights incorporated into domestic law by the Human Rights Act.[4] If he is unable to make such a statement, he must state this but that the government wishes to proceed with the bill nonetheless. At its second reading there will be a main debate upon the bill where MPs or peers will have a chance to ask questions of the government minister and argue over the merits of any particularly contentious provisions. Following the second reading the bill then goes to the committee stage. At this point a standing committee of MPs or peers will scrutinise the provisions of the bill in much greater detail. Having done this, they may propose amendments to the bill which in their view will improve it as a whole. From the committee stage the bill is then sent back to the House as a whole. This is known as the report stage and MPs or peers will engage in further debate upon the bill, and will also have the opportunity to vote to accept or reject any amendments made at the committee stage. The bill will come to its conclusion with a third and final reading, at which point there is a final debate on the contents of the bill followed by a vote. If the vote on the bill is positive, the bill is then sent to the other House of Parliament where it will go through all of the same stages once again. If any amendments are made there, it must return to the first House for these amendments to be voted upon.

Clearly, the parliamentary process is a lengthy one. There are several hurdles which a bill must overcome in both Houses before the process has been completed and the bill is close to entering the statute book as a new piece of legislation. It is important to emphasise, however, that although bills must proceed through both Houses of Parliament, it is the House of Commons which is the pre-eminent body of the two.[5] The importance of the House of Lords to the legislative process has declined considerably in the twentieth century, largely as a result of the fact that, whereas the Commons is a democratically elected, accountable and representative body, the Lords is an undemocratic, unaccountable and unrepresentative body. To restrict the ability of the House of Lords to block legislation, the Parliament Acts of 1911 and 1949 were adopted.[6] As a result of these two statutes, the House of Lords can only delay the passage of a bill into law as an Act of Parliament by one year. Thus, any bill which has been passed by the House of Commons need not necessarily receive a positive vote in the House of Lords to eventually become law. As far as 'money' bills (those which involve the raising of revenue) are concerned, the House of Lords may only delay these by a period of one month. This reflects money bills' fundamental importance to the effective functioning of government. In practice, it has not proven necessary for governments to make great use of the provisions of the Parliament Acts to force their legislative programme through the House of Lords. They have only actually been invoked on four occasions to ensure legislation could be passed in the face of a disagreeable House of Lords.[7] The first such occasion did not occur until 1991, when the War Crimes Act 1991 was passed into law. Since then, the provisions of the Parliament Acts have been utilised on a further three occasions to facilitate the passage of the European Parliamentary Elections Act 1999, the Sexual Offences (Amendment) Act 2000 and the Hunting Act 2004.

Government bills will usually pass smoothly into legislation as a consequence of the fact that governments ordinarily enjoy a majority in the House of Commons.[8] This is not always the case, however, and sometimes legislative proposals will have to be shelved where there is significant opposition including from the government's own backbenchers.

[5] This relates back directly to the question which asks you to consider the relative importance of the Commons, Lords and Sovereign to the legislative process.

[6] It is imperative that you refer to the impact of the Parliament Acts as it is these which are responsible for curbing the power of the House of Lords to block legislation, thus diminishing its relative importance in the legislative process.

[7] This is a convenient place to allude to some relevant examples to reinforce a point.

[8] This is an appropriate comment to make following discussion of the parliamentary process, evidencing awareness of the political context within which Acts of Parliament are made. You might wish to refer to the current political situation in which there is a coalition government and legislative proposals stem from compromises between the two parties.

[9] Do not forget to include coverage of this issue as the question specifically refers to it. You should demonstrate that the role of the sovereign in the parliamentary process is a mere formality.

[10] This reinforces the mere formality of royal assent. Making such a point also allows you to evidence wider knowledge of the subject area.

The final step in the making of an Act of Parliament is the granting of royal assent. This is a mere formality.[9] The monarch today enjoys no meaningful legal or political power and her consent is only required by constitutional convention. In practice, this is never refused. The last occasion on which this did happen was when Queen Anne refused to assent to the Scottish Militia Bill of 1707.[10] It is inconceivable that royal assent would be refused today, and if this did occur a constitutional crisis would be likely to ensue. The Royal Assent Act 1967 provides that royal assent is deemed to be given on the date on which this is informed to parliament. The Act of Parliament will come into force on this date unless the act itself provides otherwise, either by specifying an alternative date or leaving it to statutory instrument to bring the act into force.

 **Make your answer stand out**

- Provide some context to the question by explaining the origins of parliamentary bills, in particular the extent to which they are largely driven by government policy.
- Use examples where appropriate; for example, cases in which the Parliament Acts have been invoked to pass a bill, or a private members' bill has been successful.
- Make reference to the requirement imposed upon a minister introducing a bill into parliament by section 19 of the Human Rights Act 1998.
- Demonstrate a solid awareness of the impact of the Parliament Acts 1911 and 1949 and the norms applicable to the requirement of royal assent.

**! Don't be tempted to . . .**

- Explain only the main stages through which a bill must pass in Parliament without first providing an explanation of the origins of bills.
- Neglect to consider the role of the sovereign within the legislative process.

#  Question 4

'The mechanisms which exist for subjecting delegated legislation to scrutiny and control suffer from such limitations as to be almost meaningless as a form of exercising restraint on the exercise of discretionary law-making power.' Discuss.

# Answer plan

→ Briefly explain what delegated legislation is and the main forms which it takes.

→ Discuss the extent to which consultation requirements serve as meaningful control on the making of delegated legislation.

→ Consider the merits of the scrutiny mechanisms which new delegated legislative measures must go through before they can become law.

→ Consider the role of the courts in scrutinising delegated legislation.

→ Conclude by stating to what extent you agree with the assertion contained in the question.

# Diagram plan

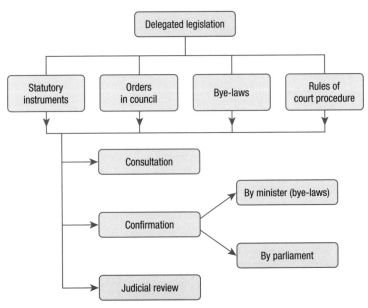

A printable version of this diagram plan is available from www.pearsoned.co.uk/lawexpressqa

# Answer

[1] You should begin by briefly explaining what delegated legislation is and the main forms which it takes, as some forms of scrutiny are specific to certain kinds of measure.

Delegated legislation refers to legal instruments made by bodies other than Parliament, either under the Royal Prerogative or powers conferred by statute, and takes several main forms.[1] Statutory instruments are made by government ministers or civil servants within their departments, the authority to make them being contained in 'enabling' Acts of Parliament. Statutory instruments will often be used to legislate on technical matters too onerous to take up Parliament's time. Orders in Council are measures theoretically made by the Privy Council, either under the Royal Prerogative or powers contained in statute, and are routinely used to give legal force to the UK's international obligations in domestic law, for example the implementation of UN sanctions or provisions of European law.[2] Bye-laws are made by local authorities or other public authorities under powers contained in statute and Courts Rules committees are empowered to make rules governing court procedure.

The significance of delegated legislation is evidenced by the fact that it far exceeds statute law in volume. For example, in 2003 there were approximately 3,500 statutory instruments enacted, yet only 45 Acts of Parliament.[3] The growth of delegated legislation has largely been a consequence of the growth of the welfare state in the post-World War Two era. As the state has undertaken more activities, it has simply not been practical for Parliament to tackle the many issues requiring legislative action. However, the increased devolution of law-making powers to unelected actors has given rise to one of the biggest criticisms of delegated legislation; that it is profoundly undemocratic and potentially susceptible to abuse.[4] The nature of delegated legislation means that it must be subject to meaningful forms of scrutiny to safeguard against abuses of delegated powers.

Arguably, delegated legislation is subject to scrutiny at three stages: before it is made, before it acquires legal force, and once it is in force.[5] Before delegated legislation is made, those responsible for making it may be required to consult specific persons or bodies likely to be affected by the proposed measures. However, consultation requirements vary from one situation to another.[6] The enabling act may require a minister to consult named organisations. For example, the National Insurance Act 1946 required draft regulations made under its powers to be submitted to the National Insurance Advisory Committee. Often it will be advantageous for law-makers to consult relevant bodies, especially where expertise in technical matters is sought. However, consultation requirements are limited as a meaningful form of control on the making of delegated legislation. They are not applicable to all instances of delegated legislation and often are phrased in such terms as to give considerable discretion to the person making it as to who, if anybody, is consulted. Furthermore,

[2] You might demonstrate your knowledge here by citing examples of these measures, for example Orders in Council implemented under the Southern Rhodesia Act 1965 to effect UN sanctions against Southern Rhodesia.

[3] It is helpful if you can cite statistical evidence of the significance of delegated legislation. This underlies the importance of ensuring that it is subject to adequate forms of scrutiny, and is central to the question.

[4] This builds upon the previous point and you make the case clearly for the importance of sufficient control being exercised over the use of powers to make delegated legislation.

[5] This is a logical way of breaking down the various forms of scrutiny which existed of delegated legislation.

[6] This is a crucial point to make and serves to reinforce the limitations of this as a meaningful restriction upon the making of delegated legislation.

that consultation takes place does not ensure that any advice or information obtained during that process will necessarily be acted upon.

The most important opportunity for scrutiny of delegated legislation takes place once it has been drafted and awaits legal confirmation. Under section 235 (2) of the Local Government Act 1972, local authority bye-laws are subject to confirmation by the relevant government minister before acquiring legal force.[7] While theoretically serving as a check upon local law-making, the sheer volume of bye-laws means that no government minister can seriously scrutinise all of them properly. In addition, recent legislative developments – the Local Government and Public Involvement in Health Act 2007 and Localism Act 2011 – have weakened the requirement for ministerial approval by expanding the number of situations where it is not necessary.[8]

Orders in Council made under the Royal Prerogative are not subject to the approval of Parliament,[9] but statutory instruments do require confirmation by Parliament, which can take one of a number of forms. The form applicable will be determined by the terms of the enabling Act which provided the authority for its enactment. Most common is the 'negative resolution' procedure.[10] Here, the statutory instrument in question is laid before Parliament for 40 days during which time any Member of Parliament may review it, and the possibility exists of either House moving to reject it. In practice this provides no meaningful form of scrutiny as the sheer volume of delegated legislation makes it unlikely that many statutory instruments will be inspected more closely. The 'affirmative resolution' procedure provides better prospects of scrutiny taking place. Under this, Parliament must positively vote in favour of the enactment of a statutory instrument, subjecting it to wider exposure. However, this procedure is rarely used and reserved for more significant matters. Likewise, the recently developed 'super affirmative resolution' procedure provides for greater scrutiny but is used only in a very limited number of cases.[11] Here, the statutory instrument in question is laid before Parliament for 60 days and two special committees must review and report upon its contents. This may lead to amendments being made by the relevant minister before the committees report back to Parliament, which must consider the report before affirming the measure.

[7] It is important that you do not overlook this requirement as it is the main requirement applicable to bye-laws once they have been drafted.

[8] It is very important to mention these developments. This demonstrates that you are aware of some of the most relevant recent developments, and these can also be cited to suggest that there has been a weakening of control mechanisms applicable to law-making on the part of local authorities.

[9] This is very important, clearly showing that there is one form of delegated legislation that is largely free of any scrutiny at this stage.

[10] As the most commonly used procedure for parliamentary scrutiny, the shortcomings of this procedure are particularly instructive and add solid weight to your arguments that scrutiny of delegated legislation suffers from serious limitations.

[11] You are able to show clearly here that even the more robust of the procedures for parliamentary scrutiny are of limited effectiveness.

Within Parliament a number of specialised committees are responsible for keeping delegated legislation under review. Most prominent of these is the Joint Committee on Statutory Instruments, but this does not have the authority to consider the merits of measures enacted. The House of Lords Merits of Statutory Instruments committee can consider their merits, but the volume of delegated legislation makes it questionable how big a contribution these committees can in practice make to the scrutiny of delegated legislation.

Once delegated legislation comes into force it can only be challenged via the courts, by way of an action for judicial review. The Queen's Bench Division of the High Court can strike down as ultra vires measures where relevant procedural requirements have not been satisfied. For example, in *Agricultural, Horticultural and Forestry Industry Training Board* v *Aylesbury Mushrooms* [1972] 1 All ER 280, a failure to satisfy statutory consultation requirements led to the annulment of resulting regulations. Delegated legislation may also be ruled substantively ultra vires the powers conferred upon the law-maker where s/he exceeds the powers conferred, as happened in *Commissioners of Customs & Excise* v *Cure & Deeley Ltd* [1962] 1 QB 340. The main difficulty with reliance on the courts to rectify problems with delegated legislation is that they can only consider these measures after they have become law and cannot pronounce on their merits.[12] Whilst ensuring legal accountability, judicial review is hardly a form of genuine scrutiny of the various implications of provisions of delegated legislation.

In conclusion, there is considerable truth in the statement. However, the sheer volume of delegated legislation makes it difficult to subject it to more robust scrutiny. It might also be noted that most delegated legislation is made in respect of non-controversial matters, suggesting that the limited forms of scrutiny available may not be as worrying in practice as they may appear in theory.[13]

[12] You can develop this point effectively by pointing to possible injustices which will already have been caused before the measure is nullified by the courts.

[13] This is a reasoned conclusion supported by the preceding discussion. It answers the question directly, while offering a balanced view of the possibilities and needs which exist for clear scrutiny of the exercise of delegated legislative powers.

**Make your answer stand out**

- Make reference to recent legislative developments which have impacted upon the scrutiny requirements for certain forms of delegated. legislation, in particular the Local Government and Public Involvement in Health Act 2007 and the Localism Act 2011.
- Explain clearly the role of judicial review in nullifying delegated legislative measures as ultra vires.
- Cite examples from statute and case law in support of your answer.
- Refer to academic commentary, for example McHarg (2006) 'What Is Delegated Legislation?', *Public Law*, v. 50, 539–61.

**!** **Don't be tempted to . . .**

- Provide a detailed account of the various forms of delegated legislation and the procedures by which they are made.
- Omit to refer to any relevant examples in support of your answer.
- Confine your discussion simply to statutory instruments.

#  Question 5

'While forceful criticisms can legitimately be levelled at the use of delegated legislation, its use is absolutely essential in modern society and it would be naïve to think it could simply be dispensed with.' Critically assess the validity of this statement.

## Answer plan

→ Briefly explain what delegated legislation is and the major forms which it takes.

→ Discuss the perceived advantages of delegated legislation.

→ Discuss the perceived disadvantages of delegated legislation.

→ Conclude by commenting upon the extent to which you agree with the statement contained in the question.

# Diagram plan

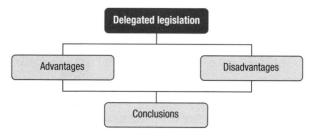

A printable version of this diagram plan is available from www.pearsoned.co.uk/lawexpressqa

## Answer

[1] Your introductory paragraph should briefly explain what delegated legislation is and the main forms which it takes. This should be brief, however, as your main focus must be to consider the advantages and disadvantages of delegated legislation.

Delegated legislation is legislation made by persons or bodies other than Parliament[1] under powers either conferred upon them by Parliament under statute or exercised under the royal prerogative. Statutory instruments are, arguably, the most prominent form of delegated legislation and consist of regulations, rules and orders made by government ministers or their civil servants under powers conferred by statute. Orders in Council are made by the Privy Council either under powers conferred by statute, in which case they are simply a form of statutory instrument, or under the Royal Prerogative. Rules of court procedure are made by the court rules committees under powers conferred by statute, and local authorities and occasionally other corporations make bye-laws in respect of matters within their areas under powers conferred by statute.

[2] This is an absolutely essential point to make. It is the most often cited reason why delegated legislation is necessary.

[3] This is a useful statistic to cite as it reinforces the point that you have just made.

Parliament simply has insufficient time to consider all matters requiring legislation and delegated legislation helpfully fills this gap.[2] The process by which an Act of Parliament is made is lengthy, consisting of several stages through which a bill must pass in both Houses of Parliament. These time constraints are evidenced by the fact that Parliament enacts very few statutes in comparison to the voluminous amount of delegated legislation that is made. For example, in 2003 only 45 statutes were enacted compared to approximately 3,500 statutory instruments.[3] It is simply impossible for Parliament to legislate itself on such an enormous amount of issues and delegated legislation fills this void.

On a related point, delegated legislation can provide detailed rules going far beyond what could be contained in statute.[4] For example, the amount of detail required to effectively legislate in respect of matters such as taxation regulations or social security benefits is far greater than can be dealt with through the parliamentary process. Even when statute is used to advance government policy objectives, it is usually necessary to leave the finer points to be implemented through delegated legislation.

Furthermore, Members of Parliament lack not only time but the specialised knowledge necessary to oversee the implementation of much legislation of a technical nature. Leaving such matters to delegated legislation enables expertise in the relevant areas to be drawn upon during its drafting.[5] Heavily technical measures in particular can be drafted within a government department where there is a pool of expertise in this area. Taking the example of entitlement to social security benefits, the necessary detailed rules can be more effectively drafted by civil servants within the Department of Work and Pensions who deal with these issues on an ongoing basis. The same point can be made of taxation rules drafted by the Inland Revenue. Where bye-laws are made by local authorities, provision exists for relevant local knowledge to inform the law-making process, again illustrating the extent to which relevant expertise or specialist knowledge can be drawn upon. Clearly, in respect of matters of primarily local concern, the relevant local authority is in a much better position to make appropriate rules than is a Parliament with little understanding of local needs and interests.

Delegated legislation can be used to change the law relatively quickly. As noted above, an Act of Parliament must go through several stages before becoming law. This will ordinarily take at least several months. By comparison, measures made through delegated legislation can be completed in a matter of weeks depending upon their relative complexity. A related final advantage of delegated legislation is that, whereas statutes cannot always anticipate future needs or changes, delegated legislation can be used to respond quickly to these. To recall an earlier example, social security benefit entitlements are likely to need to change relatively regularly in light of other factors.[6] Parliament cannot envisage how often this need

[4] Many of the arguments in support or criticism of delegated legislation are related to one another as opposed to being a series of mutually exclusive points. You should relate them to one another where appropriate. The argument made here builds upon from the previous one so make sure you show this connection.

[5] This highly important advantage of delegated legislation must be mentioned. It is helpful to refer to some relevant examples to reinforce the point that it enables technical expertise to be drawn upon.

[6] If you have difficulty thinking of relevant examples, the same example can sometimes be used to reinforce more than one argument.

may arise, so the relevant minister will be empowered to make regulations where appropriate.

Undoubtedly, there are several very strong arguments that can be made in support of the role played by delegated legislation. In particular, it is necessary to tackle the many issues which Parliament is simply unable to and allows for relevant expertise on technical and specialist matters. However, its use has been subject to criticism on a number of grounds. It is argued that there is insufficient democratic involvement or accountability within the process by which delegated legislation is made,[7] as it is made by unelected persons and bodies who cannot effectively be held to account. This strengthens the need for proper scrutiny of delegated legislation, but it has often been contended that existing measures are inadequate. Delegated legislation is rarely debated in Parliament. Although statutory instruments theoretically require the assent of Parliament, many are approved through the 'negative resolution' procedure whereby they are laid before Parliament for 40 days, at the end of which they are deemed approved in the absence of any objection being raised. It is rare for individual members to pay any real attention to a particular measure. Orders in Council made under the Royal Prerogative receive no further scrutiny, and local authority bye-laws – although ordinarily subject to confirmation by the relevant minister – are now exempt from this requirement in an increasing number of cases as a result of measures such as those contained in the Local Government and Public Involvement in Health Act 2007. The courts may nullify measures that have been made ultra vires, but this is arguably a method of control applicable in more drastic circumstances and no real substitute for effective scrutiny of the law-making process.

Another criticism of delegated legislation is that the sheer bulk in which it is produced makes it difficult to keep up to date with the introduction of new legal rules. This can be related to the constitutional principle of the rule of law, most models of which require that laws should be clear and intelligible.[8] It is understandable that keeping abreast of several thousand new pieces of legislation every year is far from easy. A related criticism is that, although measures made under delegated legislation are published, they are not publicised either before or after their implementation as widely as Acts of Parliament are, which automatically tend to receive greater media

[7] This is the most stinging criticism of delegated legislation. There is much that can be said in respect of the lack of proper scrutiny of measures of delegated legislation and, although you can only realistically give so much attention to it in a more general question on the advantages and disadvantages of delegated legislation, its inclusion is essential in your discussion of its disadvantages.

[8] This is a very effective point which evidences the ability to understand the relationship between delegated legislation and broader legal principles.

[9] This is a reasoned and logical conclusion which flows naturally from the rest of the answer. A very strong case can be made for the necessity of delegated legislation, but there remain concerns over the lack of meaningful scrutiny which takes place of it.

attention. This adds to the difficulty of keeping up to date with new legislative measures.

Arguably, there is no question of the necessity of delegated legislation for the reasons set out earlier. Critics of delegated legislation rarely suggest that it should not exist. Their arguments are more concerned with the lack of meaningful scrutiny which it undergoes and, to a lesser extent, the limited publicity which is given to its introduction. Strengthening confidence in delegated legislation requires that steps be taken to respond to these concerns.[9]

 Make your answer stand out

- Draw upon examples from relevant areas of law to reinforce your arguments.
- Relate the various advantages or disadvantages of delegated legislation to one another where appropriate, as opposed to treating them as a series of mutually exclusive arguments.
- Demonstrate awareness of the main modes of scrutiny which take place of measures of delegated legislation and their limitations.
- You might usefully illustrate the danger of delegated legislation being used to circumvent parliamentary scrutiny by reading and drawing upon some of the arguments made in relation to a specific example of a bill conferring wide delegated legislative powers in Burns (2006) 'Tipping the Balance', *New Law Journal*, v. 156, p. 787.

! Don't be tempted to . . .

- List the various advantages and disadvantages of delegated legislation with no real discussion.
- Discuss the various advantages and disadvantages of delegated legislation as mutually exclusive issues.

# 🖋 Question 6

Explain the major forms of EU law and the manner of their application within domestic law.

## Answer plan

➡ Explain that there are different forms of EU law and that their manner of application within domestic law varies, briefly illustrating the concepts of direct applicability and direct effect.

➡ Explain the application of treaties and that they are the most important source of EU law.

➡ Explain the application of regulations, highlighting their generally automatic applicability within domestic law.

➡ Explain the application of directives, highlighting the importance of direct effect for their enforceability.

➡ Briefly explain the lesser importance of decisions, opinions and recommendations as sources of EU law.

## Diagram plan

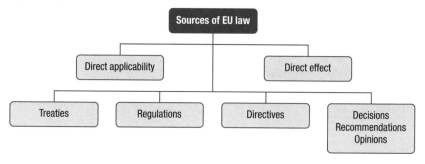

A printable version of this diagram plan is available from www.pearsoned.co.uk/lawexpressqa

## Answer

[1] You cannot explain the manner of application of the different forms of EU law within domestic law without reference to the concepts of direct applicability and direct effect. As these are relevant to the discussion of all of the major sources of law, it will be helpful to briefly explain their meaning and relevance to the application of EU law at the outset of your answer.

There are three major sources of EU law: treaties, regulations and directives. The way in which these different forms of law apply in member states varies. Before explaining the sources in further detail, it will be useful first of all to briefly explain the concepts of direct applicability and direct effect as these are central to the enforceability of EU law within domestic law.[1] A provision of EU law which is directly applicable will have automatic application within the domestic law of member states without any need for implementing measures on their part. While treaty provisions and regulations are capable of direct applicability, directives are not. Direct effect refers to the ability of provisions of EU law to be relied upon within domestic law even where they are not directly applicable and have not been implemented within domestic law. The concept of direct effect was established in the case of *Van Gend en Loos* v *Nederlandse Tariefcommissie* [1963] ECR 3,[2] where the criteria which must be satisfied for a provision to be capable of direct effect were set out, these being that the relevant provision was clear, unconditional and required no further legislation on the part of the state.

[2] It is absolutely essential that you refer to *Van Gend en Loos* in explaining direct effect and the criteria which govern its application. It is a case of huge significance.

Treaties comprise the highest source of law within the EU.[3] They set out its main aims and objectives and provide the institutional and normative framework within which EU institutions are to operate. The treaties also lay down the various rights and obligations of member states. There are several key treaties.[4] The Treaty of Rome (European Community Treaty) established the original European Economic Community in 1957. The Single European Act 1986 introduced measures as part of the process of creating a single economic market within Europe. The Treaty on European Union of 1991 created the European Union and in 1997 the Treaty of Amsterdam amended and re-numbered the European Community Treaty and Treaty on European Union. More recent treaties are the Treaty of Nice 2001 and the Lisbon Treaty 2007. *Van Gend en Loos* first established that treaty provisions are capable of enjoying direct effect if they are unconditional, clear and precise in terms of the rights and obligations which they give rise to and leave member states with no discretion as to their implementation. An example can be found with Article 139 of the European Community Treaty, which laid down the principle of equal pay for men and women. Article 139 was held to be directly effective in UK domestic law in *Macarthys Ltd* v *Smith* [1992] notwithstanding its absence in UK equal pay legislation.[5] Treaty provisions enjoy both vertical and horizontal direct effect,[6] that is to say that they can be enforced against both public (vertical direct effect) and private (horizontal direct effect) bodies. However, non-mandatory treaty provisions containing mere policy statements or objectives are not capable of enjoying direct effect.

[3] This is a key point and emphasises the relative importance of treaties within the hierarchy of sources of EU law.

[4] You can evidence wider awareness of the development of EU law by briefly mentioning some of the key treaties to have been created.

[5] There is no better way of illustrating the direct effect of treaty articles than by providing an example of an occasion on which a treaty article has been held to be directly effective.

[6] At some point you need to distinguish vertical and horizontal direct effect.

It has been said that regulations are the European source of law that most closely resemble an Act of Parliament. Regulations apply throughout the EU as soon as they come into force. They are directly applicable. They do not need to be implemented in member states by domestic legislation, and must be applied even if they conflict with domestic legislation. Regulations must be published in the *Official Journal of the European Union*. Regulations are far more common than treaties as sources of EU law. Like treaty provisions, regulations are capable of enjoying direct effect provided that they meet the *Van Gend en Loos* criteria. There was some uncertainty as to whether regulations could enjoy both horizontal and vertical direct effect, but it was confirmed by the European Court of Justice in the case of *Munoz y Cia SA* v *Frumar Ltd* (2002) Unreported, 17 September that they could.[7]

[7] Credit ought to be given for making this point. The case is not particularly well known, yet is relevant to the question and evidences a wider awareness of EU legal developments.

Directives tend to be less precise in their content than do regulations. Generally speaking, they will establish broad policy objectives which member states are to implement through methods of their own choice. As such, directives are not directly applicable within member states but depend for their application on implementation through domestic legislation. Initially it was felt that directives would be unable to enjoy direct effect. However, in the case of *Van Duyn* v *Home Office* [1974] 1 WLR 1107 it was established that unimplemented directives may be relied upon in domestic law under the principle of direct effect where they impose clear and unconditional obligations on a government.[8] Directives will only have vertical direct effect though and cannot be enforced against non-state bodies. This is largely due to the perception that it would be inappropriate to bind a private body by a measure that has yet to be implemented into domestic law and the content which it may be unaware of. However, this could potentially mean that an aggrieved party suffering loss through the failure of a government to properly implement a directive may be left without an appropriate remedy.

[8] This case is central to the enforceability of directives in domestic law and ought to be included in your answer.

[9] The application of directives gives rise to more difficult issues than do treaty provisions and regulations. You would be expected to say more about their application in domestic law as a result. It is useful to explain some of the ways in which the European Court of Justice has sought to fill the gaps left by the more limited application of directives in domestic law. This evidences wide understanding of the subject area.

The European Court of Justice has attempted to plug this gap through a range of other initiatives.[9] Firstly, a broad approach has been taken to the definition of the state and public bodies so as to maximise the range of bodies against which directives can be enforced through the principle of vertical direct effect. For example, in the case of *Marshall* v *Southampton and South-West Hampshire Area Health Authority* [1986] QB 401, a health authority was considered to constitute a public body. In *Von Colson* v *Land Nordrhein-Westfalen* [1984] ECR 1891, the European Court of Justice developed the concept of indirect effect whereby domestic legislation is to be interpreted as far as possible in accordance with directives. As the ultimate sanction, states who fail to implement directives properly within the time frame provided can be held liable and required to provide compensation to those who suffer loss as a result, under the principle of state liability established in *Francovich v Italy* [1991] ECR I-5357.

Treaties, regulations and directives are the most important sources of EU law. They are wide in their application and, in the right circumstances, can be enforced in domestic law courts. There are, however, also some less significant sources of law that ought to be briefly mentioned.[10] Decisions of EU institutions may be addressed to states or private individuals or bodies. They have the force of law under Article 249 of the European Community Treaty, but only bind their recipients. They have no general application beyond this. Recommendations and opinions of the Council and Commission, covered by Article 211 of the European Community Treaty, do not constitute binding law but may influence the conduct of member states.

[10] While the main focus of your answer should be on the major sources of EU law – treaties, regulations and directives – awareness of the complete range of sources is evidenced by brief reference to decisions, recommendations and opinions.

## ✓ Make your answer stand out

- Explain clearly the concepts of direct applicability and direct effect and show how they are relevant to the application of the major sources of EU law within domestic law.
- Highlight some examples of prominent regulations and directives which have been applied in domestic law.
- Comment on the merits of allowing directives to enjoy horizontal direct effect.
- Illustrate some of the measures taken by the European Court of Justice to fill gaps in situations where directives have not been capable of horizontal direct effect.

## ! Don't be tempted to . . .

- Simply explain what the different sources of EU law are without any explanation of the manner in which they are applied within domestic law.
- Treat directives as a less important source of law for the purpose of your answer as there is actually more to be said about issues relevant to the enforceability of directives than there is treaties or regulations.
- Confuse EU law with the European Convention on Human Rights, which is not relevant to this question.

#  Question 7

'Parliamentary sovereignty has been so significantly undermined by the impact of the UK's membership of the European Union to the extent that it has become meaningless.' Critically assess the validity of this statement.

## Answer plan

➜ Explain the doctrine of parliamentary sovereignty.

➜ Briefly refer to the development of the concept of supremacy of EU law through the jurisprudence of the European Court of Justice.

➜ Explain the importance of section 2 of the European Communities Act 1972.

➜ Illustrate the recognition of the supremacy of EU law by domestic courts with particular reference to the *Factortame* case.

➜ Conclude by commenting upon the constitutional significance of the UK's membership of the EU.

## Diagram plan

| Doctrine of parliamentary sovereignty | ➜ | Doctrine of supremacy of EU law | ➜ | s. 2, European Communities Act 1972 | ➜ | *Factortame* | ➜ | Constitutional significance of EU membership |

A printable version of this diagram plan is available from www.pearsoned.co.uk/lawexpressqa

## Answer

[1] The question asks you about the impact of EU law on parliamentary sovereignty, so you need to demonstrate that you understand what the doctrine of parliamentary sovereignty entails before you proceed to explore how it has been affected by the impact of EU law. Your first paragraph should explain the doctrine of parliamentary sovereignty.

The doctrine of parliamentary sovereignty lies at the heart of the UK constitution. It holds that Parliament may make or unmake any law whatsoever. There are no restrictions upon its freedom to legislate.[1] The unlimited scope of this power was underlined in the case of ***Madzimbamuto v Lardner-Burke & George*** [1969] AC 645, where Lord Reid expressed the view that although 'the moral, political and other reasons against . . . doing [certain things] are so strong that most would regard it as highly improper . . . this does not mean it is beyond [Parliament's] power to'. There are two core strands to parliamentary sovereignty. Firstly, Parliament may not bind its successors. It may not enact provisions preventing later Parliaments doing certain things or requiring that a special procedure must be followed to change a particular law. Secondly, the doctrine of implied repeal holds that where later Acts of Parliament conflict with earlier ones, the later Acts take effect and are said to implicitly repeal the earlier ones. Where an Act of Parliament conflicts with a provision of international law, it was established in **Mortensen v Peters** [1906] SLT 227 that the former prevails.[2] Prior to the accession of the UK to the then European Economic Community (EEC), European law was simply an alien form of international law with no binding effect on the UK. However, the UK's membership of the EU has forced a reappraisal of the extent to which Parliament continues to enjoy sovereignty within the domestic legislative process.

The notion that European law would prevail over domestic legislation in the event of a clash between the two forms of law has deep roots in the jurisprudence of the European Court of Justice where the concept of the supremacy of European law developed. In the case of **Costa v ENEL** [1964] CMLR 425 it was suggested that, in acceding to the EEC, member states had 'limited their sovereign rights . . . and . . . created a body of law which binds both their nationals and themselves . . . the law stemming from the treaty . . . could not, because of its special and original nature, be overridden by domestic legal provisions'.[3] The European Communities Act 1972 gave effect to European law within the UK.[4] The two key provisions are sections 2(1) and 2(4). Section 2(1) provides that European legislation is to be given effect to in domestic law. Section 2(4) is potentially more controversial, however, as it appears to provide that domestic legislation will be given effect subject to provisions of European law, implying the supremacy of the latter in the case of conflict. Although it would be two decades before the impact of European law upon parliamentary sovereignty was finally clarified, there were some early signs of recognition on the part of the UK courts of the monumental impact which European law would have upon the long established doctrine of parliamentary sovereignty.[5] Lord Denning, in particular, made prominent comments upon the subject. Not long after the passage of the European Communities Act, he prophesied in **HP Bulmer Ltd v J Bollinger SA (No. 2)** [1974] Ch 401, that the European Community Treaty was 'an incoming tide. It flows into the estuaries and up the rivers. It cannot be held back'. Later, in **Macarthys Ltd v Smith** [1979] 1 WLR 1189, he said, 'If . . . it should appear that our legislation is deficient or is inconsistent with Community

[2] You will not usually need to recite the facts of a case. The main point is that you understand the legal principles which emanate from cases.

[3] Reference to *Costa* v *ENEL* is helpful as it illustrates that the notion that European law would take precedence over domestic law was rooted in the jurisprudence of the European Court of Justice prior to the UK's accession to the EEC. Although you cannot be expected to quote extensively from judgments in an examination setting, it is useful if you can incorporate some passages from particularly important cases, and when writing longer essays you should do so.

[4] It is absolutely essential that you consider the impact of the 1972 Act, as this gave effect to European law within the UK and hints at its supremacy over domestic legislation.

[5] Reference to such decisions is useful as it builds up a picture of gradual recognition of the supremacy of European law on the part of the UK courts.

law . . . then it is our bounden duty to give priority to Community law. Such is the result of s 2(1) and (4) of the European Communities Act 1972'.

The impact of EU law on parliamentary sovereignty was finally confirmed in *R* v *Secretary of State for Transport, ex parte Factortame (No. 1)* [1990] 2 AC 85.[6] The case concerned a conflict between provisions of the UK Merchant Shipping Act 1988 and provisions of European law. The case was brought by the operators of fishing vessels who had been precluded by provisions of the 1988 Act from being able to register their vessels in the UK and were thus unable to fish in British waters. They claimed that the relevant provisions of the Merchant Shipping Act were in breach of European law and should therefore be disapplied by the courts. The case reached the House of Lords which ultimately ruled that the 1988 Act was in conflict with provisions of European law and consequently would be overridden. The House took the view that it had always been clear since the passage of the European Communities Act that in the case of a conflict a domestic court would be obliged to give precedence to European law. This was a landmark occasion in UK constitutional and legal history, representing the first occasion on which provisions of an Act of Parliament were set aside, and making clear that parliamentary sovereignty only exists to the extent that domestic legislation does not fall foul of European provisions.

[6] It is absolutely essential that you include coverage of the *Factortame* case in your answer. This is the most important case on the impact of European law on parliamentary sovereignty and goes to the very heart of the question, establishing firmly that European law will override conflicting provisions of domestic statutes. You need to stress very clearly the landmark status of the ruling in *Factortame*.

The impact of Factortame has been reinforced in subsequent cases.[7] For example, in *R* v *Secretary of State for Employment, ex parte Equal Opportunities Commission* [1994] 1 WLR 910 parts of the Employment Protection (Consolidation) Act 1978 were held to be incompatible with European law. More recently, the constitutional significance of the European Communities Act 1972 was commented upon in *Thoburn* v *Sunderland City Council* [2002] EWHC 195 (Admin), where it was described by Lord Justice Laws as a 'constitutional Act' which could only be repealed by express provisions of an Act of Parliament.[8]

[7] It is useful to follow up your discussion of *Factortame* by illustrating how it has been reinforced in later cases. Again, this evidences a wider understanding of the subject area.

[8] The *Thoburn* judgment is very interesting for its commentary on the constitutional significance of the 1972 Act as well as the modern relevance of the doctrine of parliamentary sovereignty. If you have time, you might embark on a lengthier discussion of this.

Parliamentary sovereignty has undoubtedly been radically affected as a result of the UK's membership of the EU. Although Parliament retains the ability to legislate on any matter of its choosing, should this conflict with a provision of European law it will be overridden by it. Parliamentary sovereignty appears to be thus heavily diminished.

However, there is a strong argument to be made for the proposition that Parliament can reclaim its complete sovereignty any time by simply repealing the European Communities Act 1972. It will be recalled that, according to the doctrine of parliamentary sovereignty, no Parliament can bind its successor. It is the 1972 Act which has given European law effect within the domestic legal system and, if a later Parliament chooses to repeal that Act, it will cease to have effect and parliamentary sovereignty will be restored to its former state. This was evidently recognised by Lord Justice Laws in the case of *Thoburn*, where he re-stated the fundamental principle that no Parliament can bind its successors meant the 1972 Act could not become entrenched in domestic law to the point where it could not be repealed. Although political factors make this unlikely, it is none-theless the case that parliamentary sovereignty can arguably be fully reasserted at any stage.[9]

[9] Your conclusion should include comment upon the extent to which parliamentary sovereignty has been undermined by the impact of European law, and whether and how full parliamentary sovereignty might possibly be reclaimed. This relates directly back to the question which you have been asked to answer.

## ✓ Make your answer stand out

- Demonstrate a clear understanding of the meaning and scope of the doctrine of parliamentary sovereignty.
- Make reference to a range of relevant cases which touch upon the impact of European law on parliamentary sovereignty.
- Comment upon the constitutional significance of the European Communities Act 1972 and the UK's membership of the European Union.
- Refer to critical commentary upon the issues raised by the question by reading and drawing upon the discussion provided in Craig (2007) 'Britain in the European Union'; and Bradley (2007) 'The Sovereignty of Parliament'; both contained in Jowell and Oliver (eds) *The Changing Constitution*, 6th edn, Oxford: Oxford University Press.

## ! Don't be tempted to . . .

- Write an answer that is entirely or almost entirely focused upon the *Factortame* case and omits discussion of any other cases.
- Write about the application of EU law within domestic law more generally.
- Discuss the impact of the European Convention on Human Rights on domestic law.

#  Question 8

Critically evaluate the role played by the key EU institutions in the making and enforcement of EU law.

## Answer plan

➡ Explain the roles of the Council of Ministers and the European Council, highlighting their different roles and the role of the Council of Ministers within the legislative process.

➡ Explain the role of the European Commission, particularly in formulating legislative proposals and the enforcement of EU law.

➡ Explain the limited role of the European Parliament within the legislative process.

➡ Explain the major functions of the European Court of Justice, distinguishing its judicial and supervisory roles.

➡ Conclude upon the relative importance of the major institutions as law-makers and enforcers.

## Diagram plan

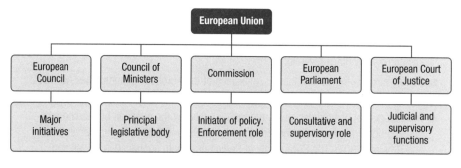

A printable version of this diagram plan is available from www.pearsoned.co.uk/lawexpressqa

## Answer

[1] The question is rather straightforward, simply asking you to explain the main functions of the key EU institutions and to comment on their roles within the law-making and enforcement process. You need to ensure that you cover the five major institutions and do this for each of them.

There are five major institutions involved in the making and enforce-ment of EU law.[1] The European Council comprises the heads of governments of member states and meets twice yearly. It has the same powers as the Council of Ministers which meets on a more regular ongoing basis and is discussed below.[2] The European Council's twice yearly meetings take the form of summits, at which decisions of a hugely significant nature will often be taken. Although the European Council does not meet very often, member state governments are represented on a regular basis through the Council of Ministers.

The Council of Ministers is the most powerful legislative body within the EU.[3] It comprises of ministers from all EU member states, although its exact membership varies with the subject matter which is under discussion at any given time. For example, if the Council was holding a meeting concerning financial matters, the finance ministers of member states would attend. If environmental issues were on the table, it would be environment ministers. The member states take it in turn to hold the presidency of the Council, which rotates every six months. As already stated, the Council of Ministers is the most powerful legislative body within the EU. Legislation on all important matters will be made within this forum. The Council has three methods of taking decisions depending on the particular issue under discussion. Some decisions must be taken unanimously, others by a simple majority and some require a qualified majority.

The European Commission is the key protagonist in the development of EU policy proposals. Each member state nominates one commissioner, although commissioners do not represent the interests of their home states but rather the interests of the EU as a whole. To some extent the Commission might be described as the closest thing to an executive body within the EU. Each commissioner is assigned an area of responsibility, for example agriculture or trade. It draws up the EU budget, negotiates external agreements and the accession of new states, and is the principal initiator of new legislative proposals, which all begin with the Commission. Although the Council of Ministers is the principal legislative body, the proposals upon which it votes are heavily shaped by the Commission from which they originate.[4] Aside from its role in the formulation of policy, the Commission is endowed with important responsibilities for enforcing EU law.[5] It investigates alleged breaches of the law by member states and is empowered to take enforcement actions against them to the European Court of Justice if it deems them to have not complied with their obligations under EU law. This power has been exercised by the Commission on a considerable number of occasions.

[2] You should refer to the overlap in roles of the European Council and Council of Ministers. Although the former has no continuous presence, the latter performs the same functions on a more regular basis.

[3] It is imperative that you emphasise the role of the Council of Ministers as the supreme legislative power within the EU. This relates back directly to the question which asks you to comment upon the role of the institutions in law-making and enforcement.

[4] This is an important point to make, as although the Commission is not the supreme law-maker within the EU, it plays a highly influential role in the legislative process through the legislative proposals which it makes. In this sense it has a direct role in the shaping of EU law.

[5] Ensure that you do not overlook the enforcement role of the Commission. It is important that you explain its functions in the enforcement of EU law.

The European Parliament is the only democratically elected EU institution, with elections being held in all member states every five years. Unlike the situation in respect of domestic parliaments, the European Parliament has very limited legislative powers. It cannot accurately be called a legislative body, but rather a consultative and supervisory body within the EU law-making process.[6] Over time the Parliament has been afforded greater input within the legislative process, but its role within this process remains largely consultative. The Parliament must be consulted on legislative proposals. The Single European Act enhanced its role in this respect. However, it is not afforded a direct say in respect of the adoption of new legal measures. The Parliament can make amendments to legis-lative proposals and is able to delay the passage of new measures, but it is not capable of blocking the introduction of new legislation *per se*. This is far removed from the situation in domestic law where parliaments can in theory block legislative proposals with ease. Despite its restricted role within the legislative process, the European Parliament performs a vital supervisory function. It has important powers over the EU budget, retaining the final say on non-obligatory expenditure. It also appoints an ombudsman who investigates cases of maladministration by EU institutions and reports to the Parliament. Perhaps the most critical power enjoyed by the Parliament is its ability to remove the Commission. This theoretically very important power, however, is undermined by the fact that the Parliament may only remove the Commission as a whole, not individual commis-sioners. Although never exercised, it was arguably indirectly influential in 1999 when the Commission resigned en masse in the midst of a series of scandals.

No discussion of the major EU institutions would be complete without coverage of the European Court of Justice (ECJ). This is the principal court of the EU, although it has been assisted by a court of First Instance since 1986 to ease its heavy workload. The European Court of Justice performs both a judicial and supervisory role in the inter-pretation and application of EU law.[7] In its judicial role the European Court of Justice hears disputes between member states or between member states and the Commission and adjudicates upon their compliance with their obligations under European law. An example of a contentious case heard by the ECJ can be found in the dispute between the UK and France over France's ban on the sale of British

[6] This is the key point to make about the functions of the European Parliament. You need to explain that it only has a limited role within the law-making process, but at the same time it does enjoy key supervisory powers over the Commission and EU budget.

[7] You need to distinguish these two functions of the European Court of Justice: it is easy to forget that it performs a supervisory function in relation to Article 234 references as well as the more traditional judicial role which it exercises.

[8] You can effectively reinforce your point by citing examples of both contentious cases and Article 234 references to have been heard by the court, while at the same point showing off clear awareness of legal developments under EU law.

beef in the aftermath of the outbreak of BSE.[8] In *Commission of the European Communities* v *France* (2001) (Unreported), the ECJ ruled that the French ban contravened EU law. The ECJ also performs a supervisory role by making preliminary rulings under Article 234 of the European Community Treaty (now Article 267 of the Amsterdam Treaty) on matters referred to it by member state courts. This occurs when a national court is uncertain as to the appropriate scope or application of EU law in a given situation. The national court may refer the matter to the European Court of Justice for a preliminary ruling in response to the national court's request. Preliminary rulings were obtained by UK courts in cases such as *HP Bulmer Ltd* v *J Bollinger SA (No. 2)* [1974] Ch 401, and *Marshall* v *Southampton and South West Hampshire Area Health Authority* [1986] QB 401.

All of the major institutions play an important role within either the law-making or enforcement process, although clearly some are more significant than others.[9] The Council of Ministers undoubtedly plays

[9] The conclusion should relate back to the question by summarising the relative importance of the key institutions within the law-making and enforcement process.

the most important role within the legislative process, although the Commission is responsible for the initiation of legislative proposals, the Parliament has a consultative function in this process and the European Council is directly involved in major legislative initiatives. The Commission plays a key role within the enforcement of EU law through its power to take member states to the European Court of Justice, which is the ultimate arbiter on their compliance with, and the correct application of, EU law.

✓ **Make your answer stand out**

- Ensure that you highlight what you consider to be the key function(s) of each of the key institutions.
- Make references to some of the limited changes made by the Treaty of Lisbon, for example in relation to the powers of the European Parliament.
- Comment upon the perceived 'democratic deficit' which exists within European legislative processes.
- Provide relevant examples of both contentious cases and Article 234 (now Article 267) references to have been heard by the European Court of Justice.

## ❗ Don't be tempted to . . .

- Provide detailed technical information on each of the institutions, such as their location.
- Explain the main functions of the institutions without commenting upon their roles within the legislative and law enforcement process.
- Confuse the EU institutions with the machinery of the European Convention on Human Rights.

**www.pearsoned.co.uk/lawexpressqa**

 Go online to access more revision support including additional essay and problem questions with diagram plans, You be the marker questions, and download all diagrams from the book.

# Judicial precedent

2

## How this topic may come up in exams

There are relatively few ways in which understanding of judicial precedent is assessed. You might be asked to generally explain how the system of binding judicial precedent operates. You may be asked to demonstrate an understanding of the ways in which judges are able to avoid the application of precedent, or the particular position of the Supreme Court or the Court of Appeal with respect to the extent to which they are bound by precedent and the circumstances in which they may depart from it. Questions which ask you to evaluate the relative merits of binding judicial precedent are also popular.

# ■ Attack the question

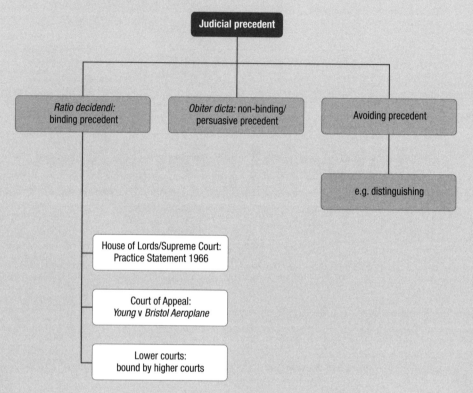

A printable version of this diagram plan is available from www.pearsoned.co.uk/lawexpressqa

# 🖎 Question 1

Discuss the extent to which the Court of Appeal is able to depart from its own previous decisions and comment upon whether it should enjoy the same position as the Supreme Court.

## Answer plan

→ Explain briefly the system of binding precedent.

→ Explain briefly the importance of the court hierarchy, and the place of the Court of Appeal within this hierarchy.

→ Illustrate the circumstances in which the Court of Appeal is able to depart from its own previous decisions.

→ Contrast the position of the Court of Appeal to that of the Supreme Court and assess whether the Court of Appeal should be similarly unbound by any of its previous decisions.

## Diagram plan

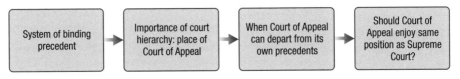

| System of binding precedent | → | Importance of court hierarchy: place of Court of Appeal | → | When Court of Appeal can depart from its own precedents | → | Should Court of Appeal enjoy same position as Supreme Court? |

A printable version of this diagram plan is available from www.pearsoned.co.uk/lawexpressqa

## Answer

The system of judicial precedent requires courts to follow decisions reached in previous cases sharing the same material facts – those facts of central importance to the decision reached – to the cases before them. It is based on the maxim of '*stare decisis*', meaning 'let the decision stand' and its rationale lies essentially in treating like cases alike.[1] It is important to distinguish between *ratio decidendi* and *obiter dicta*. The *ratio decidendi* is that part of a judgment containing the legal principle underlying the decision reached in a case; the reason for the decision. This part of the judgment forms binding precedent for future cases. The term *obiter dicta* refers to any part of a judgment not forming the *ratio decidendi*, including dissenting judgments and hypothetical scenarios. While non-binding, *obiter dicta* may form persuasive precedent in later cases.

[1] Although the question asks specifically about the ability of the Court of Appeal to depart from its own previous decisions, it is useful to explain briefly what judicial precedent is by way of your introduction. You should distinguish *ratio decidendi* and *obiter dicta* as only the former provide binding precedent.

The court hierarchy is central to the operation of binding precedent. Decisions of higher courts are binding upon those below them in the hierarchy. Thus, decisions of the Supreme Court are binding upon the Court of Appeal. The Court of Appeal's decisions bind those courts below it. However, whereas the Supreme Court need not follow its own previous decisions since Lord Gardiner's 1966 Practice Statement, generally the Court of Appeal is obliged to follow its own previous decisions.[2]

The general rule that the Court of Appeal's previous decisions bind it was re-stated in the case of *Young v Bristol Aeroplane* [1944] KB 718.[3] However, Lord Greene MR set out three exceptions where the Court of Appeal (CA) could depart from its own previous decisions. Firstly, when two previous conflicting decisions of the CA existed, it could choose which to follow and disregard the other. Such a situation arose in *Tiverton Estates Ltd v Wearwell Ltd* [1974] 2 WLR 176, a case concerning the interpretation of a provision of the Law of Property Act 1925. This exception is uncontroversial as clearly it is impossible to follow two conflicting decisions, and cannot be regarded as a meaningful exception. Secondly, when a previous decision of the Court of Appeal conflicts with a later decision of the Supreme Court, the CA should not follow its earlier decision. A case giving rise to this kind of situation was *Family Housing Association v Jones* [1990] 1 All ER 385, where an earlier Court of Appeal decision concerning the distinction between a licence and tenancy had been superseded by more recent House of Lords (now Supreme Court) decisions. Likewise, this cannot be regarded as a notable exception to the general rule as decisions of the Court of Appeal are inferior to those of the Supreme Court anyway. Finally, the Court of Appeal does not have to follow its own previous decisions which have been made *per incuriam*, meaning 'through want of care', for example when taken in ignorance of some relevant legal authority. An example of a case where such a situation arose is *Bonalumi v Home Secretary* [1985] QB 675.[4]

There are now arguably additional situations in which the Court of Appeal is not bound by its own previous decisions.[5] The European Court of Justice is now firmly ensconced at the top of the court hierarchy when matters of European law are involved and when a previous decision conflicts with a provision of EU law, the CA must ignore its earlier decision in deference to the European provision.

[2] Before launching into discussion of the circumstances in which the Court of Appeal is not required to follow its own previous decisions, it is worthwhile briefly stating the importance of the court hierarchy to the operation of binding precedent and the position of the Court of Appeal within that hierarchy, and particularly that whereas the Court of Appeal is generally bound to follow its own previous decisions, the Supreme Court is not.

[3] It is absolutely essential that you refer to *Young v Bristol Aeroplane* as this is the major case.

[4] You should avoid simply listing the exceptions. Try and provide case law examples in which they have been applied. The question asks you to 'discuss' the circumstances in which the Court of Appeal may depart from its own previous decisions, so you should try and comment on their significance or the extent to which they increase the flexibility afforded the Court of Appeal.

[5] You should make sure your answer takes account of post-*Bristol Aeroplane* developments by referring to the obvious impact of European law and possible influence of the Human Rights Act on the ability of the Court of Appeal to depart from its own previous decisions.

Section 2 of the Human Rights Act 1998 requires domestic courts to take account of the jurisprudence of the European Court of Human Rights. It does not make decisions of the Strasbourg institutions binding upon domestic courts, but they are likely over time to impact upon domestic judicial decision-making on matters which give rise to issues under the Human Rights Act. It was also held in *R (Kadhim)* v *Brent Housing Benefit Review Board* [2001] QB 955 that the Civil Division is not bound by its own previous decisions where an earlier Court of Appeal assumed a proposition of law to exist which was not subject to consideration by that court.

Although the exceptions set out in *Young* v *Bristol Aeroplane* [1944] KB 718, apply to both Civil and Criminal Divisions of the Court of Appeal, a more flexible approach is taken to the application of its own previous precedents by the Criminal Division, due to the fact that individual liberty is often at stake in criminal cases.[6] The Criminal Division stated clearly in *R* v *Spencer* [1985] 1 All ER 673, that it need not adhere to past precedent as rigidly as the Civil Division and would depart from its own decisions when an individual's liberty is at stake. This more flexible approach is likely to be strengthened as a result of the incorporation of the ECHR into domestic law, which enshrines the right to liberty in Article 5. At the same time, it has increased uncertainty in the criminal law.

Although there is some scope for the Court of Appeal to depart from its own previous decisions, this is relatively limited when its position is contrasted to that of the Supreme Court. The result of the **1966 Practice Statement** is that the Supreme Court is free to depart from its own previous decisions when it considers it appropriate to do so. There have been strong suggestions that the Court of Appeal should enjoy similar flexibility. Lord Denning, in particular, led a campaign to assert the same power for the CA, but the then House of Lords maintained in cases such as *Davis* v *Johnson* [1978] 2 WLR 553, that the Court of Appeal remained generally bound by its own previous decisions.[7] An objection to conceding such power to the Court of Appeal is that it may place it on a par with the Supreme Court, undermining the latter's status as the superior court in the country, or weaken the system of binding precedent. However, a strong argument for extending the same freedom to the Court of Appeal lies in the fact that in most cases, the CA is the final appeal court, with very few cases reaching the Supreme Court. Given that a

[6] The Criminal Division of the Court of Appeal enjoys greater flexibility to depart from its past decisions than the Civil Division. You should demonstrate that you are aware of this.

[7] The question also asks you to consider whether the Court of Appeal should enjoy the same freedom to avoid past precedent as the Supreme Court. You should provide some context to this debate.

major reason put forward in the **1966 Practice Statement** for allowing the then House of Lords to depart from its own precedent was that rigid adherence to precedent could lead to injustice, it is arguably sensible to apply the same logic in extending this flexibility to the Court of Appeal, given that few cases heard by it will have an opportunity to be heard in the Supreme Court. Furthermore, the Supreme Court's status within the court hierarchy would remain unaffected as its decisions would remain binding on the Court of Appeal and an ultimate right of appeal would lie to the Supreme Court.[8]

[8] Conclude by evaluating the arguments concerning whether the Court of Appeal should have the same freedom as the Supreme Court and answering the question directly: should it? Why/why not?

 **Make your answer stand out**

- Use case law examples where appropriate of situations in which the Court of Appeal has applied the exceptions to the rule obliging it to follow its own previous decisions.
- Point out the greater flexibility exercised by the Criminal Division of the Court of Appeal when considering whether to follow its own decisions.
- Put forward clear arguments as to whether the Court of Appeal should have the same freedom to depart from its previous decisions as the Supreme Court.
- Make reference to the campaign led by Lord Denning to loosen the restrictions placed by the doctrine of binding precedent on the Court of Appeal.

**! Don't be tempted to . . .**

- Simply explain the exceptions set out in *Young* v *Bristol Aeroplane*.
- Write an essay which is largely concerned with the court hierarchy and the Court of Appeal's place within this.

#  Question 2

Assess the extent to which judges are able to avoid applying precedent to cases before them.

# Answer plan

➡ Briefly explain the doctrine of judicial precedent and the importance of the court hierarchy to its operation.

➡ Explain when the Supreme Court and the Court of Appeal may depart from their own previous decisions.

➡ Explain the concept of distinguishing and how it empowers judges to avoid precedents.

➡ Explain other judicial techniques for avoiding unwelcome precedents.

➡ Comment upon the extent to which the system of judicial precedent operates flexibly.

# Diagram plan

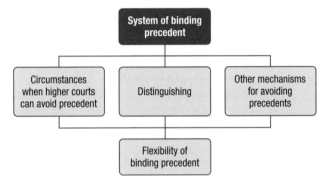

A printable version of this diagram plan is available from www.pearsoned.co.uk/lawexpressqa

# Answer

Under the system of judicial precedent, courts are ordinarily obliged to follow the decisions reached in previous cases sharing the same material facts to those of the cases before them. The hierarchy of the courts is central to its operation. Courts are bound by previous decisions of higher courts within the court hierarchy, but not lower courts. While the Supreme Court is not obliged to follow its own previous decisions, the Court of Appeal and High Court are theoretically bound by their own previous decisions subject to a number of recognised exceptions. The lower courts, while not bound by their own decisions, are bound by the decisions of the higher courts. Although a common criticism of the doctrine of judicial precedent is that it is rigid, there are various circumstances in which courts are able to avoid giving effect to precedent.[1]

[1] The introductory paragraph of the answer should briefly show that you understand what judicial precedent is, and how the court hierarchy is fundamental to its operation. This will lead nicely into the discussion to follow of the ability of the higher courts to avoid the application of precedent.

The higher courts enjoy special powers to avoid applying their own previous precedents.[2] The highest domestic court, the Supreme Court, enjoys the strongest powers to avoid being bound by past precedents. Prior to 1966, it was bound to follow its own previous decisions. However, Lord Gardiner's **Practice Statement** that year stipulated that the House of Lords would consider itself free to depart from its own previous rulings 'when it appears right to do so', thus giving it considerable scope to avoid the application of its own past precedent, which it has done in several important cases. For example, the House in *Vestey v Inland Revenue Commissioners* [1980] AC 1148 declined to follow its earlier decision from *Congreve v Inland Revenue Commissioners* [1948] 1 All ER 948, and later in *R v Shivpuri* [1987] 1 AC 1 it declined to follow a previous decision on a matter of criminal law for the first time. In another prominent case, *Murphy v Brentwood DC* [1990] 3 WLR 414, the House departed from its earlier ruling on the liability of local authorities for the inspection of building foundations, *Anns v Merton LBC* [1978] AC 728.[3]

[2] A significant part of the answer should be focused upon the higher courts because of the special position which they enjoy in terms of their ability to avoid the application of precedent.

[3] There are several examples of cases which could be cited as examples of the House of Lords (now the Supreme Court) departing from its own previous decisions. Those included here are just some possible examples that might be used.

Although in theory the Court of Appeal is generally bound to follow its own previous decisions, there are such significant exceptions to this rule as to give it considerable ability to avoid having to apply them. In *Young v Bristol Aeroplane* [1944] KB 718, Lord Greene set out three situations where the court would be entitled to depart from its own previous decisions. Firstly, when there are two previous conflicting decisions of the Court of Appeal, the court can choose which of these decisions to follow and disregard the other. The court found itself in this position in *Tiverton Estates Ltd v Wearwell Ltd* [1974] 2 WLR 176. Secondly, when a previous decision of the Court of Appeal conflicts with a later decision of the Supreme Court, the CA should not follow its earlier decision, in deference to the superior status of the Supreme Court. A case giving rise to this kind of situation was *Family Housing Association v Jones* [1990] 1 All ER 385. Finally, the Court of Appeal does not have to follow one of its own previous decisions when that decision had been made *per incuriam*, meaning the decision had been taken in ignorance of some relevant legal authority. An example of a case where such a situation arose is ***Bonalumi v Secretary of State for the Home Department***

**[4]** You are unlikely to have time to discuss further most of the case examples you cite in your answer. The main point is that you show that you are aware of actual scenarios when precedent has not been followed, and the grounds for this.

**[5]** This is a crucial point. Whereas the higher courts enjoy specific rules enabling them to avoid precedent, the concept of distinguishing is one that can be invoked by any court to avoid a decision of any court.

**[6]** You are unlikely to have sufficient time to discuss these in any detail, but should be aware of their relevance. If you are able to provide examples of any of these mechanisms being utilised by the courts, you will receive credit.

[1985] QB 675.[4]

In addition to the exceptions set out in ***Young v Bristol Aeroplane***, as a consequence of the supremacy of EU law, when a previous Court of Appeal decision conflicts with a provision of EU law, the Court will not follow its own precedent. The Civil Division is not constrained by an earlier decision where the court assumed a proposition of law to exist which was not subject to consideration by the court, as a result of ***R (Kadhim) v Brent Housing Benefit Review Board*** [2001] QB 955. Furthermore, it is important to note that the Criminal Division of the Court of Appeal takes a more flexible approach to the application of past precedents due to the fact that individual liberty is often at stake in criminal cases. As a result, it feels less restrained by its own precedents than the Civil Division. A clear statement to this effect was given in the case of ***R v Spencer*** [1985] 1 All ER 673. The divisional courts enjoy the freedom to depart from their own previous decisions in the same circumstances as the Court of Appeal (***Police Authority for Huddersfield v Watson*** [1947] 1 KB 842).

To avoid the application of precedent more generally, courts can make use of the concept of distinguishing. Distinguishing is a useful concept which potentially enables any court within the hierarchy to avoid the application of an unwelcome precedent. It usually involves a court finding that the material facts of a past decision and the present case are not sufficiently alike for the earlier decision to serve as a precedent in the present case. Any court can theoretically distinguish a decision of any other court, even if that court is higher in the hierarchy, if it can find such a distinction. For example, in ***R v Secretary of State for the Environment, ex parte Ostler*** [1977] QB 122, the Court of Appeal distinguished the earlier House of Lords decision from ***Anisminic Ltd v The Foreign Compensation Commission*** [1969] 2 AC 147. In this sense, it is the most useful tool open to the courts in general to avoid the application of precedent.[5] A court may also avoid a precedent by distinguishing an earlier decision on either a point of law or the issue to be addressed by the court, effectively proclaiming that these are not sufficiently alike in the earlier and present cases.

There are also other methods which can be employed by the courts to avoid applying precedent.[6] A court may interpret a past decision

[7] This conclusion flows logically from the preceding explanation of the circumstances in which courts can avoid the application of precedent. It shows an understanding of the implications of the various matters discussed in the essay as opposed to a simplified awareness of the rules governing the application of precedent lacking in any critical insight.

in such a way as to give it a narrow *ratio decidendi* that cannot be applied to the case before it. It may also determine that there is no clear *ratio decidendi* in the earlier case, which will be a sustainable argument in a substantial number of cases given that decisions are based upon judgments given by a number of judges who invariably place emphasis on different points in their reasoning. A court can also avoid applying an unwelcome precedent if it considers it to have been superseded by more recent precedents, to have been decided *per incuriam*, or is inconsistent with a more recent decision of a higher court which can be regarded as having implicitly overruled it.

Judicial precedent is not rigid. There are various circumstances in which particular courts may avoid binding precedent and more generally there exist tools which can be utilised by courts in general to depart from precedent when they deem it appropriate to do so.[7]

 Make your answer stand out

- Provide relevant examples from case law of situations in which courts have departed from precedent to reinforce the points you make in your answer.
- Emphasise the extent to which the various means which can be employed by courts to avoid the application of precedent make it a flexible doctrine.
- Explain clearly that the concept of distinguishing gives all courts considerable ability to avoid precedent.
- For a more sophisticated understanding of the application and avoidance of judicial precedent, read Duxbury (2008) *The Nature and Authority of Precedent*, Cambridge: Cambridge University Press and make reference to some of his arguments.

! Don't be tempted to . . .

- Focus your answer only on general tools such as distinguishing as a means of avoiding precedents, omitting consideration of the privileged position of the higher courts with respect to their ability to depart from previous precedent.
- Focus only on the position of the Supreme Court and Court of Appeal in avoiding precedent, as lower courts are able to avoid precedent also as discussion of distinguishing will demonstrate.

#  Question 3

'To remove the doctrine of binding precedent from the English common law system would be to shake the very foundations of the English legal system, which would be much weaker for its loss.' Discuss this statement.

## Answer plan

→ Briefly explain what the doctrine of binding precedent is and its centrality to the common law.

→ Discuss the purported advantages of the doctrine of binding precedent.

→ Discuss the purported disadvantages of the doctrine of binding precedent.

→ Conclude upon the likely consequences if binding precedent no longer operated within the English legal system.

## Diagram plan

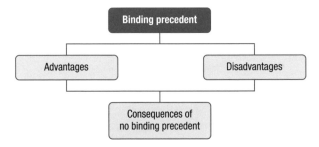

A printable version of this diagram plan is available from www.pearsoned.co.uk/lawexpressqa

## Answer

The doctrine of binding precedent is restricted to common law legal systems, yet is integral to their operation. Being that body of law found in the decisions of the courts, common law depends for its application and development upon the ability of judges to locate and follow the decisions reached by courts in previous cases sharing the same material facts as those of the cases currently before them. The doctrine of binding precedent operates by reference to the hierarchy of the courts,[1] which generally means that courts are obliged to follow relevant decisions of those courts which sit above them in the

[1] It is helpful at the outset to begin your answer by briefly explaining what the doctrine of binding precedent is and how it operates.

court hierarchy. It is important to note that while taken for granted within common law systems, binding precedent is alien to civil law jurisdictions.[2]

The operation of the doctrine of binding precedent arguably carries a number of clear advantages for parties to legal action, lawyers and judges alike. By following previous decisions, there ought to be consistency in the approach of the courts to cases that are alike. This promotes a sense of both formal and substantive justice in the law.[3] It would clearly be undesirable if cases that were essentially the same gave rise to different outcomes. Consistency in judicial decision-making in turn produces certainty,[4] as reference to relevant precedents will enable parties and their lawyers to predict with considerable confidence the likely outcome of litigation in most cases. This saves time and reduces costs for all participants within the legal system. Judges' time is saved as they are simply required to follow earlier rulings and would-be parties are less likely to pursue action where past decisions suggest their chances of success are slim, saving not only themselves time and expense, but the legal system in general which is not cluttered up with actions that are doomed to fail. However, critics of the doctrine of binding precedent would dispute its alleged strengths of consistency and certainty as a result of the mechanisms available to the courts for avoiding adherence to it,[5] a point to which we will return.

Binding precedent is also said to provide the development of detailed practical rules to govern the application of the law beyond the more skeletal framework laid down by statute. Whereas statutory provisions cannot contemplate every eventuality in which their correct application may arise, the common law is able to fill this gap and add flesh to the bones of statute law. For example, judges are required to interpret statutes. These interpretations state the correct position of the law, which is then uniformly and consistently applied through precedent.[6] The doctrine of binding precedent is also flexible. In order to prevent against rigidity in the common law, through techniques such as distinguishing, the courts can avoid being bound by past decisions in cases where this may be undesirable.[7] As a consequence of the 1966 **Practice Statement** [1966] 1 WLR 1234, the Supreme Court may depart from its own previous precedents when it considers it right to do so, and the Court of Appeal can avoid

[2] This is an important point. By reinforcing the fact that binding precedent is not a universal feature of legal systems, you strengthen the case for evaluating its merits.

[3] This is one of the key strengths of binding precedent. By making reference to the demands of formal and substantive justice you demonstrate clearly the importance of consistency while evidencing wider understanding of key legal concepts.

[4] Together with consistency, the perceived benefit of certainty rests at the very heart of the case for binding precedent. It is important that you make reference to it and the resulting positive benefits it brings of saving time and expense for judges, lawyers and parties.

[5] A number of the claimed disadvantages of binding precedent are reverse arguments of its purported strengths. You should demonstrate this.

[6] You should not overlook the role of binding precedent in developing detailed practical rules to supplement the legal provisions contained in statute. By referring to the practice of statutory interpretation you demonstrate awareness of ways in which this actually happens in practice.

[7] While it is important that you explain judges have methods of avoiding the application of precedent where the outcome will be undesirable, you should not enter into a detailed explanation of these. This question is not about the avoidance of precedent.

its own precedents in certain circumstances first set out in **Young v Bristol Aeroplane Co Ltd** [1946] AC 163.

The doctrine of binding precedent is not without its critics. Several of the core criticisms of the doctrine are reverse arguments of some of its alleged strengths. It is claimed that its consistency and certainty, arguably its most appealing features, cannot be too readily assumed for a number of reasons. The sheer complexity and volume of case law means that judges and lawyers cannot be aware of all relevant past decisions, making it questionable whether the outcomes of cases can be as confidently predicted as is claimed to be the case. In **R v Erskine** [2009] All ER (D) 142, the Court of Appeal actually stated that lawyers needed to carefully select the cases they referred to, or the justice system would be suffocated. The need to have regard to such a vast body of earlier cases might also mean the process of litigation is actually more costly and time-consuming.[8] Furthermore, while the ability of judges to distinguish past decisions in order to avoid the obligation to follow precedent may endow the common law with flexibility, it also casts doubt upon the certainty and consistency which the doctrine of binding precedent produces.

[8] This is a very good example which can be cited in support of the criticism of binding precedent that it depends on a complex and voluminous body of case law. It adds weight to your argument by illustrating that the courts themselves are aware of this problem.

The doctrine of binding precedent is attacked for being rigid, the need to follow past decisions allowing 'bad law' to stand unchallenged for lengthy periods of time. An often cited example is the law on marital rape; in spite of changing social and moral attitudes, it took until **R v R** [1991] 4 All ER 481 for the courts to depart from a body of past decisions which had held that a man could not commit the offence of rape within marriage.

[9] This is a very effective point. It acknowledges this criticism of binding precedent while simultaneously making the point that it is also a necessary and inevitable feature of the doctrine.

[10] You can use this case example effectively here to evidence your understanding of developments related to wider issues which the doctrine of binding precedent gives rise to, as well as dismissing one of the criticisms made of the doctrine.

It might be contended that the doctrine of binding precedent represents judicial law-making. There is some truth in this. Parliament's statutes cannot cover every eventuality and it is inevitable that the courts will have to develop the legal principles to fill gaps;[9] at least the operation of precedent ensures that this is done in a relatively consistent and certain fashion. At the same time, it has been argued that where courts create a new precedent they are making law retrospectively, as the legal principle at stake did not exist prior to the case in question coming to court. However, in **SW v UK** [1995] 1 FLR 434, it was ruled that the courts' development of the law on marital rape did not infringe Article 7 of the European Convention on Human Rights' protection against retrospective application of law.[10]

[11] This concludes the answer logically. The case for binding precedent has been made, while acknowledging its limitations, and the conclusion strikes a reasoned balance in maintaining the desirability of its operation subject to ensuring that some of its drawbacks do not undermine its core strengths.

The logic of binding precedent is clear enough: Justice requires that like cases should produce the same outcomes. In this sense, the English legal system would be much the worse for its absence. The doctrine is not perfect, as the criticisms detailed illustrate. Doubts over the merits of binding precedent arise in large part because of the various mechanisms which exist for its avoidance, calling into question its supposed key strengths. However, without these there is in turn a risk that binding precedent may be applied too rigidly, resulting in injustice. As long as binding precedent is generally followed and the exceptions to its application used sparingly, it is a valuable component of the English legal system which should be preserved.[11]

---

 Make your answer stand out

- Provide some context to your answer by explaining that binding precedent is a practice restricted to common law systems, thus showing that it is not an unquestioned feature of legal systems in general.
- Show how some of the various advantages or disadvantages of binding precedent are related to one another and not a series of mutually exclusive merits or drawbacks.
- Explain that some of the strengths of binding precedent also have the potential to operate as its weaknesses.
- Make reference to relevant case law in support of your answer.

---

! Don't be tempted to . . .

- Simply note the advantages and disadvantages of binding precedent without any further explanation.
- Assess the merits of the system of binding precedent simply by counting its various advantages and disadvantages.

---

**www.pearsoned.co.uk/lawexpressqa**

 Go online to access more revision support including additional essay and problem questions with diagram plans, You be the marker questions, and download all diagrams from the book.

# Statutory interpretation 3

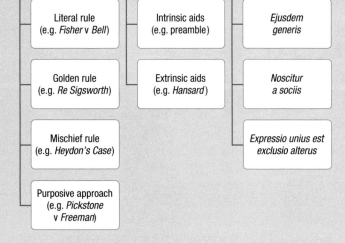

| | | |
|---|---|---|
| Literal rule (e.g. *Fisher* v *Bell*) | Intrinsic aids (e.g. preamble) | *Ejusdem generis* |
| Golden rule (e.g. *Re Sigsworth*) | Extrinsic aids (e.g. *Hansard*) | *Noscitur a sociis* |
| Mischief rule (e.g. *Heydon's Case*) | | *Expressio unius est exclusio alterus* |
| Purposive approach (e.g. *Pickstone* v *Freeman*) | | |

A printable version of this diagram plan is available from www.pearsoned.co.uk/lawexpressqa

 # Question 1

Discuss the three traditional rules of statutory interpretation used by the courts and their relative merits.

## Answer plan

➡ Explain briefly why judges need to interpret statutes and that traditionally there have been three main rules of interpretation applied by the courts.

➡ Explain, in turn, what is entailed by the literal, golden and mischief rules and give examples of their application. For each rule briefly discuss its major perceived advantages and disadvantages.

➡ Conclude on whether you consider any one rule to be superior to the others, and if so, why.

## Diagram plan

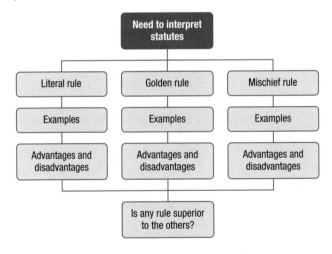

A printable version of this diagram plan is available from www.pearsoned.co.uk/lawexpressqa

## Answer

The judiciary's role is to apply laws made by Parliament. However, this is not always a straightforward task. Poor drafting of statutes may create ambiguity which the courts will need to resolve. Furthermore, language is naturally imprecise on occasion. Words may have more than one meaning and a court may need to impose

[1] It is useful to begin by explaining why judges are required to interpret statutes. This provides context to the discussion of the traditional rules of statutory interpretation.

[2] The question asks you to explain the traditional rules of statutory interpretation used by the courts. This requires that you discuss the three traditional rules of interpretation – literal, golden and mischief – and this should form the focus of your answer. You are not asked about the newer, purposive approach or rules of language and aids to interpretation, so you do not need to enter into discussion of these.

[3] Use case law examples throughout to illustrate the rules in operation. This demonstrates a sound understanding of what the rules entail and how they are applied in practice, and the citation of examples can also help to illustrate the weaknesses or strengths of the different rules.

[4] The question asks that you explain the relative advantages and disadvantages of the rules, so ensure that you are able to highlight at least one advantage and disadvantage of each rule.

one. It is not always possible to have every future eventuality in mind when drafting a statute. Sometimes draftsmen deliberately leave ambiguity in provisions in order to enable courts to tailor them to future situations that cannot yet be anticipated.[1]

Traditionally, the courts have relied on three main approaches to interpret statutes: the literal, golden and mischief rules.[2] A court may follow any approach and will not necessarily explain which it is using or why.

The literal rule requires that words are given their ordinary, grammatical meaning, even if this produces an absurd outcome. An example of the literal rule in operation is found in the case of *Fisher v Bell* [1960] 3 All ER 731. A shopkeeper was charged under the Restriction of Offensive Weapons Act 1959 with offering for sale a prohibited knife. He was acquitted as under contract law the display of an item did not constitute an offer for sale but an invitation to treat, even though the Act had been created to restrict the sale of such items. Similarly, in *Whiteley v Chappell* (1868) LR 4 QB 147, a person charged with 'impersonating any person entitled to vote' at an election was acquitted because the person impersonated was deceased, and thus not entitled to vote. These cases illustrate the major criticism of the literal rule, that its emphasis on adherence to the literal interpretation of statutes results in absurd outcomes not intended by Parliament.[3] Furthermore, words cannot be understood literally, but only in the wider context within which they are used as they often carry multiple meanings. Defenders of the literal rule argue that it respects parliamentary sovereignty by focusing upon the words used by Parliament rather than attempting to second guess its intentions in enacting the relevant provision. Furthermore, by focusing upon the literal meaning of words, the courts have less ability to interfere with the application of legislation. However, words are imprecise tools and courts will continue to need to ascertain the meaning of particular words used by Parliament.[4] The literal interpretation of just one word can yield several different outcomes, giving courts considerable discretion even using this theoretically narrow approach to statutory interpretation.

The golden rule is an extension of the literal rule and was set out by Lord Wensleydale in *Grey v Pearson* (1857) 6 HL Cas 61. Essentially the literal meaning of a provision should be applied unless producing absurdity or repugnance. The golden rule is often divided into narrow and wider meanings.[5] The former occurs when two alternative meanings can be applied to a provision, one of which will result in absurdity or repugnance. The court is to apply the meaning which will not have this effect. An example is **Adler v George** [1964] 1 All ER 628, where it was an offence to obstruct a member of the armed forces in the vicinity of designated locations. The defendant was actually caught within such a location. A literal interpretation of the provision would acquit the defendant, as he was actually in the place in question rather than its vicinity. This would be absurd given the rationale for the legislative provision. The term 'vicinity', therefore, was taken to extend to the specified place itself. The wider meaning applies when there is only one meaning to the provision which will result in absurdity or repugnance. The court may then substitute an alternative meaning. This occurred in **Re Sigsworth** [1935] Ch 89 where intestacy rules entitled the defendant to inherit the estate of his mother who he had murdered, obviously regarded as a repugnant outcome. An alternative meaning to the relevant provision was substituted so that he could not inherit. The golden rule has the benefit over the literal rule of avoiding absurd results which cannot have been intended by Parliament, by looking at the actual effect of particular interpretations. However, critics of the golden rule argue that there is no agreement on what constitutes absurdity. This may be so to some extent, but it would be difficult to argue with decisions in cases such as **Adler v George** and **Re Sigsworth**, where the application of the literal rule would clearly have produced undesirable outcomes.

The mischief rule originates from **Heydon's Case** (1584) 3 Co Rep 7a. The court is directed to ask four questions to ascertain the state of the common law before the enactment of the statutory provision, the mischief in the common law which the statute sought to remedy, the remedy for this mischief provided by Parliament and the true purpose of this remedy. The core aim is to give effect to the purpose underlying the provision. The mischief rule was applied in **Smith v Hughes** [1960] 2 All ER 859 where prostitutes were convicted of soliciting in the street under the Sexual Offences Act 1959. Although the statute made it an offence to solicit 'in the street', the prostitutes actually solicited men who were in the street from a window overlooking the street. The court looked towards the 'mischief' the Act

[5] It is useful to recall that the golden rule is taken as having both a narrow and wider meaning. This evidences understanding.

[6] It is often difficult to remember quotations that may be appropriate for citation in an examination answer, but credit is normally given when you are able to do so. The Law Commission's view of the mischief rule is worth remembering and quoting if you are asked to comment on its merits.

[7] In your conclusion attempt to briefly summarise the relative merits of the different rules and, if you have a view on what is the preferred rule, give it.

[8] The question does not ask you to give consideration to the newer, purposive approach to statutory interpretation. However, it is worth briefly mentioning its increased importance in your conclusion, as it would suggest that, of the traditional rules, the mischief rule comes closest to this increasingly significant approach to statutory interpretation. Should it? Why/why not?

was intended to remedy – solicitation by prostitutes – and convicted the defendants. The Law Commission in 1969 commented that the mischief rule was a 'rather more satisfactory approach' than the other two established rules.[6] It is arguably more likely to affect the legislative purpose of a statute and, therefore, avoid absurdity. However, it has been suggested that at the time of **Heydon's Case** it was much easier to ascertain the previous law and the statute's purpose due to the more minor role which statute law played. Identifying the purpose of legislation today may not always be so straightforward.

Each of the rules of statutory interpretation has its merits and drawbacks. A court may use any of the rules.[7] The literal rule may suit many non-controversial cases, but is arguably badly suited to those where it produces absurd outcomes contrary to the purpose of the statutory provision in question. The golden rule may remedy the shortcomings of the literal rule, but does not really consider the legislative purpose underlying the statute. The mischief rule is per-haps the most satisfactory approach, as it attempts to understand the purpose underlying the provision in question. Indeed, largely as a result of European influences, the courts are increasingly utilising a purposive approach to statutory interpretation which emphasises a provision's legislative purpose when interpreting it. This increasingly important approach is more closely connected to the mischief rule of the traditional approaches to statutory interpretation.[8]

 Make your answer stand out

- Use case law examples to illustrate the rules in operation and their relative merits.
- Provide a reasoned opinion on what rule of statutory interpretation is to be preferred.
- Show that you understand the connection between the mischief rule and the purposive approach.
- In considering the reasons why statutory interpretation can be problematic, particularly in an extended essay, you may find it useful to read and refer to Bennion (1978) 'Statute Law: Obscurity and Drafting Parameters', *British Journal of Law and Society*, v. 5, n. 2, 235.

> ## ! Don't be tempted to . . .
>
> ■ Simply state the rules of statutory interpretation without any consideration of their merits.
> ■ Try and cover all of the tools which make up the courts' approach to statutory interpretation – rules of language, intrinsic and extrinsic aids to interpretation, presumptions, etc.

#  Question 2

Discuss the extent to which it can be said that no external aids to statutory interpretation have been as significant as *Hansard* and the Human Rights Act 1998.

## Answer plan

→ Briefly explain why it is necessary for judges to interpret statutes.
→ Explain, with examples, what external aids to statutory interpretation are.
→ Explain when *Hansard* may be used as an aid to interpretation and comment upon its relative utility.
→ Explain how the Human Rights Act 1998 serves as an aid to interpretation and the effect of this.
→ Conclude upon the relative significance of the emergence of these aids to interpretation.

## Diagram plan

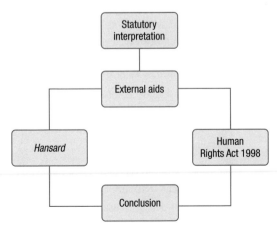

A printable version of this diagram plan is available from www.pearsoned.co.uk/lawexpressqa

# Answer

While the doctrine of the separation of powers holds that Parliament is responsible for making the law and the role of the judges is merely to apply it to the cases before them, for various reasons it is sometimes necessary for judges to interpret provisions of statutes the meaning of which is not clear.[1] The natural ambiguities of language, drafting defects, and the failure or inability of draughtsmen to foresee all future circumstances in which the legislation in question may be invoked contribute towards the need for judges to interpret statutes.

To assist them in the interpretation of statutes, judges have a number of tools which they can have regard to. These include rules of interpretation, rules of language, presumptions, and internal and external aids to interpretation. Internal aids to interpretation refer to the various parts of the statute of which a provision is being interpreted and include such things as preambles, headings and explanatory notes. By contrast, external aids refer to things not contained within the statute but which may help to ascertain the meaning of its provisions where this is not clear.[2] External aids to interpretation have long included dictionaries, textbooks, government reports and white papers, treaties, statutory instruments, the historical setting, and other statutes including the Interpretation Act 1978.

Several of these various external aids are of very limited utility.[3] For example, dictionaries may be helpful in establishing the meaning of particular words but not necessarily their use in the wider context of a statutory provision. Similarly, despite its title the Interpretation Act 1978 only provides meanings for commonly used words. Treaties may only be helpful where issues of International or European law arise. Other external aids are arguably more useful in helping judges to interpret statutes. For example, reference to a statute's historical setting or a white paper preceding its enactment may shed some light on the underlying objectives of its provisions, as may statutory instruments adopted under the Act.

Arguably, however, *Hansard* is an even more helpful external aid to interpretation.[4] *Hansard* is the official record of Parliamentary debates and until the case of ***Pepper v Hart*** [1993] 1 All ER 42 could not be referred to as an aid to the interpretation of statutes. Arguably, the decision in ***Pepper v Hart*** marked a major development

[1] Although a lengthy discussion of the reasons why judges are called upon to interpret statutes is not necessary, it is helpful to briefly explain why the need for statutory interpretation arises in order to reinforce the role of external aids in this process.

[2] You should demonstrate that you are aware of the various external aids. Although the focus of the question is on *Hansard* and the HRA, it refers to them in the context of external aids more generally. You can only assess them as external aids by making some reference to other aids as well.

[3] Building upon the previous point, while you cannot embark upon a lengthy discussion of the various external aids you should highlight some of their limitations. This will make it easier to demonstrate the significance of the emergence of *Hansard* and the HRA as external aids to interpretation.

[4] It is important that you explain when *Hansard* can be used as an aid to interpretation and explain its utility in assisting judges to identify the purpose of a particular provision. This goes to the very heart of the question. In an extended essay you might discuss how the courts have defined further the circumstances in which reference can be had to *Hansard* and any possible consequences of this.

in statutory interpretation. There, the House of Lords ruled that judges may consult *Hansard* in cases where a statutory provision was ambiguous or obscure, or its literal meaning leads to an absurdity; the material relied on consists of statements by a minister or other promoter of the bill; and the statements relied on are clear. The main rationale for permitting judges to refer to *Hansard* is that, as the official record of parliamentary debates, it may provide some evidence of the intention of government ministers or MPs introducing and/or voting for the bill in question, which is potentially helpful if doubts arise over the meaning of particular provisions. Given that judges are already exposed to media coverage of events in Parliament, the situation pre-*Pepper* v *Hart* whereby they were unable to have recourse to these in seeking to understand statutes made little sense.

The use of *Hansard* has not been without criticism. It has been contended that this adds time and expense to the process of judicial deliberation, and that while recording the statements of some ministers or MPs, *Hansard* does not necessarily evidence the intention of Parliament as a whole in voting for a statute's enactment. Nonetheless, while all external aids come with their limitations, *Hansard* comes the closest to providing evidence of the purpose of statute through the record it offers of the process by which it was made.[5] Its utility is evidenced through its citation in subsequent cases such as **Warwickshire County Council v Johnson** [1993] 1 All ER 299 and **Three Rivers DC v Bank of England** [1996] 2 All ER 363.

[5] To give a balanced treatment to the issue you should make reference to the criticisms of the use of *Hansard*. You can do so here while making the case for its strengths over other external aids to interpretation.

It is important to emphasise that the Human Rights Act 1998 was not enacted specifically as an aid to statutory interpretation. Rather, its effect is to incorporate into domestic law the substantive rights contained in the European Convention on Human Rights and to allow individuals to invoke them in any case which comes to court. Where there is an allegation that a particular statutory provision violates a convention right, the Human Rights Act provides two main mechanisms which the courts can utilise in order to resolve the matter. Although section 4 allows the higher courts to issue a declaration of incompatibility, which is effectively a judgment that the provision in question is not compatible with the convention right invoked, such a declaration can only be given if the requirements of section 3 cannot be satisfied. Section 3 imposes a duty of interpretation upon courts which requires that as far as possible they are to interpret legislation

[6] This is the key issue here. The question does not ask for general consideration of the HRA but refers to it as an aid to interpretation. Section 3 clearly aids interpretation in directing judges to approach the construction of legislation which potentially impacts upon human rights in the way specified.

[7] This is an essential point and you will receive credit for making it. There is scope for contrasting the relative difference of *Hansard* and the HRA as external aids, as both rest upon different presumptions.

[8] You can illustrate the significance of section 3 best by citing examples of cases in which the courts have successfully given effect to the duty of interpretation by construing legislation in a manner which conforms with convention rights.

[9] This is a natural conclusion to the preceding discussion which you demonstrated the different nature of the significance of the emergence of *Hansard* and the HRA as external aids to interpretation.

in a manner which ensures its provisions are compatible with convention rights.[6] Essentially, if a provision can be given more than one meaning, that which affords respect for convention rights should be applied.

The impact of the Human Rights Act as an external aid to interpretation is very different from that of pre-existing aids.[7] Whereas these can be principally seen as providing mechanisms by which courts attempt to ascertain the meaning or purpose of particular provisions, section 3 of the Human Rights Act does not purport to do this. Rather its objective is to ensure that statutory provisions are applied in a way which affords respect for convention rights irrespective of the original purpose of these statutory provisions. The courts have given effect to section 3's duty of interpretation in a number of cases.[8] For example, in *R v A* [2001] 2 WLR 1546, the conformity of provisions of the Youth Justice and Criminal Evidence Act 1999 with Article 6's guarantee of the right to a fair trial was in question. The House of Lords managed to interpret the statutory provisions so as to allow the admission of evidence considered necessary by the trial judge to make the trial fair.

It would appear that no external aids to interpretation have been as significant as the two considered specifically here, albeit for different reasons.[9] The use of *Hansard* arguably goes further than other aids in enabling judges to ascertain the underlying purpose of statutory provisions, whereas section 3 of the Human Rights Act is remarkable in placing conformity with convention rights at the heart of the interpretative function of judges where human rights issues arise.

✓ **Make your answer stand out**

■ Explain clearly the different nature of *Hansard* and the Human Rights Act 1998 in terms of their influence upon the process of statutory interpretation.

■ Illustrate the courts' approach to section 3 of the Human Rights Act through reference to case law examples.

■ Illustrate the use of *Hansard* through reference to case law examples.

■ Refer to academic commentary on the use of Hansard as an aid to interpretation, for example, Steyn (2001) '*Pepper* v *Hart*: A Re-examination', *Oxford Journal of Legal Studies*, v. 21, n. 1, 59.

# 🖎 Question 3

Discuss, with examples, the rules of language and presumptions applicable to statutory interpretation.

## Answer plan

➜ Explain that three main rules of language and a series of presumptions are used by judges in interpreting statutes.

➜ Explain the main rules of language and provide examples of their use from relevant case law to illustrate how useful they are in practice.

➜ Explain some of the main presumptions applied by the courts when interpreting statutes and provide examples of some of these being applied from relevant case law to show their significance.

➜ Conclude on the significance of the rules of language and presumptions in aiding statutory interpretation.

## Diagram plan

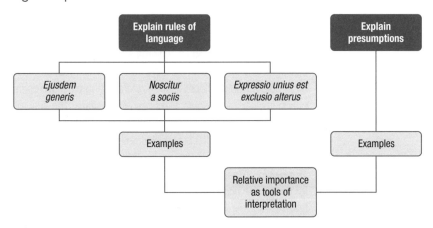

A printable version of this diagram plan is available from www.pearsoned.co.uk/lawexpressqa

## Answer

Judges use various mechanisms in order to ascertain the appropriate meaning to be given to uncertain statutory provisions. In addition to intrinsic and extrinsic aids to interpretation, judges employ three

[1] In the introduction, the wider context to statutory interpretation – of which rules of language and presumptions are a part – is alluded to. Like intrinsic and extrinsic aids, these are also effectively means of assisting judges to understand the appropriate meaning to give to statutory provisions.

[2] By providing examples you show clearly how the rules of language apply in practice, and also evidence that you are aware of the operation of these rules. Citation of relevant cases evidences both knowledge and understanding.

[3] Most of the cases concerning the rules of language being applied are not particularly widely known. You will need to ensure you have some relevant examples in mind beforehand. Knowledge of a good range of cases on this area is very impressive.

main rules of language and a series of presumptions in interpreting statutes.[1]

The first rule of language used by judges is the *ejusdem generis* rule, meaning that when words with a general meaning follow a list of specific words within a statute, those general words are to be construed to apply only to things of the same type as the specific words used. Examples illustrate the rule well.[2] In **Powell v Kemptown Park Racecourse** [1899] AC 143, the phrase 'house, office, room or other place' could not extend to an outdoor betting ring. The specific words listed were all indoors, so 'other places' was to be construed to encompass only indoor places. Similarly, in **Wood v Commissioner of the Police of the Metropolis** [1986] 2 All ER 570, a weapon was defined as 'any gun, pistol, hangar, cutlass, bludgeon or other offensive weapon'. A piece of glass could not be regarded as an 'other offensive weapon', as the specific weapons listed were all of a type designed specifically for use as a weapon, which a piece of glass was not.

The *noscitur a sociis* rule provides that a word is known by the company it keeps. Words in lists having related meanings are to be interpreted in relation to each other, so in **Pengelley v Bell Punch Co** [1964] 1 WLR 1055, a requirement that 'floors, steps, stairs, passages and gangways' be kept free from obstruction was not applicable to factory floors used for storage, the other words in the provision clearly envisaging areas used for passage. The final rule of language is the *expressio unius est exclusio alterus* rule, meaning that to express one thing is to exclude others. If a number of specific things are expressed, others are implicitly excluded. For example, in **Tempest v Kilner** (1846) 3 CB 249, a provision relating to contracts for the sale of 'goods, wares and merchandise' was taken to exclude contracts for the sale of stocks and shares by implication. Similarly, in **R v Inhabitants of Sedgley** (1831) B & Ald 65, it was held that a poor rate levied on owners of 'lands, houses, tithes and coal mines' did not apply to owners of limestone mines. The express inclusion of coal mines explicitly excluded limestone mines.[3]

A series of presumptions is made by judges when interpreting statutes. In the absence of clear evidence to the contrary, these apply. It is presumed that Parliament does not intend to alter the common law. In **Beswick v Beswick** [1968] AC 58, the House of

Lords refused to interpret section 56 of the Law of Property Act 1925 to overturn the long established common law doctrine of privity of contract, in the absence of any express intention by the statute to do so. There is also a related presumption that statutes do not intend to exclude the jurisdiction of the courts.[4] The courts have proven willing to construe provisions as far as they can to preserve their jurisdiction. Even where ouster clauses have been used, they have endeavoured to construe statutory provisions to allow judicial review, as for example in **Anisminic Ltd v Foreign Compensation Commission** [1969] 2 AC 147.

There is a series of presumptions particularly relevant to criminal law and individual rights.[5] It is presumed that a mental element (*mens rea*) is required for criminal liability. This can be rebutted by express words or implication in offences of strict liability, and the courts will consider all relevant factors. The presumption is strongest in cases of a truly criminal character. For example, in **Sweet v Parsley** [1970] AC 132 it was held that a landlord was not criminally liable for the use of cannabis by tenants in her property in the absence of any knowledge of the commission of the offence on her part. The courts will also presume that statutes do not intend to interfere with private rights or deprive individuals of their property. Wherever possible, statutes will be interpreted to respect these rights. It is presumed that statutes do not intend to deprive individuals of their liberty. If a statute is designed to deprive individuals of their liberty, clear words must be used to this effect. It is significant that, even when statutes evidence an intention to interfere with individual liberty, the courts have sought to construe the statute's provisions as narrowly as possible so as to permit only the least possible interference. This has happened in a number of cases brought under mental health legislation.

There are three further notable presumptions made by the courts. It is presumed that statutes are not intended to have retrospective effect. This reflects the ideal of the rule of law, a key principle of which is that law should only apply prospectively. However, this presumption may be rebutted by the inclusion of express words. For example, the War Crimes Act 1991 made acts committed a half century earlier criminally punishable. Statutes are not presumed to apply to the Crown unless they are expressly stated to do so or necessary implication requires this. The Crown is expressly bound by the terms of statutes such as the Occupiers Liability Acts 1957 and

[4] As there are several presumptions worth discussing, it is worthwhile to group them together. In this paragraph you explain two related presumptions. For each, again you are showing knowledge and understanding through the choice of examples provided.

[5] Again, related presumptions are tackled together with relevant examples being cited. This flows on nicely from the preceding paragraphs and the essay is being developed naturally and within a logical structure.

[6] The discussion of presumptions is concluded in the same vein as it has been tackled in the preceding two paragraphs. Throughout, the discussion has also shown how presumptions are relative concepts which can be dispensed with when there is clear statutory intention to override them. This will lead nicely into the overall conclusion to the answer.

1984, the Equal Pay Act 1970 and the Sex Discrimination Act 1975 amongst others. Finally, it is presumed that Parliament does not intend to legislate in breach of the UK's obligations in international law. However, as established in **Mortensen v Peters** (1906) SLT 227, the effect of parliamentary sovereignty is that a clear statutory provision which clashes with a provision of international law will be afforded precedence.[6]

[7] The conclusion follows naturally from the main body of the answer. The earlier discussion of rules of language illustrated through the case examples cited that these are mainly a means of understanding particular words in statutory provisions and the conclusion here reinforces that.

[8] Likewise, this concluding comment on the use of presumptions flows naturally from their discussion within the main body of the answer. They serve a valuable function without impinging upon parliamentary sovereignty.

The rules of language used by judges are clearly helpful in clarifying the meaning of particular provisions, as the examples cited illustrate. To some extent they represent a commonsense approach to interpreting statutes where the correct scope of particular words or phrases can be understood by reference to the broader provision of which they are a part. However, their value is likely to be limited to those scenarios where it is possible to understand a word or phrase by reference to the context within which they appear. This will not always be possible, for example where the meaning of an entire provision is ambiguous, and judges may need to have recourse to other aids in order to interpret it appropriately.[7] The presumptions made by judges are not absolute. They serve as a useful starting point to guard against statutes having a more radical impact than may have been intended, while still being rebuttable when the underlying aim of a statute was clearly to override a particular presumption.[8]

## ✓ Make your answer stand out

- Cite a good range of relevant examples from case law and/or statute to illustrate the rules of language and presumptions being utilised in practice and to support any points that you make.
- Emphasise the balance which the relativity of presumptions made by the courts when interpreting statutes allows to be struck between preventing against unintended radical effects of statutes, and respecting Parliament's ability to make any law it wishes when this is its clear intention.
- Demonstrate that rules of language have limited value, being applicable to words or phrases that can be interpreted by reference to the wider provision of which they are part.
- Make reference to the importance of some of the presumptions made by the courts from a human rights perspective.

## ! Don't be tempted to . . .

- Simply list the rules of language and presumptions.
- Confuse the rules of language with the well-known rules of interpretation (the literal rule, golden rule and mischief rule).

# 📝 Question 4

'Although it is now clear that *Hansard* can be referred to in order to find evidence of parliamentary intention, there is still much debate as to how useful it is', Elliott and Quinn (2010) *English Legal System* (11th edn), p. 68. Discuss.

## Answer plan

→ Briefly explain what *Hansard* is and that until the decision in *Pepper* v *Hart*, courts were not permitted to use it as an aid to statutory interpretation.

→ Discuss the main arguments in favour of and against the use of *Hansard* as an aid to interpretation.

→ Explain the decision in *Pepper* v *Hart*.

→ Consider how the courts have refined the decision in *Pepper* v *Hart* in subsequent cases.

→ Conclude upon the extent to which the courts make appropriate use of *Hansard* as an aid to interpretation.

## Diagram plan

| Hansard: pre-*Pepper* v *Hart* | → | Arguments for and against use of *Hansard* | → | Decision in *Pepper* v *Hart* | → | Case law post-*Pepper* v *Hart* | → | Conclusion |

A printable version of this diagram plan is available from www.pearsoned.co.uk/lawexpressqa

## Answer

*Hansard* is the official daily report of parliamentary debates. Prior to the decision in **Pepper v Hart** [1993] 1 All ER 42, the courts were not permitted to refer to *Hansard* in order to obtain any assistance

[1] It is useful by way of introduction to briefly explain what *Hansard* is and the traditional position in respect of its use as an aid to statutory interpretation.

with the interpretation of statutory provisions.[1] However, as courts began to adopt a more purposive approach to statutory interpretation, in which they increasingly sought to ascertain the intention of Parliament when enacting a particular statutory provision, calls grew for the prohibition on the use of *Hansard* as an aid to interpretation to be relaxed. Lord Denning especially argued strongly for the use of *Hansard* as an aid to interpretation, and indeed made use of it in *Davis v Johnson* [1978] 2 WLR 553, although he was heavily criticised for doing so by the House of Lords.

The principal reason advanced for the use of *Hansard* rests upon the assumption that allowing judges to consult debates from the time when a provision was approved by Parliament may be helpful in assisting them to clarify its intended meaning.[2] Lord Denning

[2] The quotation which you are asked to discuss is rather general and essentially raises the issue of the extent to which *Hansard* is useful in enabling judges to ascertain the parliamentary intention underlying statutory provisions. You can begin your answer by considering the main arguments advanced as part of this debate, beginning with the case for *Hansard*'s use. You may draw upon the views of judges like Lord Denning to reinforce the reasons why judges should be able to consult *Hansard*.

adopted such reasoning in *Davis v Johnson* [1978], where he commented that to ignore things said in Parliament would be to 'grope in the dark for the meaning of an Act without switching on the light'. As Lord Griffiths acknowledged in *Pepper v Hart* [1993], the courts now adopt a purposive approach when interpreting statutes. Thus, it would appear nonsensical to deprive them of the use of a key source of information to assist in understanding the purpose underlying particular legislative provisions, especially when they may consult other extrinsic aids such as government white papers and other law reform proposals. Reference to legislative debates have long been an established source for consultation by the judiciary in other jurisdictions. Furthermore, proceedings in Parliament are widely reported in the media, to which the judiciary is as exposed as anyone else. To ignore *Hansard* essentially would involve the judiciary turning a blind eye to the obvious.

However, although a prima facie case can be made for the utility of *Hansard* to judges, there are grounds to be cautious about the extent to which it assists in ascertaining the purpose underlying a particular provision.[3] *Hansard* only reveals the views of a small minority of MPs

[3] You must clearly articulate the reasons why reference to *Hansard* may not provide a reliable means of ascertaining parliamentary intention. Again, cite relevant judicial/academic opinions in considering these points.

on any one issue, and the statement of any one member can never be definitive of the views of Parliament as a whole. Even looking to the views expressed by a minister introducing a bill in Parliament has its difficulties, as it cannot be assumed that these are shared by other MPs. Furthermore, statements in Parliament do not always provide a clear perspective of the intended objective of legislative provisions, a point commented on by Lord Scarman in *Davis v*

# QUESTION 4

*Johnson* [1978], where he noted that anything said in the cut and thrust of public debate was not 'conducive to a clear and unbiased explanation of the meaning of statutory language'. A further objection to the use of *Hansard* is that it increases the time and expense spent on litigation. This was mentioned by Lord Steyn in a 2001 article (Steyn 2001), where he suggested that much of appellate courts' work is now more concerned with the interpretation of documents than examining precedents.

The House of Lords, in ruling that judges could use *Hansard* as an aid to interpretation in **Pepper v Hart** [1993], seems to have recognised that, whereas it may prove useful in some circumstances, its unrestricted use would be undesirable for the reasons discussed above. The House ruled that, for *Hansard* to be consulted, the provision in question must be ambiguous, obscure or result in an absurdity if given its literal meaning, the material relied upon must only consist of statements of the minister or promoter sponsoring the legislation, and that such statements must be clear. Thus, it could only be consulted in a limited range of circumstances, in which a clear ministerial statement would shed light on the appropriate application of an unclear provision.[4] The use of *Hansard* in this case was particularly useful as the kind of situation raised by the case had been specifically mentioned by the relevant minister at the time of the statute's passage. *Hansard* was referred to in several subsequent cases, beginning with **Warwickshire County Council v Johnson** [1993] 1 All ER 299. Its use was extended in **Three Rivers DC v Bank of England** [1996] 2 All ER 363 to cover situations where legislation itself is not ambiguous but might be ineffective in its intention to give effect to EC directives, and reference to *Hansard* may assist in determining the provision's actual purpose.

That the courts entertain doubts over the utility of *Hansard* in deciphering the intention of Parliament has become more apparent in subsequent cases where they have restricted its usage.[5] For example, in **Melluish (Inspector of Taxes) v BMI (No. 3)** [1995] 4 All ER 453, it was held that only ministerial statements at the time of the statute's passage can be considered, and not anything said subsequently about the purpose of the Act, and in **R v Secretary of State for the Environment, Transport and the Regions, ex parte Spath Holme** [2001] 2 AC 349, it was ruled that only statements pertaining to the meaning of a statutory provision could be consulted,

[4] While you need to explain the decision in *Pepper* v *Hart*, it is very important that you emphasise that the House of Lords did not permit unrestricted reference to *Hansard*. This is central to the issue raised by the question, and shows that even at this stage the courts entertained reservations over the extent to which *Hansard* provided a reliable means of identifying Parliament's intention in enacting statutory provisions.

[5] By considering some of the post-*Pepper* v *Hart* case law you are able to make connections between theory and practice in relation to the use of *Hansard*. You can illustrate effectively that the courts' restrictive approach to the extent to which judges may consult it, demonstrates that the question of its utility as a means of identifying parliamentary intention continues to influence judicial thinking.

and not those relating to matters of policy. The clear implication of recent case law is that use of *Hansard* as an aid to interpretation should be the exception rather than the rule. This was reinforced in **Wilson v Secretary of State for Trade and Industry** [2003] UKHL 40, where the House of Lords stressed that courts must be careful not to regard ministers or sponsors' statements as being indicative of the objective intention of Parliament, and that *Hansard* could only be used to interpret the meaning of words in legislation, and not the reasons for the legislation.

[6] Your conclusion should refer back to the original quotation and draw together the arguments made throughout the answer in summarising whether you agree with it or not.

In conclusion, the quotation bears much truth.[6] Whilst *Hansard* may prove very useful to courts in certain circumstances, in assisting them to interpret the underlying intention behind specific statutory provisions, there are limitations to the extent to which it can provide them with reliable means of ascertaining the purpose of a provision, and thus should not be regarded as foolproof. The problems associated with the use of *Hansard* appear to have been recognised in the approach of the courts since **Pepper v Hart**, as they have attached much caution to *Hansard's* use by restricting the circumstances in which recourse may be had to it as an aid to statutory interpretation. While it can be useful to the courts, it should not be assumed that this will always be so, hence the restrictive approach of the courts which consider its use as being exceptional rather than the norm.

✓ Make your answer stand out

- Make the connections between the theoretical debate over the merits of allowing judges to use *Hansard* to ascertain the intention of Parliament and the courts' approach to its usage in practice.

- Make comparisons between the utility of *Hansard* as an aid to interpretation and other aids to interpretation.

- Consider specifically whether *Hansard* can be taken as reflecting the intentions of Parliament as a whole when voting in favour of a bill.

- Refer, where appropriate, to the opinions of judges and/or academics upon the utility of *Hansard* in helping judges to discover the intention underlying a particular statutory provision, for example, Steyn (2001) '*Pepper* v *Hart*: A Re-examination', *Oxford Journal of Legal Studies*, v. 21, n. 1, 59.

! **Don't be tempted to . . .**

■ Focus simply on *Pepper* v *Hart* without considering how later cases have contributed to the development of the debate over *Hansard's* utility.

■ Discuss only the relative merits of *Hansard* as an aid to statutory interpretation in abstract form, without making reference to the relevant case law on the issue.

# ◢ Question 5

'The role of the judiciary may theoretically be to apply the law, but the reality is that judges in fact do also make law.' Discuss.

## Answer plan

→ Briefly explain the doctrine of separation of powers whereby Parliament makes the law and the role of judges is simply to apply it.

→ Discuss the role played by the judges in the development of the common law.

→ Discuss the ability of the judges to determine the meaning of statutes.

→ Refer to some of the most significant cases where judicial decisions have had the effect of changing the law.

→ Conclude by commenting upon whether judges make law.

## Diagram plan

A printable version of this diagram plan is available from www.pearsoned.co.uk/lawexpressqa

## Answer

According to the doctrine of the separation of powers, Parliament makes the law and the role of the judiciary is simply to apply the law to the cases which come before them. Unelected judges do not, and should not, become involved in law-making which is the constitutional

[1] In your introduction you
should make brief reference
to the traditional notion that
judges merely apply the law,
before stating that in practice
their role is much more
significant than this. This
sets the scene nicely for
the arguments to follow.

[2] This is an essential point
to make. The common law
is the most obvious example
of judges making law and
you can provide examples
of huge areas of law which
are governed by principles
developed by judges.

[3] This reinforces the
significance of judicial
decisions. Where there is no
clear legal position, judicial
rulings on the matter are
tremendously important.

[4] This builds upon the points
made above. By referring to
the considerable uncertainty
in the law, you show that
in making their rulings on
unsettled issues, judges are
effectively determining what
the relevant legal position
will be.

preserve of the democratically elected Parliament. However, notwithstanding conventional theory, the fact is that judges play a significant role in the development of the law which goes beyond simply applying an objectively definable set of legal rules to the cases before them.[1]

Much law is not actually found in statute, but rather is contained in the common law, the legal principles which have emerged from judicial decisions.[2] Considerable branches of law, for example contract and tort, consist predominantly of principles developed within the common law. Murder is also a crime found in common law. It is difficult to claim that judges play no part in law-making given the huge volume of common law which exists. The actual content of the law here is the product of judicial decisions. Through the system of judicial precedent, higher courts are able to establish legal principles which are to be followed by lower courts in similar cases, thus theoretically creating a degree of certainty within the common law and restricting the ability of judges to depart from established legal principles. In practice, however, judges have considerable flexibility to avoid being bound by precedent, in particular through the process of distinguishing cases from earlier ones. This can create much uncertainty in the common law. Often there will be no clear precedent to govern a particular issue, and a court's ruling will have the practical effect of declaring the relevant legal position for the first time. This occurred in *Airedale NHS Trust v Bland* [1993] AC 789,[3] where the House of Lords had to determine whether it was lawful to stop artificially feeding a patient in a coma. That many Supreme Court or Court of Appeal decisions are settled by narrow margins demonstrates that there is much judicial disagreement as to the correct state of the law. Often the question of 'what is the law?' on a matter will only be answered following a lengthy court process. While judges may argue that rather than 'making' law they are actually 'declaring' or 'finding' the law, the fact that much judicial disagreement exists upon the correct state of the law demonstrates that judicial decisions can have the practical effect of creating new legal rules.[4]

Even where Parliament has legislated upon a particular matter, it is naive to say that the judiciary are simply tasked with giving effect to its enactments. Statutory provisions are sometimes ambiguous or unclear in their meaning. In such cases the judiciary have to interpret their meaning. While it is often said that this process involves the judiciary attempting to discover the intention of Parliament, which would imply that the judiciary seeks to avoid playing the role of 'law-maker' when interpreting statutes, the reality is that there is a series of different approaches to statutory interpretation which a court might take with radically different outcomes in terms of a statutory provision's practical application.[5] For example, whereas literally interpreting statutory provisions may be appropriate in many cases, applying a literal approach to some statutory provisions may result in the court giving a provision an absurd meaning which Parliament clearly did not intend it to have. For example, in *Fisher v Bell* [1960] 3 All ER 731, the display of flick knives in a shop window was held not to amount to the offence of offering such weapons for sale contrary to the Restriction of Offensive Weapons Act 1959 as under principles of contract law such a display was regarded as an invitation to treat. This outcome clearly ran counter to the objectives of the relevant legislation. Although the court could argue it simply interpreted the law, the fact is that its interpretation determined how the provision in question would be applied, effectively giving it a practical application of its choosing. The courts have moved increasingly towards the adoption of a purposive approach to statutory interpretation, in which their main objective is to identify the purpose behind a particular provision. The decision in *Pepper v Hart* [1993] 1 All ER 42, to allow judges to consult *Hansard* when interpreting statutes, reinforced this. While a more purposive approach to statutory interpretation might be felt to minimise the danger of judges giving meanings to provisions at odds with their intended objectives, there remain difficulties in ascertaining the intention of Parliament, and judges nonetheless retain the discretion to use any approach to statutory interpretation which they wish. Although they may simply be interpreting the law, the approach which they choose to take will in practice determine what the law is understood to be.

Case law is replete with examples of situations in which the judiciary have effectively rewritten the law through their development of common law principles, particularly in order to accommodate societal changes.[6] For example, the landmark case of *R v R* [1991] 3 WLR 767 overturned a century of acknowledged precedents to establish that a man could commit the offence of rape against his wife. More recently, in *R v Dica* [2004] QB 1257, the Court of Appeal determined

[5] Be careful not to enter into a discussion of the various rules of statutory interpretation. The main point to make is that judges have some input into the practical application of statutory provisions, which may vary depending upon the particular approach which they utilise.

[6] If you have time, you could make more of this point through the provision of a greater range of examples. These highlight the landmark effects of judicial rulings upon the state of the law.

that a person could be criminally liable for recklessly infecting someone with HIV. In both cases a legal position is declared by the court which had not previously been assumed to exist, without any legislation having been enacted by Parliament to change the law. The conclusion that judges had effectively made new law here would appear difficult to rebut.

While some would argue that judges clearly make law, others would prefer to say that judges simply 'discover' the law, they ascertain its correct meaning and apply it to the cases before them. Arguably, it is not so important which of these summations of the role performed by the judiciary is accepted.[7] There is no real disagreement that judges play a significant part in the development of the law. They develop the principles contained in the common law and give practical meaning to statutes. The actual content of the law is not a clear cut matter, as the amount of non-unanimous decisions reached by the higher courts should make apparent. The decisions reached by judges ultimately tell us what the law is, and whether those judges have made or simply interpreted the law is irrelevant to those who are disadvantaged by their rulings. The reality is that judges have a huge bearing upon the law's content and practical application.

[7] This is a balanced conclusion which relates back to the quotation and reinforces the main points made in the answer.

## ✓ Make your answer stand out

- Use practical examples to reinforce your points.
- Emphasise the importance of the practical application of the law, which takes effect through judicial decisions.
- Refer to theoretical debates over the way in which judges interpret statutes.
- Read and make reference to academic commentary on judicial law-making, for example, Griffith (1997) *The Politics of the Judiciary*, London: Fontana.

## ! Don't be tempted to . . .

- Describe in detail the main principles of judicial precedent and statutory interpretation.
- Engage in more general discussion on the appropriate constitutional role of the judiciary.

# Human rights and the constitution

## How this topic may come up in exams

Examination questions pertaining to human rights are likely to test your understanding of the main features of the Human Rights Act, its manner of operation, the remedies which are available for infringements of human rights, or more specifically the impact of the Act on human rights protection in the UK. More general constitutional questions may test your understanding of the doctrine of separation of powers in relation to the role of the judiciary, executive and legislature in law-making, or may seek to assess your awareness of events of topical interest, such as changes introduced by the Constitutional Reform Act 2005.

## ■ Attack the question

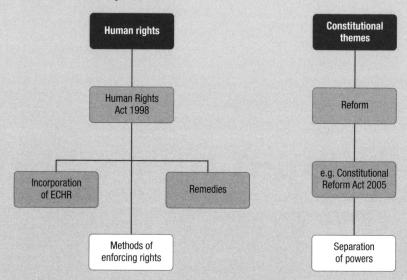

A printable version of this diagram plan is available from www.pearsoned.co.uk/lawexpressqa

#  Question 1

'Only an entrenched bill of rights can adequately protect human rights.' Discuss with reference to the limitations of the Human Rights Act 1998.

## Answer plan

→ Explain what an entrenched bill of rights is.

→ Explain the basic features of the Human Rights Act, illustrating its limitations.

→ Discuss the main strengths of an entrenched bill of rights.

→ Discuss the major problems which an entrenched bill of rights gives rise to.

→ Conclude upon the relative merits of an entrenched bill of rights and the extent to which the Human Rights Act model addresses some of the limitations of an entrenched bill of rights.

## Diagram plan

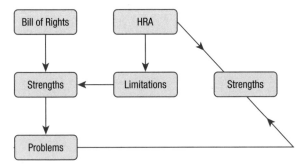

## Answer

[1] You need to explain clearly at the outset what an entrenched bill of rights is. As the question asks for some comparison with the Human Rights Act, it is essential that you can point out the distinctive features of an entrenched bill of rights. Most important is its superior status to 'ordinary' law.

An entrenched bill of rights is essentially a legal document which guarantees a series of fundamental individual rights that can be enforced by individuals against the state. Bills of rights are commonly found within the written constitutions of states, the most prominent example being that of the US Bill of Rights which forms the first ten amendments to the American Constitution. An entrenched bill of rights enjoys a status that is superior to that of ordinary law, and where its provisions conflict with those of ordinary law, the bill of rights prevails.[1] Whereas most democratic states have a written bill of rights of some form, the UK does not. Instead, protection of human rights is entrusted to the mechanism introduced by the Human Rights Act 1998.

Section 1 of the Human Rights Act incorporates within UK domestic law the substantive rights contained in the European Convention on Human Rights, and under section 6 obliges public authorities not to act in a way incompatible with any Convention rights. Section 7 then allows individuals to bring proceedings against public authorities alleging a breach of their rights under the Convention or to rely upon them in any legal proceedings. It is important to note that the Convention rights only form part of the ordinary law and are not elevated to a superior status which enables them to override other legal provisions which conflict with them. The courts have two main tools for giving effect to individual rights under the Human Rights Act.[2] Whereas secondary legislation conflicting with Convention rights can be ruled ultra vires, primary legislation cannot be invalidated by the courts. Section 3 imposes a duty of interpretation upon the courts to interpret existing legislation to conform to Convention rights as far as possible. Where this is not possible, the higher courts may issue a declaration of incompatibility under section 4. This has no effect upon the validity of the legislation in question, but the political embarrassment caused by such a declaration may result in a government deciding to amend the offending legislation through the fast-track procedure provided for by section 10.

The major limitation of the Human Rights Act lies in the fact that it affords no legal guarantee of the protection of individual rights. Legislative provisions which encroach upon Convention rights remain valid and the courts cannot override them in the name of enforcing human rights.[3] Governments remain theoretically free to enact measures which infringe human rights by virtue of their domination of Parliament and the courts have no power to intervene in such cases.

An entrenched bill of rights offers a number of theoretical advantages over the model contained in the Human Rights Act. Most importantly, it would enable the courts to properly subject the actions of government to adequate control. The bill of rights would be superior to any legislation passed by Parliament. Any legislative provisions which ran counter to the rights which it guaranteed could be struck down as invalid by the courts,[4] thus giving the courts the tools necessary to protect against any situation which might arise in which

[2] This reinforces the differences between an entrenched bill of rights and the HRA. You contrast the two models effectively by explaining the mechanisms used by the HRA for protecting individual rights.

[3] This is the main criticism of the HRA. You might explore this further, however, by considering the extent to which UK governments have failed to act upon courts' declarations of incompatibility under the HRA.

[4] This follows on from the earlier point in relation to the major limitation of the HRA. Arguably, it is the strongest argument for an entrenched bill of rights and you should say so.

[5] In strengthening this argument you might make reference to the political debates which have taken place in recent years, for example the Conservative Party's call for the HRA to be repealed and replaced with a 'British bill of rights'.

[6] This is an argument which you might explore further in an extended essay by reference to material concerning the role of the judiciary more generally, thus demonstrating an ability to link different topics within the ELS syllabus.

[7] You can reinforce this point by referring to some examples of political divisions underpinning US Supreme Court decisions, for example the 2000 *Bush* v *Gore* decision which effectively decided the outcome of that year's Presidential election. It is, however, also useful to query the extent to which the US model provides pointers for elsewhere given the different experiences of many other countries which have entrenched bills of rights.

[8] You usefully illustrate this point with a practical example. You might consider, however, in an extended essay how at the same time rights are capable of evolution notwithstanding the existence of an entrenched bill of rights. Examples from the US such as segregation and abortion can be used to illustrate this point.

[9] Within the context of the English legal system, this is arguably the key criticism of the introduction of an entrenched bill of rights. You can make this point more effectively by detailing further the meaning and operation of the doctrine of parliamentary sovereignty.

government embarked upon a series of repressive measures. Secondly, the protection of human rights would no longer be dependent upon political considerations. Currently, Parliament can legislate in violation of convention rights and even where a court issues a declaration of incompatibility, whether a government chooses to remedy the offending provision is a decision which will rest upon political factors. Under an entrenched bill of rights, the protection of human rights would depend solely upon legal considerations on the part of the courts.[5] Finally, it has been suggested by the likes of Griffith that the courts in the UK have traditionally adopted a deferential stance towards governments in judicial review cases. The introduction of an entrenched bill of rights would arguably raise the status of the UK judiciary and would empower them to take a more robust stance in holding government to account through the role which it would play in the enforcement of human rights.[6]

However, notwithstanding its apparent advantages, there are clear practical difficulties associated with an entrenched bill of rights. Firstly, there is a risk that it serves to politicise the judiciary by empowering them to strike down legislation made by a democratically elected legislature. Although they theoretically make judgements on legal grounds, one only has to look at the experience of the US Supreme Court, the members of which are chosen by Presidents for their perspectives upon major constitutional questions.[7] It can be reasonably argued, however, that the American situation is relatively unusual in terms of the profiles enjoyed by its most senior judges. The senior judiciary in most states is far more low key. Secondly, an entrenched bill of rights may result in the rigid application of outdated interpretations of particular rights.[8] For example, in the US judicial interpretations of the 'right to bear arms' has served as a barrier to some efforts to introduce tougher gun control legislation. It is easier for rights to evolve to meet changing societal priorities where they are not entrenched. However, the most serious practical criticism of any attempt to create an entrenched bill of rights for the UK rests upon the proposition that it would be impossible to do so under the terms of the UK Constitution. Parliamentary sovereignty means that no legal instrument can be enacted which cannot subsequently be repealed.[9] Entrenchment is simply not an option, barring some form of political revolution which gave rise to a new constitutional settlement.

[10] The conclusion relates back nicely to the question by summarising the extent to which the merits and drawbacks of the entrenched bill of rights and HRA models are effectively the reverse of one another. The conclusion is sensible in highlighting the relative insignificance of the various arguments in light of our constitutional model, evidencing ability to think critically.

To some extent the strengths respectively of an entrenched bill of rights and the Human Rights Act address the weaknesses of the other. There are clear merits to an entrenched bill of rights, not least being its empowerment of the judiciary to hold government to account for human rights violations through the power to strike down offending legislation. The problems of an entrenched bill of rights are often advanced based upon analyses of the US experience – with particular emphasis upon controversial areas such as the right to bear arms – for which reason they may be overstated. In any event, such problems are merely academic in nature when we consider the UK's constitutional framework makes an entrenched bill of rights unviable. For all its limitations, the Human Rights Act is as strong a mechanism as can be achieved.[10] Notwithstanding the inability of judges to nullify legislation which violates human rights, the political embarrassment and resulting pressure for rectification means that it is likely to result in the protection of fundamental rights in most cases.

## ✓ Make your answer stand out

- Draw upon comparative material, for example from the US experience, in discussing the merits of an entrenched bill of rights.
- Make reference to the practical constitutional problems posed by the doctrine of parliamentary sovereignty to the feasibility of an entrenched bill of rights being introduced in the UK.
- Make reference to academic commentary on the limitations of the Human Rights Act, for example Vick (2002) 'The Human Rights Act and the British Constitution', *Texas International Law Journal*, v. 37, n. 2, 329–72.
- Make reference to academic commentary on the bill of rights debate, for example, Macklem (2006) 'Entrenching Bills of Rights', *Oxford Journal of Legal Studies*, v. 26, n. 1, 107–29.

## ! Don't be tempted to . . .

- Enter into a lengthy description of the provisions of the Human Rights Act and case law brought under the Act.
- Base your answer around a simple critique of the US Bill of Rights, neglecting to make reference to the Human Rights Act.

# 🔖 Question 2

Discuss the range of remedies available to an individual whose human rights have been infringed by a public authority.

## Answer plan

➡ Briefly explain that an individual may bring an action against a public authority alleging a violation of his Convention rights, or rely upon the Convention rights in any legal proceedings.

➡ Briefly explain the nature of the courts' power to award remedies under section 8 of the Human Rights Act 1998.

➡ Explain the major private law remedies which might be awarded to a victim of a human rights violation.

➡ Explain the major public law remedies which might be awarded to a victim of a human rights violation.

➡ Explain that non-judicial remedies may also be available in cases of human rights violations.

## Diagram plan

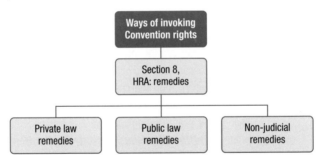

A printable version of this diagram plan is available from www.pearsoned.co.uk/lawexpressqa

## Answer

Although Parliament is not obliged to legislate in accordance with rights contained in the European Convention on Human Rights and incorporated into domestic law by the Human Rights Act 1998, an obligation is placed upon public authorities to act in accordance with these rights by section 6 of the Act. An individual who feels that his Convention rights have been infringed may initiate legal proceedings against a public authority alleging that such an infringement has

[1] Your introductory paragraph should refer to the key provisions of the Human Rights Act relating to remedies against public authorities. You should explain clearly that section 8 empowers the courts to award any remedy 'just and appropriate' to the victim of a human rights infringement, thus illustrating the wide range of remedies available in such cases.

[2] You must ensure that you give some attention to the remedy of damages as it is arguably the most significant private law remedy available for human rights violations.

[3] This is a useful point to make as it illustrates the wide range of situations in which an action constituting a human rights violation will also give rise to liability, and thus a remedy, under the civil law.

[4] To illustrate the relevance of damages it is important that you are able to explain that they are not simply available as a matter of course, but must be just and appropriate in the circumstances. Your explanation of damages as a remedy will benefit from the inclusion of examples from the case law of occasions upon which courts have awarded them or declined to do so.

taken place, or may alternatively rely upon these rights in any proceedings (section 7). Section 8 of the Act governs remedies in cases where a violation of a Convention right is found to have occurred and provides that a court may award any remedy within its powers which it considers to be just and appropriate. Thus, a wide range of remedies is available in cases of human rights infringements. Whether a particular remedy is just and appropriate in a given case will hinge upon the powers of the court hearing the case, the route through which the case has come to court and the circumstances relevant to the individual case itself.[1]

There is a series of private law remedies open to the courts to award in cases where a public authority violates a Convention right. The most relevant to human rights cases will often be the common law remedy of damages,[2] which can be awarded in any case where a civil wrong has been committed. Many actions which amount to an infringement of a Convention right will also constitute a civil wrong.[3] To give just two examples, an action constituting the tort of false imprisonment may at the same time amount to the denial of the right to liberty under Article 5 of the Convention, whereas an act which amounts to inhuman or degrading treatment contrary to Article 3 might also take the form of the tort of trespass to the person. Section 8 of the Human Rights Act does provide that damages are only to be awarded where this is necessary to afford just satisfaction to the victim of the human rights violation,[4] and the courts have emphasised in a number of cases that damages should not be simply available as a matter of course. For example, damages were not considered just or appropriate in **R (IH) v Secretary of State for the Home Department** [2003] *The Times*, 14 November, where the violation in question had already been publicly acknowledged and put an end to. By contrast, in **R (Bernard) v Enfield LBC** [2003] HRLR 4, damages were awarded for a violation of Article 8 of the Convention when the claimants had been left in unsuitable accommodation for 20 years.

Several equitable remedies are available in private law proceedings, of which arguably the most useful to victims of human rights infringements is that of injunction.[5] An injunction is essentially a court order to refrain from doing something and will be useful where a public authority intends to take an action which might amount to the infringement of a Convention right. For example, in **Doherty v Birmingham City Council** [2009] 1 AC 367, caravan dwellers

QUESTION 2

[5] There is no need to enter into any detailed discussion of most equitable remedies as most are of only minimal relevance in the context of human rights violations. Injunctions are worth mentioning, however, as they have a clear relevance which you may be able to illustrate with examples from case law.

[6] Credit should be given for your ability to mention that prerogative orders are available when a case has been brought through the route of judicial review. You are unlikely in an examination setting to have time to enter into a lengthy discussion of their utility, but if you do have time could do so with reference to cases in which they have been awarded for violations of Convention rights.

[7] The question does not restrict itself to judicial remedies. Therefore, it is highly relevant to explain that some important non-judicial remedies may be of value to victims of human rights infringements in certain circumstances.

sought an injunction to prevent the local authority from evicting them, alleging that to do so would violate their right to respect for privacy and family life under Article 8 of the Convention. Injunctions will be particularly relevant in situations where a particular infringement is taking place on a persistent basis and the most suitable means for responding to it is to prevent its continuation. Other equitable remedies are generally of less significance in the human rights context, although specific performance might be awarded where a public authority's failure to fulfil an obligation will result in the infringement of an individual's Convention rights. An award of specific performance would require the authority to fulfil its obligations, thus remedying any infringement.

Where an action against a public authority is brought by way of an application for judicial review, an additional series of public law remedies – known as prerogative orders – are available if the authority is found to have acted unlawfully.[6] A quashing order has the effect of quashing the decision of a public authority where that decision is found to be invalid. A quashing order is potentially available in any judicial review action where a public authority has made a decision which is incompatible with any Convention rights, given the obligation placed upon public authorities by section 6 of the Human Rights Act. A prohibiting order prohibits public authorities from taking decisions or actions which will amount to them exceeding their jurisdiction. It will be relevant in the human rights context where a public authority plans action which will result in it infringing upon Convention rights. By prohibiting planned action it prevents the infringement occurring in the first place. A mandatory order directs public authorities to perform legal duties. In the human rights context a mandatory order can be used to ensure that a public authority performs a duty which, if it failed to perform, would result in the infringement of a convention right.

Although the full range of judicial remedies may be made available in cases where a public authority has violated Convention rights, it is important to note that some significant non-judicial remedies are also available in certain circumstances.[7] In the context of the criminal law, statutory compensation schemes exist for both the victims of violent crime and miscarriages of justice. Where a human rights violation takes the form of a violent criminal action which causes injury to the victim, for example severe mistreatment at the hands of the police, compensation may be available under the Criminal

_ 81

Injuries Compensation Scheme. Where the violation of an individual's Convention rights results in him being wrongly convicted of a criminal offence, most commonly because the Article 6 right to a fair trial has been compromised, he may be eligible for compensation under section 133 of the Criminal Justice Act 1988 which makes compensation available to victims of miscarriages of justice. Some public authorities' functions are also subject to the jurisdiction of an ombudsman, to whom complaints of maladministration against such authorities can be referred. This is a limited form of remedy, however, as the ombudsman's powers are declaratory and recommendatory only, and do not include the power to award compensation.

Victims of human rights violations potentially can avail themselves of the full range of judicial remedies under the law, as well as a series of non-judicial means of redress. While the remedy suited to each case will vary with its circumstances, there are several means through which a just and appropriate form of redress can be afforded to the victim of a human rights infringement.[8]

[8] The conclusion flows naturally from the discussion within the answer. It was explained at the outset that potentially a victim of a human rights infringement can avail themselves of the full range of remedies under the law, and the answer has highlighted the most relevant of these.

## ✓ Make your answer stand out

- Demonstrate that victims of human rights infringements can potentially benefit from both private and public law remedies.
- Refer to some of the non-judicial remedies which may be of potential relevance to victims of human rights infringements.
- Compare situations in which remedies can effectively halt human rights infringements with those in which they are of no effect in rectifying past acts.
- Read Leigh and Lustgarten (1999) 'Making Rights Real: The Courts, Remedies and the Human Rights Act', *Cambridge Law Journal*, v. 58, n. 3, 509–45, and draw upon some of the critical insights into the remedies provided for by the Act.

## ! Don't be tempted to . . .

- Explain or refer to every judicial remedy available under the general law, as not all will be as relevant in the human rights context.
- Explain the various forms of legal action through which individuals may allege a violation of their Convention rights.

#  Question 3

'The creation of the Human Rights Act 1998 has resulted in greater conflict between the executive and legislature with the judiciary.' Assess the validity of this statement.

## Answer plan

→ Explain the limited ability of the judiciary to pronounce upon the conformity of government actions or legislative provisions with recognised human rights norms prior to the introduction of the Human Rights Act.

→ Explain the main mechanism which the Human Rights Act affords courts to rule upon the conformity of government actions or legislative provisions with the European Convention on Human Rights.

→ Discuss examples of cases where the courts have issued declarations of incompatibility, or interpreted provisions in a way which conforms to the ECHR.

→ Assess the extent to which the Human Rights Act has brought government and the judiciary into greater conflict.

## Diagram plan

Limited power of judiciary pre-HRA → Mechanism in HRA for pronouncing on conformity with ECHR → Use of declarations of incompatibility + interpretation to comply → Greater conflict?

A printable version of this diagram plan is available from www.pearsoned.co.uk/lawexpressqa

## Answer

[1] At the outset it is useful if you briefly explain the limited means available to judges prior to the HRA to rule on human rights issues. This will then reinforce the significance of the powers entrusted to the judiciary under the terms of the HRA.

Prior to the entry into force of the Human Rights Act 1998 (HRA), the UK was only bound by the European Convention on Human Rights (ECHR) in international law. As a consequence, the judiciary had only very limited means with which to pronounce upon the protection of human rights in domestic law.[1] They could have some recourse to the ECHR as an aid to statutory interpretation in light of the presumption that Parliament is presumed not to want to legislate in breach of the UK's international obligations. However, in general if government acted or Parliament legislated in a manner contrary to an ECHR provision, there was very little the courts could do.

The HRA, while incorporating the ECHR into domestic law, does not empower courts to strike down legislative provisions. It does, however, enhance the authority of the courts in human rights matters in some important respects.[2] Most significantly, while courts should try to interpret domestic legislation in a manner compatible with the ECHR as far as possible (section 3), where this cannot be achieved higher courts may issue a declaration of incompatibility. That is to say, they can proclaim legislation to be in contravention of ECHR rights. Although this has no automatic consequences, it is likely to result in pressure for reform and gives the judiciary the power to expose shortcomings by government in the human rights field. Furthermore, the courts have the power to award any of the full range of remedies where a human rights violation is found to have occurred.

[2] Before considering the extent to which the judiciary has come into conflict with the executive and legislature, you should briefly explain the powers given to judges by the HRA to rule upon the compatibility of measures with the ECHR.

The courts have proven willing to issue declarations of incompatibility in respect of a number of legislative provisions.[3] The first such instance came in *R (on the application of H) v Mental Health Review Tribunal for North and East London Region* [2001] EWCA Civ 415 where the Court of Appeal determined that sections 72–3 of the Mental Health Act 1983 were incompatible with Articles 5(1) and 5(4) of the ECHR. In *Wilson v First County Trust* [2003] EWCA Civ 633, the House of Lords declared a provision of the Consumer Credit Act 1974 to be incompatible with the ECHR, and in *Bellinger v Bellinger* [2003] 2 WLR 1174 issued a declaration of incompatibility in relation to transsexuals' rights.

[3] You should ensure that you provide examples of declarations of incompatibility issued by the courts in order to show that you are aware of instances of possible conflict between the judiciary and legislature or executive.

A notable area of conflict between courts and government has been in relation to anti-terrorism provisions.[4] Section 23 of the Anti-Terrorism, Crime and Security Act 2001 made provision for the Home Secretary to order the detention of foreign nationals suspected of involvement in terrorist activities indefinitely and without charge. The government entered a derogation under the ECHR on the grounds that the threat of terrorism constituted an emergency threatening the life of the nation. The issue came to a head in the case of *A and others v Secretary of State for the Home Department* [2004] UKHL 56, where the House of Lords declared the relevant provision to be incompatible with Article 5's right to liberty and Article 14 (non-discrimination in protection of rights) on the principal ground that it was discriminatory and illogical – any concern over the threat of terrorism would surely necessitate that the provision be applied to

[4] This is an area which you might wish to explore in greater depth, particularly in an extended piece of work on this subject. The example provided here is one of the most notable instances of the judiciary finding itself at odds with the government of the day over one of its policies due to the human rights implications.

UK and foreign nationals alike, who were both capable of terrorist activity. Furthermore, any subject of a derogation order was free to leave the country (and potentially engage in terrorism against the UK from abroad), undermining the argument that the provision was necessary to protect against the terrorist threat. Following the outcome of this case, the offending legislative provisions were replaced by the Prevention of Terrorism Act 2005 which created control orders. These gave rise to new tensions over the extent to which restrictions might be placed upon terrorist suspects, and in the case of **Secretary of State for the Home Department v JJ** [2007] UKHL 45, the orders imposed upon six suspects were judged by the House of Lords to amount to a breach of Article 5's right to liberty.

The cases referred to above would appear to indicate growing tension between the courts and government over human rights issues. However, it is very rare for a court to issue a declaration of incompatibility. Section 3 of the HRA obliges them to interpret legislative provisions to conform with the ECHR insofar as this is possible, and the broad nature of the rights protected by the ECHR gives them much scope for interpretation. In the overwhelming majority of cases brought under the HRA, the courts have either found that there is no prima facie contravention of the ECHR, or have been able to interpret the applicable legislation under section 3 in a manner compatible with the Convention.[5] For example, in **Brown v Stott** [2001] 2 WLR 817 the Privy Council held that Article 6's guarantee of a fair trial was not an absolute right and dismissed arguments that section 172 of the Road Traffic Act 1988 contravened it. Similarly, in **R v Benjafeld and others** [2001] 3 WLR 75, both the Court of Appeal and House of Lords dismissed arguments that powers of confiscation enjoyed by the state were incompatible with the ECHR.

[5] This is a very important point which you need to make in order to provide a balanced discussion. You must not focus solely on instances of conflict between the judiciary and executive or legislative, but must demonstrate that such instances are far from representing the norm.

The courts have used section 3 of the HRA in a number of cases to interpret statutory provisions in a manner which will not bring them into conflict with the ECHR. For example, in **R v A** [2001] 2 WLR 1546, a challenge was launched to restrictions placed upon the admission of certain evidence in rape trials by section 41 of the Youth Justice and Criminal Evidence Act 1999, which the House of Lords tackled by interpreting the provision in a manner compatible with the ECHR. In **Mendoza v Ghaidan** [2002] EWCA Civ 1533, the Court of Appeal used section 3 to interpret a right conferred upon partners to inherit statutory tenancies under the Rent Act 1977 to

[6] You should make reference to some instances where the courts have interpreted legislation to conform to the ECHR. There is scope to provide more detailed discussion of the cases cited in an extended piece of work.

extend to same-sex partners.[6] A final example can be found with *R v Secretary of State for the Environment, Transport and the Regions,* ex parte *Holding & Barnes plc and others* [2001] 2 WLR 1389, where aspects of the planning system were alleged to contravene Article 6's right to a fair trial. The court disagreed, finding the planning system to be entirely compatible with Article 6.

In conclusion, the statement is arguably misleading. Undoubtedly, the HRA has given the judiciary a tool with which it can rule upon the compatibility of legislative and executive actions with the ECHR, and indeed it has made effective use of its power to issue declarations of incompatibility in some prominent cases. However, through the mechanism of judicial review the courts have always been in the position of ruling upon the legal validity of government actions more generally. The HRA has not led to a flood of cases in which the courts have found the ECHR to have been breached. In fact, such findings have been very few and as some of the cases referred to illustrate, the courts attempt to find compatibility with the ECHR wherever possible, and for the most part appear to do so.[7]

[7] This is a reasoned, logical conclusion which flows naturally from the discussion contained in the essay.

## ✓ Make your answer stand out

- Refer to a range of case law in order to illustrate the courts' use of declarations of incompatibility and section 3 to interpret statutory provisions to conform to the ECHR.
- Make reference to the doctrine of separation of powers and the role of the courts in the application of the law.
- Contrast the role of the UK judiciary in enforcement of Convention rights with that of the US judiciary in enforcing the US Bill of Rights.
- Read Kavanagh (2009) 'Judging the Judges under the Human Rights Act: Deference, Disillusionment and the "War on Terror"', *Public Law*, 287–304 for some critical insights into the judiciary's approach to human rights issues which have arisen in relation to anti-terrorism legislation to which you can make reference in your answer.

## ! Don't be tempted to . . .

- Focus only on instances of cases where the courts have issued declarations of incompatibility.

#  Question 4

Discuss the significance of the major reforms introduced by the Constitutional Reform Act 2005.

## Answer plan

➜ Briefly explain that the changes brought about by the Constitutional Reform Act 2005 formed part of the government's constitutional reform agenda and are especially significant for their impact upon the separation of powers within the UK.

➜ Discuss the changes introduced to the role of the Lord Chancellor.

➜ Discuss the creation of the new Supreme Court to replace the House of Lords as the highest domestic court.

➜ Discuss the changes introduced to the judicial appointments process.

➜ Conclude by commenting upon the constitutional significance of the Act.

## Diagram plan

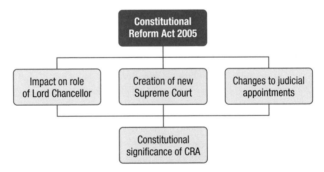

A printable version of this diagram plan is available from www.pearsoned.co.uk/lawexpressqa

## Answer

The Constitutional Reform Act 2005 formed part of the Labour government's constitutional reform agenda enacted during its first two terms in office. The Act impacts upon the court apparatus and judiciary of the UK legal system and has been of particular significance for the considerable impact which it has been perceived as having on the separation of powers in the UK. In terms of the major reforms introduced by the Act, arguably three matters are of such

[1] The introductory paragraph sets the scene for the remainder of the essay. It clearly shows what are considered to be the most important reforms introduced by the Constitutional Reform Act and provides a structure to be followed in answering the question.

significance to warrant explanation and comment.[1] Firstly, the Act impacted considerably upon the role and status of the Lord Chancellor within the judicial system. Secondly, the Act created a new Supreme Court for the UK which has replaced the Judicial Committee of the House of Lords as the final appellate court within the domestic legal system. Thirdly, the Act introduces new provisions to govern appointments to the judiciary. Each of these reforms introduced by the Constitutional Reform Act will now be considered in turn.

Prior to the Constitutional Reform Act, the role of Lord Chancellor was especially controversial due to his concurrent involvement in all three powers, through serving as a cabinet minister, speaker of the House of Lords and head of the judiciary all at the same time. He could sit in judgment upon cases brought before the Judicial Committee of the House of Lords and was also capable of exercising considerable influence on judicial appointments. One of the main concerns over the former overlapping functions of the Lord Chancellor, apart from its violation of the doctrine of the separation of powers, was that it seriously impinged upon the principle of the independence of the judiciary, considered by most constitutional scholars to constitute a core requirement of the rule of law.

[2] This paragraph effectively explains the main changes to the role of the Lord Chancellor. It is important to stress their relevance by reference to the extent to which they strengthen the independence of the judiciary.

Motivated by such concerns, the role of the Lord Chancellor is radically altered by the provisions of Part 2 of the Constitutional Reform Act.[2] While the official title of Lord Chancellor remains and is conferred upon the government minister responsible for the administration of justice, the judicial functions of the Lord Chancellor have ceased to exist. While in his capacity as a government minister the Lord Chancellor will by convention sit within the Houses of Parliament, he is no longer required to be a member of the House of Lords under section 2 of the Act. When taking upon the post of Lord Chancellor, combined with that of Secretary of State for Justice, Jack Straw became in 2007 the first MP to hold the title of Lord Chancellor. The Lord Chancellor no longer holds judicial office and has been replaced as head of the judiciary by the Lord Chief Justice, under section 7(1) of the Act. The removal of the judicial functions of the Lord Chancellor serves to reinforce the independence of the judiciary. This is underlined by provisions such as section 3 which obliges the Lord Chancellor, as well as other government ministers, to uphold the independence of the judiciary. The Lord Chancellor, even if he happens to be a member of the House of Lords, no longer holds the post

[3] This point is easy to overlook, but is worth mentioning also in the context of changes to the role of Lord Chancellor.

of Speaker within that chamber of Parliament.[3] Due to changes initiated by section 18 and Schedule 6, the members of that body now independently select their own speaker, bringing it in line with the House of Commons. This arguably reinforces the perception that although Parliament, in practice, tends to be dominated by the government of the day, it ought to retain at least some degree of independence from government.

Part 3 of the Constitutional Reform Act is concerned with the new Supreme Court for the UK, which section 23 creates. Under section 40, the Supreme Court's jurisdiction is essentially that formerly exercised by the House of Lords, serving as the ultimate appellate court for the UK.[4] Despite its name, it has no special constitutional role, in the absence of a codified constitution. The first members of the court were those serving as Lords of Appeal in Ordinary at the time of its commencement of business on 1 October 2009. Although the creation of the Supreme Court to some extent appears to have been a cosmetic exercise, given the fact that it simply takes upon a role previously exercised by the House of Lords comprised of the same judges, there is at least one notable difference. Whereas the Lords of Appeal in Ordinary, the 'Law Lords' who sat upon the Judicial Committee of the House of Lords, were also entitled to sit and vote in the legislative chamber of the House of Lords, this privilege is not afforded to members of the new Supreme Court. Section 137 provides that any judge of the Supreme Court is disqualified from sitting or voting in the House of Lords while he holds judicial office.[5] This change is notable in that it removes the overlap which previously existed between the judiciary and legislature and serves to strengthen the separation of powers model in the UK, reinforcing the independence of the judiciary from the politically driven legislative process.

[4] This is a key point to be made about the new Supreme Court. In terms of its functions, there is little to distinguish it from the House of Lords.

[5] This is an obvious significant change brought about by the Act and ought to be mentioned. It reinforces the argument made at the outset of the answer: that the act has impacted considerably upon the separation of powers and independence of the judiciary.

[6] You are unlikely to have time to explain these various provisions in any technical detail, but the important point is that you emphasise the role of the newly created Judicial Appointments Commission and relate this back to the importance of the independence of the judiciary.

There are detailed provisions in the Constitutional Reform Act concerning judicial appointments processes.[6] The main objective of these new provisions has been to strengthen the independence of appointments processes and minimise the influence of government over these. Prior to the Act, the Lord Chancellor had a huge input into decisions over judicial appointments. Appointments to the High Court and lower courts were made by the Queen on his advice, and those to the Court of Appeal and House of Lords on the advice of the Prime Minister, who acted in turn on the Lord Chancellor's advice. Section 61 of the 2005 Act created an independent Judicial Appointments

Commission which is charged with the responsibility of recommending suitable candidates to fill judicial vacancies which arise. Although the Lord Chancellor may reject the first nomination for a post, he cannot substitute his own choice of nominee or reject more than one nominee per post. Supreme Court appointments will be effectively chosen by the Lord Chancellor from a list put forward by a temporary appointments commission formed for this purpose. Although some scope remains for government influence over judicial appointments, the changes brought about by the Act clearly provide for a much greater degree of independence in judicial appointments.

[7] This is a logical conclusion which relates back to the argument advanced at the outset of the answer and which has been reinforced throughout the following discussion.

In conclusion, the major reforms introduced by the Constitutional Reform Act 2005 are of huge significance. Their impact upon the role of the Lord Chancellor, functions of Supreme Court judges and judicial appointments considerably strengthen the separation of powers within the UK and reinforce the independence of the judiciary.[7]

## ✓ Make your answer stand out

- Clearly emphasise the importance of the Constitutional Reform Act in terms of its impact upon the separation of powers and independence of the judiciary. For some critical insights on these matters, you may find it helpful to read Windlesham (2005) 'The Constitutional Reform Act 2005: Ministers, Judges and Constitutional Change, Part 1', *Public Law*, 806.
- Demonstrate a clear understanding of the situation which existed before the reforms introduced by the Act came into force, in order to reinforce its significance.
- Make reference to wider constitutional themes, such as the separation of powers and the independence of the judiciary, and relate the impact of the reforms to such concepts.
- Consider the argument that many of the changes brought about by the CRA are of greater theoretical than practical significance.

## ! Don't be tempted to . . .

- Concentrate your answer simply on the changes made to the role of the Lord Chancellor.
- Attempt to reel off numerous provisions of the Act, rather than focusing on the few most significance changes it has brought about.

# Personnel within the English legal system

## 5

## How this topic may come up in exams

Examination questions will typically require you to demonstrate an understanding of the process by which judges, solicitors and barristers are appointed or become qualified, and the main functions which they perform. Specifically, you may be asked to comment upon the composition of the judiciary or consider the case for a unified legal profession. You might also be tested on your understanding of the function of lay participants – magistrates and juries – in the legal system, their relative merits, and the process by which they are selected. You may also be asked to assess the role of the government's law officers.

# ■ Attack the question

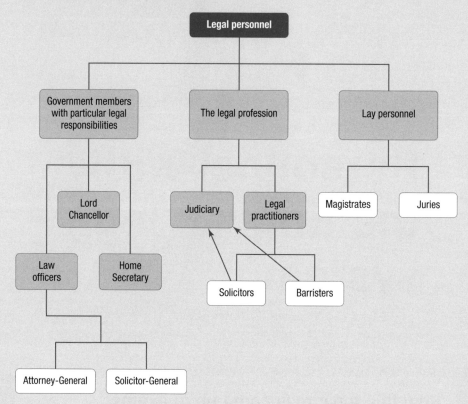

A printable version of this diagram plan is available from www.pearsoned.co.uk/lawexpressqa

#  Question 1

(A) What requirements must a candidate for the judiciary satisfy?

(B) Discuss the extent to which the current judiciary is representative of society.

## Answer plan

➡ Briefly explain how judicial appointments are made.

➡ Explain what qualifications must be satisfied by candidates for judicial posts, ensuring that you mention some of the recent reforms which have broadened the pool from which appointments must be made.

➡ Make some observations upon the current composition of the judiciary with reference to gender, race, age and background.

➡ Briefly refer to some of the initiatives which have, or may, impact upon levels of diversity among the judiciary.

## Diagram plan

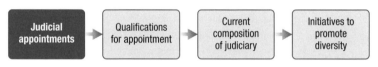

A printable version of this diagram plan is available from www.pearsoned.co.uk/lawexpressqa

## Answer

[1] Before considering the qualifications to be satisfied by candidates for the judiciary, it is helpful to briefly explain how judicial appointments are made by way of background to your answer. The role of the Judicial Appointments Commission is particularly relevant, as it has played an important role in developing some of the necessary qualifications.

The Constitutional Reform Act 2005 created the Judicial Appointments Commission, which is the principal body responsible for most judicial appointments.[1] It is responsible for soliciting applications for judicial vacancies and evaluating the merits of candidates for posts, before putting forward a nominated candidate for confirmation or rejection by the Lord Chancellor. As the Lord Chancellor may only reject one candidate for each vacant post, his role in the appointments process is clearly limited and the Judicial Appointments Commission's choice of candidates to fill vacant posts will generally stand. A more complicated process governs appointments to senior judicial posts, where temporary commissions are formed to consider the merits of candidates. For appointments to the Supreme Court, the Lord Chancellor is presented with a choice of candidates from which a vacancy can be filled. For any candidate to be considered for appointment to a judicial post, however, certain qualifications must be satisfied.

The qualifications for holding judicial office essentially fall into two categories. Firstly are those qualifications which any potential judge must be able to satisfy.[2] Under section 63(3) of the Constitutional Reform Act, judicial appointees are required to be of 'good character'. The Judicial Appointments Commission has set out guidelines which will inform its judgments upon the question of whether candidates are of 'good character'. These include consideration of the criminal convictions, insolvency history and disciplinary records of candidates. Candidates for judicial office must also be citizens of the UK, Ireland or a Commonwealth country, and be under the judicial retirement age of 70. To assess candidates for vacancies, the Judicial Appointments Commission has also identified five core qualities and abilities which are required for judicial office. These consist of intellectual capacity, personal qualities, an ability to understand and deal fairly, authority and communication skills and efficiency.

In addition to satisfying these various general qualifications, specific statutory requirements apply to each judicial post concerning the minimum degree of experience necessary for candidates seeking that particular post.[3] Until relatively recently, eligibility for appointment to judicial posts was based on the number of years during which a candidate had enjoyed rights of audience. As a result, barristers accounted for the overwhelming majority of new appointments to the judiciary. However, the Tribunals Courts and Enforcement Act 2007 made eligibility for more posts dependent upon a candidate's number of years' post-qualification experience as opposed to rights of audience.[4] Thus, more solicitors will now be eligible for consideration for appointment to judicial posts. Due to provisions of the 2007 Act, legal executives are now also able to apply for certain judicial posts, as are government lawyers. The pool of potential judicial appointees, therefore, is wider than it has ever been before. Generally speaking, a candidate for judicial office must have a minimum of five to seven years' post-qualification experience at the level for which they are seeking a judicial position. Longer minimum periods of qualification are required for appointments to the more senior judicial posts.[5]

It is widely acknowledged that the judiciary within the UK are not particularly representative of the wider society. The composition of

[2] It is useful to distinguish judicial qualifications into those which apply generally to all posts and those specific to particular posts.

[3] You need to demonstrate that different levels of experience are required for different judicial posts within the court hierarchy, in addition to the general qualifications required of all candidates for judicial office.

[4] This is a very important point to make. It shows awareness of relatively recent developments but is directly relevant to the issue of the composition of the judiciary to be addressed later in the answer.

[5] Within the constraints of an exam setting it is not necessary to describe the various minimum periods of qualification required for appointment to each judicial office. The key point is that you demonstrate that you are aware of the existence of these. You could perhaps provide an example, say, of the minimum requirements for appointment to a senior court, such as the Supreme Court or Court of Appeal.

the judiciary is regularly subject to criticism on the grounds that it is disproportionately white, male, middle-class and middle-aged. Some commentators have also called into question the political values which they feel are held by most judges. Statistically, there is little case for disputing the narrow composition of the judiciary.[6] The judiciary is overwhelmingly white. In 2004, only 3% of judges came from ethnic minority groups, despite the fact that ethnic minorities accounted for 8% of the population of the UK. The gender imbalance within the judiciary is also evident. Although the population is split approximately evenly by sex, women only held 16% of judicial posts in 2004. In terms of senior posts, they were even less well represented, holding just 9% of those positions. The narrow class background from which judges are drawn is blatantly obvious when it is considered that since 1997 approximately 80% of the holders of judicial office received a public school education. The average age of judges is 58, confirming that judges are by and large middle-aged. Having considered the statistical evidence, it is difficult to refute the commonly held perception that judges are indeed white, male, middle-class and middle-aged.

[6] You can most effectively illustrate the extent to which the judiciary is not representative of wider society through the citation of some relevant statistics.

It can be asked whether it particularly matters that the judiciary are unrepresentative of the wider society.[7] In his famous work *The Politics of the Judiciary* (1997), Griffith suggests that the narrow range of backgrounds from which members of the judiciary are drawn has resulted in the existence of a judiciary which is biased in favour of conventional and established interests, and cites a number of areas of the law where he perceives the courts as having given effect to such interests. At the same time, defenders of the judiciary would argue that, notwithstanding their unrepresentative composition, the judiciary are fiercely independent and exercise balanced judgments upon sensitive political matters. In support of this view they might make reference to various examples in the area of judicial review where the courts have held to account the actions of governments of both political persuasions. Arguably, the major concern over the unrepresentative composition of the judiciary is that it threatens to undermine public confidence in the judicial system. If the population at large are unable to relate to the judiciary because they are not perceived to reflect the diversity of the population, a resulting perception that the judiciary lacks legitimacy would not be surprising. Reinforcing such arguments, in a 2002 article concerned with the

[7] This is a relevant point to raise. If the judiciary is unrepresentative, it is worth considering briefly why this might matter before looking at how it might be made more representative.

under-representation of women in the judicial ranks, Baroness Hale argues that a more representative judiciary is necessary for imperatives associated with the promotion of equal opportunities and bolstering the judiciary's legitimacy.

[8] You should conclude your answer by briefly considering whether any steps have been taken to improve the diversity of the judiciary. At this point you can relate back to your earlier discussion of the qualifications necessary for judicial appointment, as recent changes in that respect offer some prospects of improving the diversity of those appointed to judicial office.

Some steps have been taken to improve the diversity of the judiciary.[8] Under section 64 of the Constitutional Reform Act, the Judicial Appointments Commission must have regard to the need to encourage diversity in judicial appointments. In pursuit of this, the Commission may undertake various initiatives, for example, launching campaigns to encourage under-represented groups to apply for judicial posts. The Lord Chancellor can also issue guidance on promoting diversity within the judiciary. It should not be overlooked that recent changes to necessary qualifications for appointment to judicial posts will hopefully also go some way towards improving diversity within the judiciary. By widening the pool of potential candidates, whereby more solicitors (or even legal executives) – who comprise a more diverse group than do barristers – are likely to assume judicial posts, gradually there should be more women, ethnic minorities and those with non-public school educational backgrounds holding judicial office.

✓ Make your answer stand out

- Demonstrate how the judicial appointments process has been opened up to allow for a wider pool of potential categories of people to be eligible for appointment to judicial posts.
- Make comparisons with judicial appointments processes in other countries.
- Refer to academic debates on the composition of the judiciary in considering the importance of a diverse bench, for example the discussion provided by Hale (2002) 'Equality and the Judiciary: Why Should We Want More Women Judges?', *Public Law*, 489.
- Consider how the diversity of the judiciary might be enhanced.

! Don't be tempted to . . .

- Describe in detail the minimum qualifications applicable to each single judicial post.
- Treat the two parts of the question as mutually exclusive questions.

 # Question 2

'Solicitors and barristers share in common basic legal qualifications and the fact that they work in the law. However, that is where their similarities end.' Discuss in relation to the roles performed by solicitors and barristers respectively.

## Answer plan

→ Briefly explain the division of the legal profession within the UK.

→ Explain the different routes through which solicitors and barristers qualify.

→ Explain the nature of the work undertaken by solicitors and the environment within which they work.

→ Explain the nature of the work undertaken by barristers and the environment within which they work.

→ Conclude by commenting upon the extent to which the roles performed by solicitors and barristers respectively are different.

## Diagram plan

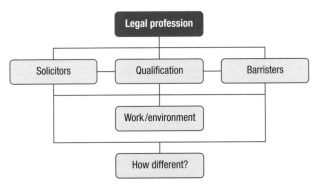

A printable version of this diagram plan is available from www.pearsoned.co.uk/lawexpressqa

## Answer

[1] By alluding to the nature of the main differences between the two professions at the outset, you set the scene nicely for the main contents of the answer to follow.

Compared to many jurisdictions the UK is somewhat unusual in lacking a single legal profession. The distinction between the roles of solicitors and barristers is of historic origin, and to this day the two professions are distinct from one another in their routes to qualification, the nature of the work they perform and the environments within which they operate.[1]

The normal route for entry to either of the legal professions begins with the requirement of either a qualifying law degree, or a degree in another subject followed by the successful completion of the graduate diploma in law (formerly known as the common professional examination). This requirement can be dispensed with in some circumstances but these are rare and exceptional. Following completion of this stage, the routes to qualification of solicitors and barristers proceed down different paths, as the quotation implies.[2]

[2] It is important that you show the similarities and differences in the qualifying routes for both professions. You are able to refer back to the question here in agreeing that in terms of qualifying routes, solicitors and barristers only share basic legal qualifications in common, after which they must pursue different paths. You should ensure that you explain both the formal qualifications and necessary training which must be satisfied by solicitors and barristers.

To qualify as a solicitor, a student must first complete the legal practice course before obtaining a training contract. The training contract is effectively the apprenticeship stage of training and involves spending two years as a trainee solicitor, ordinarily in a firm of solicitors, but the training contract might alternatively be served with a government department or public sector body. During the training contract, the trainee solicitor will gain practical experience of the work undertaken by solicitors, but will also complete several days of practical skills courses. After successful completion of the training contract, a trainee becomes a fully fledged solicitor and can apply to the Master of the Rolls to be entered onto the roll of qualified solicitors. Instead of taking the legal practice course, a person wishing to qualify as a barrister must undertake the bar vocational course. Upon completion, an aspirant barrister will need to obtain a pupillage. This is a one-year position effectively assisting a practising barrister and, as the term implies, the objective is for the 'pupil' to gain experience and understanding of the functions of a barrister by learning from the experienced 'master' barrister. Upon completion of the pupillage stage of training, the candidate is called to the bar, meaning that he is recognised as qualified to practise as a barrister. Trainee barristers must join one of the four inns of courts and must dine there 12 times before being eligible to be called to the bar. The route to qualification is clearly very different for solicitors and barristers. However, post-qualification both professions are expected to undertake continuing training and education on an annual basis.[3]

[3] This is a useful point to make as it illustrates the fact that training does not end upon qualification. If you have time you might explain in a little more detail the specific continuing professional development requirements of each profession.

It has been suggested that solicitors perform a 'general practitioner' role within the provision of legal services.[4] They are involved in the provision of all forms of legal service, covering such diverse forms of work as conveyancing, probate, drafting contracts, provision of advice to suspects in police custody, and advocacy. In practice, an individual solicitor is likely to specialise in one or a few areas of law.

[4] This is a very important point. You need to illustrate the diverse range of services provided by solicitors as this is a key factor distinguishing them from barristers.

Solicitors enjoy considerable direct contact with their clients. Most solicitors spend much of their time concerned with various forms of paperwork undertaken for private clients, with only a minority of solicitors being involved in advocacy. The traditional role of solicitors has been challenged by some key changes in recent years.[5] In 1985, solicitors lost the monopoly which they had long held upon conveyancing, this being opened up to non-solicitors. On the other hand, solicitors have seen their rights of appearance in the courts substantially increased. Although traditionally solicitors would represent defendants in most criminal proceedings, as the overwhelming majority of cases were dealt with in the magistrates' courts, barristers effectively had a monopoly on advocacy in higher courts. However, the Courts and Legal Services Act 1990 conferred greater rights of audience upon solicitors, which were then increased by section 36 of the Access to Justice Act 1999, as a result of which solicitors now enjoy full rights of audience, subject to having the necessary qualifications and training. Increasingly solicitors are now undertaking advocacy work.

Solicitors are able to form partnerships,[6] and since 2001 have been able to form limited liability partnerships, which they are increasingly doing. With the exception of a small number of solicitors working alone, solicitors invariably work within a firm of solicitors, which range from huge commercial firms in London employing thousands of staff to smaller practices where the staff number single figures. The Law Society is the professional body of solicitors, although the regulation of solicitors is now the responsibility of the Solicitors Regulatory Authority.

Unlike solicitors, barristers only undertake advocacy and related work, such as the preparation of materials for court proceedings.[7] In contrast to the perception of the solicitor as a 'general practitioner, the barrister is very much a 'specialist'. Furthermore, most barristers specialise in particular areas of law. After ten years of practice, a barrister may apply to become a Queen's Counsel (QC), a title which is used to distinguish an elite group of the most highly regarded barristers. Unlike solicitors, barristers enjoy only limited direct access to clients. Traditionally, clients are referred to a barrister through a solicitor. The ban on direct access to clients was relaxed in 2004, but direct access is restricted and is only permitted where a barrister has been in practice for three years. Barristers are bound by the 'cab rank' rule, whereby they are obliged to take on any case which they

[5] Credit should be given for coverage of this issue. By referring to some of the ways in which the traditional role of solicitors has undergone change, you evidence awareness of wider debates over the future roles of the legal profession and can refer back to this in your conclusion.

[6] The difference between solicitors and barristers is further highlighted by reference to the environments within which they work. By clearly explaining the working environment of solicitors here, you can contrast this to that of barristers later in your answer.

[7] In explaining the nature of the work undertaken by barristers, you should be able to refer back to points you have already made about solicitors to reinforce the differences between them.

are asked to unless they are already committed to another case for the time in question.

Unlike solicitors, barristers may not form partnerships. They are instead required to be self-employed.[8] However, barristers are based in premises shared with other barristers known as chambers. A barrister, once qualified, must obtain a tenancy within a chambers in order to practise. Although each individual barrister is self-employed, each chambers will have a shared clerk of chambers who will be responsible for ensuring the smooth running of the chambers and for allocating cases to barristers. The professional body of barristers is the Bar Council, with the regulation of barristers being undertaken by the Bar Standards Board.

[8] Again, you are able to contrast the working environment of barristers with that of solicitors to reinforce the major differences between the professions.

Solicitors and barristers are undoubtedly very much distinct from one another. They qualify through different routes, are regulated by different bodies, work in different environments and undertake different work. The quotation, thus, bears much truth. However, there has been a growing debate in recent years over possible moves towards a fusion of the two professions, and measures such as the granting of full rights of audience to solicitors may be taken as evidence of increasing overlap between the professions. That said, there clearly remain such significant differences between them that the creation of a unified legal profession would constitute a very radical step indeed.[9]

[9] Having considered the major differences between solicitors and barristers, it is helpful to add some context to this in your conclusion by referring to debates over possible fusion of the two professions. You can refer back to your earlier discussion of changes to the role performed by solicitors in considering the extent to which there has been some convergence between the professions.

✓ Make your answer stand out

- Make reference to the increased rights of audience now enjoyed by solicitors to illustrate the extent to which there is now greater overlap between the legal professions.

- Ensure that your answer covers not only the differences in the necessary training of, and nature of work undertaken by, solicitors and barristers, but also the different nature of their working environments.

- Consider the challenges posed to the role particularly of solicitors by the growth of alternative business structures.

- Provide greater context to your answer by reading Abel (1987) 'The Decline of Professionalism', *Arbitration*, v. 53, n. 3, 187, and making reference to the historical and social background to some of the distinctions between the two legal professions.

> **! Don't be tempted to . . .**
>
> ■ Explain the main features of the two professions without making any comparison between them.
> ■ Become sidetracked by considering the arguments over merging the legal professions.

# Question 3

Discuss the case for a merged legal profession to replace the separate status of barristers and solicitors.

## Answer plan

➜ Briefly explain the major differences between the nature of the work undertaken by barristers and solicitors.

➜ Discuss the arguments in favour of a merged legal profession.

➜ Discuss the arguments against a merged legal profession.

➜ Conclude by commenting upon whether you consider the case for a merged legal profession to be sufficiently compelling.

## Diagram plan

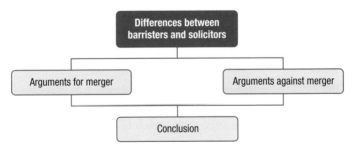

A printable version of this diagram plan is available from www.pearsoned.co.uk/lawexpressqa

[1] Begin your answer by providing some context, demonstrating the extent to which solicitors and barristers are very different in some key respects.

## Answer

The legal profession within the UK is divided into two significantly different branches, solicitors and barristers.[1] They have different routes to qualification, their working environments are different, they have their own professional and regulatory bodies and, whereas solicitors are engaged in the provision of the full range of legal services, barristers only undertake advocacy work. Notwithstanding these significant differences, there has been a growing debate over the merits of creating a single unified legal profession. Recent developments, such as the greater rights of audience afforded solicitors by the Courts and Legal Services Act 1990 and Access to Justice Act 1999, have arguably added further momentum to this debate.

[2] This is a prominent argument that you should refer to.

A major argument for creating a unified profession is that this will reduce the cost of litigation.[2] The traditional restriction upon the ability of potential litigants to approach barristers directly means that ordinarily a solicitor will be contacted in the first instance, who will probably undertake some work upon the case in hand before, when appropriate, instructing a barrister who will represent the client in court proceedings. The client is, thus, essentially required to pay two lawyers for work on the same matter. It has been suggested that the creation of a unified legal profession could minimise the costs faced by potential litigants, who would be able to approach the same person to undertake all of the work in a shorter period of time as any duplication would also be removed. It has been suggested that generally barristers are likely to be cheaper than solicitors due to the lesser overheads which they incur. However, such estimates are based upon the current differing natures of the working environments of solicitors and barristers and it is less clear exactly how more economical the services of a single legal profession would be for litigants.[3]

[3] Here you counterbalance the argument you have just considered by highlighting its possible limitations. You should do this for each argument considered in your answer, where appropriate.

[4] This argument is closely connected to the one considered previously. You should make connections between the various arguments where you can. They are not mutually exclusive.

A related argument is that the present existence of two separate professions produces inefficiency due to the unnecessary duplication of much work.[4] Prior to a barrister becoming involved in a particular case, a solicitor will already often have undertaken a considerable amount of preparatory work. Often the barrister will have actually had very little input into the case prior to the time at which it reaches court and will have to familiarise himself with all the relevant information and materials which have already been prepared and understood by the solicitor. The existence of a single legal profession would remove this duplication, as the same person who began work on the case could take it through to its conclusion in litigation. Duplication aside, it is also sometimes felt that barristers are insufficiently involved in the preparatory work for cases, meaning that they are perhaps sometimes insufficiently acquainted with a case to argue its merits in court.[5] Many clients only meet their barrister for the first time at the 'last minute', immediately before a case commences in court.

[5] This is a key point that can be drawn from the more general argument. Be prepared to try and identify these where they exist and clearly state them.

The above arguments only really apply where litigation is concerned.[6] The enhanced rights of audience afforded solicitors by the Access to Justice Act 1999 mean that increasingly solicitors will be able to steer cases to and through court litigation. A more general argument for a unified profession is that currently much talent goes to waste,[7] with law students having to choose their career path at a very early stage, potentially depriving each profession of the talents of those who have embarked upon the other career path. This argument is now harder to sustain in respect of solicitors who may be effective advocates, as it has become much easier for solicitors to take upon advocacy work that was once solely the domain of barristers. However, barristers are very much limited to advocacy work and any competences they may have for other forms of legal work currently go unrecognised and unusable. The argument can be made that other countries do not tend to divide the legal profession as the UK does, but this is hardly a good reason in itself why the UK should not do so.

[6] Here you are recognising the limitations of some of the arguments that you have considered. This demonstrates that you are taking a balanced approach to the question.

[7] Again, here is an argument that you can take and subject to a counter-argument.

It is argued that the existence of separate legal professions allows for specialisation.[8] However, solicitors are generalists in performing the full range of legal services. Whereas barristers are specialists in advocacy, the gradual extension of advocacy rights for solicitors appears to undermine the importance of specialism. In any event, even within a unified legal profession lawyers would be likely to continue to specialise in particular forms of services or areas of law, just as they do now.

[8] You are now addressing the arguments against the creation of a unified profession, yet are continuing to subject each argument to critique.

A related argument is that the importance of good advocacy demands that there be a specialist body performing this service.[9] However, there is no evidence that solicitors who currently perform advocacy are less competent than barristers. Advocates must be able to satisfy minimum periods of training and/or qualification. Within a unified legal profession there is likely to be a body of lawyers who specialise in advocacy. There is no reason why the quality of advocacy would decline.

[9] Again, you present a key argument and effectively counterbalance it with a relevant point.

It has been suggested that accessibility of advocates would be threatened by the creation of a single profession as many top barristers could move to join a few large elite commercial firms, who would dominate the advocacy market.[10] However, a market would inevitably continue to exist for more affordable advocacy services and, while access to the most high-profile advocates may be restricted by economic factors, this is arguably already the case with leading barristers being far more expensive than their lower-profile peers.

[10] Some of the arguments to be considered are based on a degree of speculation. While this may be a ground for criticism of them, you may also need to think speculatively in order to rebut or accept them.

A final argument against the creation of a single legal profession is that it may threaten the independence of advocates.[11] Barristers are bound by the 'cab rank' principle and may not form partnerships, whereas neither rule would be likely to apply to those practising advocacy as part of a single legal profession. However, this argument is overstated as barristers currently deploy certain devices to circumvent the 'cab rank' principle and thousands of solicitors employed by partnerships are gradually taking on greater advocacy rights.

[11] Here you are able to effectively rebut an argument by reference to some factual evidence, in this case the increased advocacy role undertaken by solicitors.

Strong arguments can be advanced both for and against the creation of a unified legal profession. Although the arguments in favour of retaining the status quo are not entirely convincing, many of the arguments for merger concern benefits for litigants from reduced duplication of work and costs. Reforms granting greater rights of audience to solicitors have arguably gone some way towards addressing some of these concerns and it may be asked whether there is any need to proceed to a complete merger of the professions. Given the radical step which a merger would constitute, the case for such a move needs to be more compelling than it appears to be.[12]

[12] This is a logical conclusion which relates back to the opening paragraph's explanation of the significant differences between the two branches of the profession, and the balanced discussion which followed of the various arguments over merging them.

---

 Make your answer stand out

- Add some context to your answer by highlighting at the outset the significance of the differences between the two branches of the legal profession.
- Incorporate some reference to reforms which have closed the gap between the respective roles of barristers and solicitors in the provision of advocacy services.
- Make reference to studies undertaken on the case for fusion of the professions, such as that of the Inns of Court working party (2000).
- Consider whether the emergence of a single profession is made more likely as a result of the increase in alternative business structures.

! **Don't be tempted to . . .**

- List the various arguments for and against the creation of a single unified legal profession as a series of bullet points.
- Try to cover every argument you may have read on this debate if this risks you having insufficient time to properly explain the most compelling arguments.

 **Question 4**

Discuss the main functions of those members of the government with particular responsibility for the administration of justice.

## Answer plan

→ Briefly explain who the government's law officers are and which government members have particular responsibility for the administration of justice.

→ Consider the main responsibilities of the Lord Chancellor/Secretary of State for Justice.

→ Consider the main responsibilities of the Home Secretary.

→ Consider the main responsibilities of the Attorney-General and Solicitor-General and their relationship with one another.

→ Make reference to the arguments that have been made concerning the possible politicisation of the Attorney-General's functions and proposals for reform.

## Diagram plan

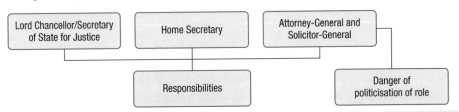

A printable version of this diagram plan is available from www.pearsoned.co.uk/lawexpressqa

# Answer

[1] You should begin your answer by stating which government members have particular responsibility for the administration of justice.

The Attorney-General and Solicitor-General are generally referred to as the government's law officers.[1] They are government members drawn from either House of Parliament and appointed by the Prime Minister. In addition to these, although many government ministers have legal functions of some form, two have responsibilities that are particularly central to the administration of justice. These are the Lord Chancellor and the Home Secretary.

[2] In explaining the functions of the Lord Chancellor, you should briefly explain the major changes that have taken place to his role relatively recently. This serves to reinforce that you understand his modern day functions by also showing what functions he no longer performs.

Historically, the Lord Chancellor's position compromised the principle of the separation of powers, him simultaneously sitting within the executive as a cabinet member, the legislature as speaker of the House of Lords, and the judiciary as its head capable of sitting on cases brought before the Judicial Committee of the House of Lords. However, the Constitutional Reform Act 2005 removed the latter two of these functions.[2] The Lord Chancellor may now be drawn from either House of Parliament, and in 2007 Jack Straw became the first MP appointed to the post. Today, the Lord Chancellor heads the Ministry of Justice and is more commonly referred to by his other title, Secretary of State for Justice. The Lord Chancellor and his ministry have overall responsibility for the operation of the legal system in general, which includes the organisation and management of the courts and tribunals, the administration of legal aid and judicial appointments.[3] The Ministry of Justice also has specific responsibility for criminal law legislation and constitutional reform. Recently, it took on responsibility for prisons and the probation service, areas which had until then been within the remit of the Home Office.[4] While the Lord Chancellor retains much responsibility for the administration of the court system, the effect of the 2005 Act is that he no longer has any judicial role.

[3] This, in essence, summarises the key responsibilities of the Lord Chancellor and the Ministry of Justice today. In an examination setting you are unlikely to have the time to embark upon a detailed discussion of any of these.

[4] This is a relevant point which evidences awareness of recent developments and leads into the next paragraph's treatment of the Home Secretary.

[5] This is the main point to be made in respect of the Home Secretary's responsibilities for the administration of justice.

Despite losing responsibility for prisons and the probation service, the Home Secretary continues to be a key governmental figure as far as the administration of justice is concerned, in particular as a result of the fact that he retains overall responsibility for the police.[5] The Home Secretary is also responsible for various crime related matters, such as government policy on drugs and the national identity card scheme. Since losing its responsibility for prisons and probation the Home Office's priorities have increasingly focused upon counter-terrorism, national security, immigration and asylum. The Home Secretary's responsibilities are very much of an executive nature and do not tread upon judicial territory.

The Attorney-General is the government's main legal adviser on both matters of domestic and international law. The Solicitor-General serves as his deputy, although since section 1 of the Law Officers Act 1997 permits the Solicitor-General to perform any of the functions of the Attorney-General,[6] the two can in practice agree upon a suitable division of labour between themselves.

As noted, the Attorney-General is the government's principal legal adviser.[7] He is responsible for advising the government upon the legal implications of government action or policy. This can occasionally lead to the Attorney-General becoming embroiled in a degree of controversy where the validity or objectivity of his advice is called into question. This occurred over the government's decision to participate in the invasion of Iraq in 2003, when the then Attorney-General, Lord Goldsmith, advised the government in a well publicised memo that there was justification under international law for the action, advice which was regarded by many as representing a U-turn from advice he had reportedly given earlier in which doubt was cast upon the legality of the government's intended course of action. The lingering assumption was that the Attorney-General changed his advice as a result of political considerations.

The Attorney-General is responsible for representing the government in major litigation, both domestically and internationally. He may also take action to restrain vexatious litigants and can intervene in the public interest in certain family and charity cases.[8] The various prosecutorial bodies fall under the oversight of the Attorney-General, most notably the Crown Prosecution Service, whose head, the Director of Public Prosecutions, is directly answerable to the Attorney-General.

The Attorney-General enjoys various specific powers in relation to the criminal justice process, which are exercised in the public interest. A varied range of offences, as diverse as those covered by the Genocide Act 1969 and the Highways Act 1980, require the Attorney-General's consent for prosecution to commence, and the Attorney-General may also grant immunity from prosecution in certain circumstances.[9] He may also intervene to stop prosecutions in certain cases. Where media coverage of a trial risks jeopardising

6 You should begin your answer by stating which government members have particular responsibility for the administration of justice.

7 This is arguably the principal function of the Attorney-General and must be mentioned. Reference to the case of Iraq is useful in demonstrating that you are aware of situations in which the Attorney-General has advised the government on controversial matters.

8 You are unlikely to have time within an examination setting to discuss in great detail the various functions of the Attorney-General. You should attempt to outline these briefly and focus upon those that are particularly interesting, topical or controversial to evidence wider understanding of the Attorney-General's role.

9 You need to make it clear that the Attorney-General enjoys specific powers in relation to the prosecution process and that you understand what the most noteworthy of these powers entail. Where possible, cite examples to illustrate situations where these powers may arise.

the right to a fair trial, the Attorney-General may bring contempt of court proceedings. Whenever there has been an acquittal in a criminal case, the Attorney-General can refer any relevant points of law to the Court of Appeal. Significantly, the Attorney-General can also appeal to the Court of Appeal against what he considers are lenient sentences handed down to those convicted of certain criminal offences. This power only applies, however, in respect of more serious offences and must be exercised within 28 days of the sentence having been imposed. The importance of this power is underlined by the fact that about 80 cases were referred to the Court of Appeal under this power during 2008 and approximately three quarters saw an increase to the original sentence.[10]

[10] Here you are focusing upon a particular power enjoyed by the Attorney-General and citing statistical evidence to illustrate its significance.

There has been some concern that some of the Attorney-General's functions may become politicised due to the fact that the post-holder is a government member.[11] For example, the need for the Attorney-General's consent for prosecution to commence in certain cases may be compromised by political considerations. If the example is taken of the police investigation into the 'cash for honours' scandal during 2006–7 in which the Prime Minister himself was questioned by police, should the Attorney-General have been presented with the decision over whether to initiate any prosecution, it would have been difficult to dispel any suggestion that his decision was politically motivated. (In the event, the police concluded there was insufficient evidence to commence any proceedings.) Controversially, in 2007 the Attorney-General decided not to sanction prosecution against BAE Systems over possible bribes to the Saudi Arabian royal family in order to procure a contract. In response to concerns over the risk of politicisation of the Attorney-General's role, the government put forward proposals in a 2008 white paper to remove his power to decide whether prosecution should proceed in individual cases except for the most exceptional and serious of matters. The Director of Public Prosecutions would become responsible for making the decision whether to prosecute in virtually all cases. Such a reform would, arguably, be welcome as it would remove any danger or perception of political considerations shaping the prosecution process and strengthen public confidence in the criminal justice process.

[11] You should conclude your discussion of the role of the Attorney-General by considering the charges which have been levelled at the possible politicisation of his role, and proposals to remove some of his powers where these may give rise to allegations of being subject to political influence. Refer to some practical examples to reinforce the issues raised.

## ✓ Make your answer stand out

- Make reference to the debate over the risk of politicisation of the role of the Attorney-General.
- Make reference to the government green and white papers, *The Governance of Britain: A Consultation on the Role of the Attorney-General* (2007) and *The Governance of Britain: Constitutional Renewal* (2008) and comment upon the possible reforms to the role of Attorney-General which they contained.
- Illustrate the functions of the personnel covered by the question by citing examples of particular measures which they have been responsible for.
- Refer to the importance of the separation of powers in relation to the roles performed by the Lord Chancellor and Attorney-General.

## ! Don't be tempted to . . .

- Attempt to explain every single responsibility of each of the personnel covered by the question.
- Interpret the question narrowly and cover only one or two of the personnel that are relevant to your answer.

# 🖎 Question 5

Explain the role performed by lay magistrates and the process by which they are appointed. To what extent are lay magistrates representative of society?

## Answer plan

➜ Explain that lay magistrates are non-legally qualified, part-time judges who preside over cases in the magistrates' courts.

➜ Outline the main categories of cases which lay magistrates hear and the limited sentencing powers which they enjoy.

➜ Explain the eligibility criteria for appointment as a lay magistrate.

➜ Explain the process by which magistrates are appointed and the training which they receive.

➜ Conclude by commenting upon the narrow range of backgrounds from which lay magistrates are invariably drawn.

# Diagram plan

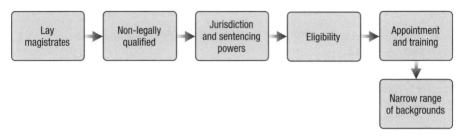

A printable version of this diagram plan is available from www.pearsoned.co.uk/lawexpressqa

## Answer

[1] Your introductory paragraph should briefly summarise the non-legally qualified, non-salaried, voluntary nature of lay magistrates. This leads into the following paragraphs' explanation of their jurisdiction and the manner by which they are appointed.

Lay magistrates are non-legally qualified, part-time judges who preside over cases heard in the magistrates' court.[1] Their involvement in the administration of justice dates back to the Justices of the Peace Act 1361. Lay magistrates are not salaried, but may receive expenses to reimburse them for costs incurred in the performance of their duties. There are approximately 28,000 lay magistrates currently sitting in about 700 different courts. They normally sit in panels of two or three, and each lay magistrate is expected to sit for a minimum of 26½ days each year. Being non-legally qualified, lay magistrates rely considerably upon the assistance of the justices' clerk, who is a legally qualified officer of the court and will advise them on any legal issues which they need further guidance upon, as well as the extent of their sentencing powers.

[2] Although you do not need to go into great detail on the jurisdiction enjoyed by magistrates, the crucial point is that you make clear that they are primarily concerned with the administration of the criminal law, in particular lower level criminal offences. This paragraph gets this point over clearly and also demonstrates an awareness of magistrates' powers as far as sentencing offenders is concerned.

Although lay magistrates have limited jurisdiction over civil matters, for example exercising licensing powers, they are primarily concerned with the administration of the criminal law.[2] All trials for summary offences are heard in the magistrates' court and it can also hear those 'triable either way' offences, listed in Schedule 1 to the Magistrates' Courts Act 1980 or contained under various individual statutes. The vast majority of criminal cases are in fact concluded in the magistrates' court. Essentially, magistrates are concerned with relatively minor offences, and approximately 50% of their time is spent on motoring offences. Lay magistrates have limited sentencing powers, although these were increased by the Criminal Justice Act 2003 to a maximum of 12 months' imprisonment for a single offence and 65 weeks where more than one consecutive custodial sentence is imposed for multiple offences. If it is felt that a particular defendant is deserving of a tougher sentence, sentencing will need to be passed over to the Crown Court where judges enjoy the full range of sentencing powers. Magistrates also have the responsibility of granting bail and issuing search warrants in certain circumstances.

[3] In explaining the process by which lay magistrates are appointed you should begin by setting out the eligibility criteria.

There are relatively few requirements to be satisfied by a person wishing to be appointed as a lay magistrate.[3] Candidates for the magistracy must be under the age of 65 at the time of appointment, although serving magistrates may continue to sit until the age of 70, they must live within 15 miles of the area for which they will serve and must be available to sit for a minimum of 26½ days annually. Although magistrates do not technically retire, they are placed upon the 'supplemental list' once they reach the age of 70 which means that they are no longer eligible to sit on the magistrates' bench. Magistrates may be dismissed earlier on certain specified grounds listed under section 11 of the Courts Act 2003, such as misconduct. In 1998 a 'job description' for magistrates was introduced, which sought to outline the qualities necessary of a magistrate. These included good character, social awareness, maturity and sound temperament, commitment and reliability. Certain categories of people are excluded from eligibility to serve as magistrates.[4] These are those whose status may lead to conflicts of interest or bias in performing the role, such as members of the police, traffic wardens, those convicted of criminal offences and bankrupts. Others are precluded from serving because their status undermines their ability to serve effectively, namely members of the armed forces and those with certain disabilities.

[4] This builds upon the previous point. It is helpful if you are able to explain briefly the rationale for such classes of people being ineligible for appointment as a lay magistrate.

[5] Local advisory committees play an important role in the appointment process and it is important that they are not overlooked in your answer. You might relate the point made here about the kinds of groups which put forward names for appointment to the lay bench to the issue discussed later of the narrow composition of the bench.

The appointment of lay magistrates is formally made by the Lord Chancellor on behalf of the Queen, under section 10(1) of the Courts Act 2003, although appointment procedures may soon fall under the remit of the Judicial Appointments Commission which was created by the Constitutional Reform Act 2005. Appointments are made following consultations with local advisory committees, the membership of which is appointed by the Department of Justice. Local advisory committees nominate candidates for vacancies.[5] In putting forward names for appointment, they are to have regard to the composition of the area for which the magistrates are to be appointed, in order to ensure a relatively representative lay bench. Local advisory committees will sometimes advertise available posts, for which various locally active groups, such as political parties, trade unions and community groups may put forward names.

[6] Although training comes upon appointment, it is worth mentioning in your answer and should receive some credit. By briefly alluding to the limited training given to lay magistrates you can reinforce their status as non-legally qualified adjudicators.

Upon appointment, lay magistrates receive relatively little training.[6] Although it is a statutory requirement under section 19 of the Courts Act 2003 that the Lord Chancellor arrange for suitable training, the training which new magistrates receive is rather basic, covering issues such as procedure, chairing hearings, jurisdiction and sentencing powers. Training places special emphasis upon the equal treatment of those who come before them in court.

A major criticism of lay magistrates is that they are drawn from a narrow sector of British society. Although there is a roughly even number of men and women sitting as lay magistrates, they do tend to be middle aged, white and come from professional backgrounds. Politically, the lay magistracy is thought to be more conservative than the population at large.[7] Arguably, more needs to be done to diversify the composition of the lay magistracy if they are to enjoy public confidence in their ability to perform their functions effectively and not be seen as 'out of touch' with the realities of everyday life experienced by others. However, it is arguable that to some extent the very nature of the lay magistrate's role can be used to account for the narrow composition of the bench. For example, older people are more likely to be retired from full-time employment and have the necessary time to devote to the work of a magistrate. Professionally employed people are also more likely to either be able to take time off work, or have retired earlier. By contrast, those employed in working-class jobs have traditionally found it more difficult to take the time off work necessary to take on roles such as that of a lay magistrate. Although there is a right to be released from work to undertake the duties of magistrate, contained in section 50 of the Employment Rights Act 1996, there is no obligation upon the part of employers to pay employees during this time, a problem more likely to affect those employed in lower-paid occupations. Although increasing the diversity of lay magistrates is not likely to be an easy task, the importance of doing so was underlined by the fact that the Auld Review (2001) made some suggestions for ways in which the composition of the lay bench may be diversified, and in 1999 a campaign was launched to diversify recruitment to the lay bench.

[7] This is a very good point on which to conclude your answer. By raising the narrow range of backgrounds from which the composition of the lay bench is drawn, you are able to indirectly raise questions about the process of appointment. Depending upon time constraints you may be able to make more of this issue and possibly make some proposals for reforms which might help to diversify the composition of the lay magistracy.

## ✓ Make your answer stand out

- Make reference to debates over the perceived narrow range of backgrounds from which lay magistrates are appointed.
- Refer to the recommendations of the Auld (2001) *Review of the Criminal Courts in England & Wales* for improving the diversity of the lay magistracy.
- Consider the merits of the functions performed by lay magistrates and whether the role of the magistracy ought to be reformed.
- Consider some of the criticisms of lay magistrates, such as the disparity in sentences handed down between different regions.

## ! Don't be tempted to . . .

- Confuse lay magistrates with District Judges, who are legally qualified full-time judges who sit in the magistrates' courts.
- Attempt to set out every individual matter over which magistrates have jurisdiction. You will not have time and it will suffice to summarise their jurisdiction more generally.

## 🖎 Question 6

Is it fair to say that there are so many exceptions to the requirement to perform jury service, and so many cases where juries are not used, that the principle of 'trial by one's peers' in criminal cases is seriously undermined?

## Answer plan

→ Briefly explain the main function of the jury within criminal trials.
→ Explain the criteria for eligibility for jury service.
→ Discuss the factors which disqualify a person from eligibility for jury service and consider how wide they are.
→ Discuss the grounds upon which exemption from jury service can be granted and consider how wide they are.
→ Consider the extent to which juries are actually used within criminal trials.
→ Conclude by providing a direct answer to the question.

# Diagram plan

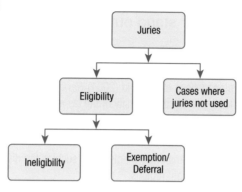

## Answer

[1] You should briefly begin your answer by stating the functions of the jury. While its official function is obvious, you should also mention its role in providing for trial by one's peers which is not only a longstanding principle of the criminal justice system but is also referred to in the question. Having set out the jury's functions you can proceed to assess the extent to which juries are utilised to fulfil these.

[2] Here you begin consideration of eligibility for jury service by stating the general position, from which you can move on to consider the exceptions to this principle.

[3] It is important to refer to the wide range of persons excluded from jury service prior to the 2003 Act as this will help you to reinforce the point that the pool of persons liable to perform jury service when summoned has actually increased considerably.

The use of a jury in criminal trials is a longstanding feature of the English criminal justice system. The jury system was described by Lord Devlin as 'the lamp that shows freedom lives' and arguably has two main functions.[1] Firstly, the official function of the jury is to determine whether the defendant is guilty or not of the offence with which s/he is charged, after having heard all evidence in the case. Secondly, the jury is widely regarded as providing an opportunity for lay participation within the legal system and enabling those accused of having committed an offence to be tried by their peers.

Eligibility for jury service is governed by section 1 of the Juries Act 1974, as amended by the Criminal Justice Act 2003. As a general rule all persons appearing on the electoral register aged 18–70 and having been resident in the UK for the previous five years are eligible to perform jury service and will be expected to do so if summoned.[2] However, while this effectively covers the entire working age adult population, the law makes provision for certain categories of person to be disqualified from serving as jurors or granted exemption.

Prior to the Criminal Justice Act 2003, several categories of people were excluded from eligibility for jury service.[3] These included mentally disordered persons, those holding certain criminal convictions or sentences, the clergy, and those concerned with the administration of justice. This latter heading was applied broadly to exclude barristers, solicitors, police officers and prison wardens from jury service. The Auld Review of the Criminal Courts (2001) suggested that the wide grounds for exclusion from jury service deprived juries of a wide range of skills and experience and recommended that disqualification from jury service should apply only to mentally disordered persons and a small number of persons with certain criminal convictions or sentences.[4] These recommendations were incorporated in the Criminal Justice Act 2003 and now only a tiny number of people are disqualified from jury service.

[4] This is very important. You directly relate your answer to the question by showing that there are now very few people who will not be expected to perform jury service, challenging one of the assertions advanced by the question asked.

Although a relatively flexible approach is taken towards the deferral of jury service to a later date to accommodate such factors as child-care commitments, pre-booked holidays and enrolment on educational courses, it is rare for a court to grant exemption from jury service altogether to someone who has been summoned. Again, post 2003 the position in this respect has been tightened so as to ensure that as small a group of people as possible can avail themselves of an exemption from jury service.[5] Prior to 2003 people employed in a range of occupations considered 'important', including doctors, nurses, Members of Parliament and military personnel, could opt out of jury service, as could anyone over the age of 65. In line with his attempt to broaden the pool of those from whom juries could be formed, Sir Robin Auld's 2001 review proposed to abolish these rights of exemption. In adopting this change, section 8 of the Criminal Justice Act 2003 only permits exemption from jury service to those who have performed it within the previous two years or are currently in military service.[6] These much narrower grounds for exemption arguably acknowledge that it may be unfair to expect someone to perform jury service on a regular basis while many others will not be summoned, and that it may be impractical to expect some serving military personnel to attend for jury service, particularly where stationed overseas. In addition, judges may grant exemption on a case by case basis where there are doubts over the ability of the juror to perform his/her role effectively, for example because of a poor grasp of the English language or a severe medical condition.

[5] This builds upon your previous point by reinforcing the reduction in the circumstances in which jury service can be avoided. In an extended essay you might say a little more about the rationale for the pre-2003 grounds for exemption and offer some critique of these.

[6] Again you show very clearly the narrow grounds which now exist for exemption. By explaining their rationale you can demonstrate their practical purpose while reinforcing the point that the current law places great emphasis upon the importance of having as wide a pool of available jurors as possible.

While it is apparent that the pool of persons who will be expected to perform jury service if requested has been widened considerably in recent years, there is some evidence to suggest that the number of criminal cases in which juries will actually be used has been reduced. It should be noted that juries are only actually used in about 1% of criminal cases. Very few criminal cases ever reach the Crown Court where juries are used. About 95% of cases are concluded in

[7] This is a crucial point to make. Although you can point to examples of the use of juries being reduced through enactments such as section 44 of the Criminal Justice Act 2003, the key limitation on the relevance of juries to the criminal justice system lies in the fact that they only hear cases in the Crown Court where a defendant contests the charges brought against him/her.

[8] Here you should emphasise that the 2003 provisions have no significant bearing on trial by jury, as one reform has since been repealed and the other applies very exceptionally.

[9] The conclusion effectively answers the question directly. It has already been demonstrated that scope for exemption from jury service has been narrowed so much as to apply only rarely. Thus, it is accurate to assert that the right to trial by one's peers has actually been strengthened.

[10] This is a balanced argument to assert. While there has been little reduction in the use of trial by jury, it is true that it has never been a feature of most criminal cases coming to court for reasons you have explained.

the Magistrates' court and in most of those which do reach the Crown Court the defendant pleads guilty, removing any need for a jury.[7] The Criminal Law Act 1977, in making many offences summary only, reduced the number of cases in which juries might be used. More recently, the Criminal Justice Act 2003 prescribed two situations in which a trial in the Crown Court would take place without a jury. Under section 43, a jury could be dispensed with when the case involves complex financial arrangements, principally applying to serious fraud cases. The implication was that most jurors will not be able to properly understand the issues raised in such cases. However, section 43 was never actually implemented and was ultimately repealed by section 113 of the Protection of Freedoms Act 2012. Of greater significance is section 44 which provides that a jury shall not be used where in the opinion of the trial judge there is a serious risk of jury tampering. It is envisaged that this provision will be applied in the most exceptional of circumstances and certainly should not be regarded as leading to a considerable reduction in the use of trial by jury.[8] Section 44 was first applied in the case of *R v Twomey* [2009] EWCA Crim 1035.

In direct response to the question, two assertions can be made. Firstly, exceptions to the duty to perform jury service have been so heavily curtailed by recent reforms that, if anything, the principle of trial by one's peers has actually been strengthened.[9] In theory, the widening of the pool of eligible jurors and the reduced scope for exemption means that juries will be potentially more representative of society at large than was previously the case. Secondly, although recent changes appear to prima facie restrict the number of cases in which juries will be used, the reality is that section 44 will only apply in very few cases. The fact is that trial by jury has always only ever applied to a small proportion of criminal cases, although importantly it continues to apply in the overwhelming majority of contested trials heard in the Crown Court.[10]

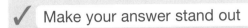

✓ **Make your answer stand out**

■ Make reference to the main recommendations of the Auld (2001) *Review of the Criminal Courts in England and Wales.*

■ Give consideration to the merits of the various former and current exemptions from the obligation to perform jury service.

■ Cite statistical evidence on the use of juries to support your arguments.

■ Make reference to academic commentary, particularly on the 2003 reforms, for example Lloyd-Bostock (2007) 'The Jubilee Line Jurors: Does Their Experience Strengthen the Case for Judge-only Trials in Long and Complex Fraud Cases?', *Crim LR*, 255.

! **Don't be tempted to . . .**

■ Enter into discussion of the merits of jury trial.

■ Describe in detail the process by which jurors are selected and summoned.

■ Confuse issues relating to eligibility for and exemption from jury service with juror vetting and dismissal.

# ✍ Question 7

Discuss the arguments for and against the abolition of juries.

# Answer plan

➡ Briefly explain the role performed by juries and refer to recent debates over their merits.

➡ Discuss the main arguments for the abolition of juries.

➡ Discuss the main arguments against the abolition of juries.

➡ Conclude upon the merits of the jury system.

# Diagram plan

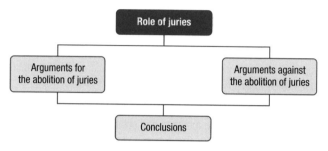

A printable version of this diagram plan is available from www.pearsoned.co.uk/lawexpressqa

## Answer

Juries are randomly selected from the electoral register and are principally used in criminal trials heard in the Crown Court, charged with responsibility for determining the guilt of the defendant.[1] There have been ongoing debates for some time as to the merits of the jury system. Sir Robin Auld's review of the criminal courts (2001) gave some attention to juries and his proposals led to the abolition of many of the previous grounds for exemption from jury service, as well as removing the need for juries to be used where a serious risk exists of jury tampering or the case involves complex financial arrangements (ss. 43–44, Criminal Justice Act 2003).

Some of the arguments that have been advanced for the abolition of juries are not particularly convincing.[2] For example, it has been claimed that it would be both cost- and time-efficient to dispense with their use. However, the counter-argument can be made that such considerations should be irrelevant to decisions over how to try cases where the interests of justice and individual liberty are at stake. It has also been argued that juries may find certain trials distressing, for example those involving offences against children. In some high profile cases, for example the James Bulger murder case, jurors have required post-trial counselling. However, such cases account for a small minority of those coming to trial and, while perhaps a reason to limit the kinds of cases which juries hear, it does not constitute a good argument for the abolition of juries *per se*. The verdicts of juries are not accompanied by any explanation, which it

[1] You should provide a little context to your answer in the first paragraph by briefly stating the principal function of jurors and referring to recent debates over the merits of the jury system. It is appropriate to focus your discussion upon the use of juries in criminal trials given that this is primarily where they are used.

[2] In discussing the arguments for the abolition of juries, it makes sense to begin with the less convincing arguments before building up to the strongest arguments, upon which you can more effectively conclude the case for abolition.

is alleged makes it difficult to formulate appeals against conviction. However, it would be impractical to expect a group of lay people to draft a reasoned justification of their findings. Furthermore, the alternative argument is that the very nature of juries' verdicts endows them with certainty and creates no risk of misunderstanding.[3]

Although the above arguments are not particularly convincing, other arguments lend greater support to the case for the abolition of juries. Jurors are lay people who will ordinarily have very little understanding of the law. As a consequence of this limited competence, many jurors may find it difficult to understand complex cases or the full nature and implications of their functions as jurors.[4] This risk was highlighted in *R v Young* [1995] QB 324, where the jury held sessions with a ouija board in an attempt to contact the victim in a murder case. The Roskill Committee (1986) concluded that in complex cases the interests of justice were not best served by jury trial. However, several studies have suggested that juries are generally capable of comprehending complex cases, for example fraud. On a related point, it has been submitted that their limited competence makes juries more prone to being influenced by others.[5] The trial judge, prosecution and defence counsel and other more vocal jurors can all potentially exert considerable influence, or even intimidation, over jurors.

Another criticism of juries is that their random, lay composition will often result in a lack of objectivity which leads to them reaching what might be regarded as perverse verdicts.[6] These arise where a jury acquits a defendant who has no defence for his actions in law, but with whom the jury has some sympathy, for example because they feel the law he has fallen foul of is an unjust one. It is a statistical fact that juries acquit a higher proportion of defendants than magistrates do, with Home Office research suggesting acquittal in jury trials is twice as likely. The biases of individual jurors may produce juries that are more sympathetic or hostile to a defendant than an objective understanding of the case would warrant. Research into acquittals by Baldwin and McConville (1979) suggested that up to a quarter of them were questionable. Although supporters of jury trial would argue that the biases of individual jurors should theoretically balance one another out, this will not always be the case as the random selection of the jury can as easily produce an unrepresentative cross-section of society as it can a representative sample. The

[3] Some of the arguments for and against the abolition of juries are opposites of one another. You should emphasise this when applicable, as here.

[4] This is one of the major criticisms of the use of juries and you must ensure that you discuss this in your answer. There are various bodies of research which you could refer to in your discussion, such as the findings of the Roskill Committee.

[5] This is another key criticism of the use of juries. You might be able to find some case examples where jurors in reaching their verdict have acted under influence exerted by others to reinforce this point.

[6] This is the final key criticism of the use of juries which you should include in your answer. Again, there are various examples of research into the area which you can cite to reinforce this point.

most recently considered arguments suggest that a fair case can be made for the abolition of the jury system. They emphasise quite clearly the limited capabilities of lay people to adjudicate properly on what may be difficult legal questions free of prejudice or influence. As will be seen, however, the ability of juries to render perverse verdicts has often been acclaimed as a virtue of the jury system.

[7] As with the criticisms of juries, you should begin your discussion of the arguments in favour of retaining juries with any arguments you consider to be unconvincing. You should ensure that you make reference to the public participation argument as it is one of the most often cited.

Defenders of the jury system maintain that it generates public participation within the legal system.[7] Trial by one's peers is a long-standing feature of the English legal system. Although research has found that most jurors have a positive experience of, and attitude towards, jury service, whether lay involvement in the legal system is particularly beneficial is debatable given some of the perceived weaknesses of the jury system referred to above and the highly important task with which they are charged. It would never be suggested that lay people should be involved in the provision of medical treatment! The argument that the prejudices of twelve people will mitigate one another has already been called into question above.

[8] This argument should be supported by reference to relevant examples from case law. You should ensure that you refer to the downside of this argument, which is the risk that jurors fail to effectively discharge their duty to judge a defendant according to the relevant law.

A final possible argument in support of the preservation of the jury system is that, as ordinary people, jurors are able to judge according to their conscience,[8] meaning that on occasion they can effectively serve as a barometer of public opinion against what may be perceived as unduly harsh consequences of the law. For example, in *R v Ponting* [1985] Crim LR 318, a civil servant had passed confidential information to the media which exposed the government over the misleading of Parliament. To many this disclosure was in the public interest and Ponting was acquitted of breaching the Official Secrets Act in what was widely perceived to be a politically motivated prosecution.

[9] The balance of the arguments considered in the answer tend to tilt in favour of the case for abolition of juries, although not overwhelmingly so. The conclusion reflects this and makes the relevant point that juries are such a longstanding feature of the legal system that it is difficult to foresee their abolition without much greater consideration of their merits first taking place.

In conclusion, some strong arguments can be made for the abolition of juries, principally those relating to their limited competence and lack of objectivity. The reasons for maintaining their use, while not without any merit, do not appear particularly compelling. However, that juries have endured for so long in common law systems suggests that their abolition will only ever occur after far greater analysis has taken place of their merits.[9]

## ✓ Make your answer stand out

■ Refer to some of the recent debates over the merits of the jury system and some of the changes to have taken place to the extent to which they are used, for example sections 43–44 of the Criminal Justice Act 2003.

■ Where relevant, refer to case examples, statistical evidence or research studies to reinforce your arguments.

■ Read and make comment upon the arguments over the merits of juries discussed by Darbyshire (1991) 'The Lamp that Shows that Freedom Lives – Is It Worth the Candle?', *Crim LR*, 740.

■ Consider proposals for improving the efficiency of jury trial, such as those of Auld (2001). You do not have to simply accept the case for the jury system as it is presently practised or its abolition.

## ! Don't be tempted to . . .

■ Discuss each single argument that appears in any textbook discussion of the merits of the jury system.

■ Reach your conclusion based upon the number of arguments which you consider for each side of the debate.

---

**www.pearsoned.co.uk/lawexpressqa**

 Go online to access more revision support including additional essay and problem questions with diagram plans, You be the marker questions, and download all diagrams from the book.

# Appeals and judicial review

## How this topic may come up in exams

Examination questions on appeals are likely to focus specifically upon either the civil or criminal appeals processes and test your understanding of the circumstances in which appeals can be made from lower court decisions and the criteria governing them. Within an ELS syllabus, any question on judicial review is likely to be fairly general and may test understanding of the judicial review procedure including standing of applicants and bodies susceptible to judicial review, the grounds upon which judicial review may be sought, and the remedies available following a successful judicial review action.

# Attack the question

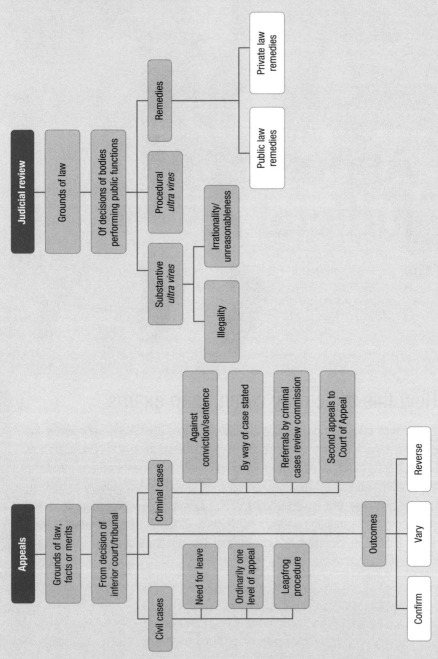

A printable version of this diagram plan is available from www.pearsoned.co.uk/lawexpressqa

#  Question 1

Explain the system governing appeals in civil cases.

## Answer plan

→ Briefly explain the nature and purpose of appeals in civil cases.

→ Explain the general requirement for leave to be obtained to appeal and that ordinarily there is only one level of appeal.

→ Briefly explain when and to where appeals against decisions of the magistrates' and county courts may be made.

→ Explain the procedure governing appeals from the High Court and the circumstances in which the 'leapfrog procedure' can be used.

→ Briefly explain the procedure followed by the Court of Appeal when hearing appeals and the scope that exists for further appeals to the Supreme Court.

## Diagram plan

A printable version of this diagram plan is available from www.pearsoned.co.uk/lawexpressqa

## Answer

[1] At the very outset of your answer you should briefly explain the nature and purpose of appeals. This will provide helpful background before you go on to explain more substantive points.

The main purpose of appeals procedures is to provide a mechanism through which incorrect decisions can be rectified.[1] Wrong decisions may be the result of errors of fact or law, or may be flawed due to a court's failure to follow the correct procedures in hearing the case. Within a civil case either party may appeal against a decision, although in response to a considerable increase in the number of appeals the Access to Justice Act 1999 introduced reforms which sought to reduce the circumstances in which appeals could be made.

A couple of important principles apply to civil appeals in general. As a result of section 54 of the Access to Justice Act 1999, permission to appeal is now required in almost all cases and must be obtained

125

[2] Before embarking upon explanation of the different routes of appeal in different cases, you should demonstrate your knowledge of the fundamental principles which govern the civil appeals process as these generally apply across the board irrespective of where a case is appealed from or on what grounds.

[3] This is an important principle governing civil appeals and it is therefore important that you mention it, while indicating where exceptions to this rule may be made.

[4] Most civil cases are initially heard in the county court or High Court. You would not be expected to entertain any real discussion of appeals from civil rulings of the magistrates' court, although in order to be comprehensive, a brief comment upon these could be made.

[5] It is essential that you demonstrate an understanding of the circumstances in which appeals from County court and High Court decisions can be made, given that these account for most civil appeals.

[6] As the major appellate court for civil cases, you should ensure that you provide an explanation of the possible outcomes of appeals to the CA. This follows on logically from your earlier explanation of the main principles governing appeals, the grounds on which they can be made and to where.

from either the court of first instance or the appellate court.[2] Permission to appeal will normally be given where the appellant has a realistic chance of success or there is some other compelling reason why the appeal should be heard. In exceptional circumstances, permission to appeal is not required. These are those in which individual liberty is at stake, such as habeas corpus applications and secure accommodation orders for children, being regarded as sufficiently serious to dispense with the ordinary requirement for leave to appeal. Motivated by the desire to reduce the number of civil appeals, section 55 of the Access to Justice Act provides that there will normally be only one level of appeal in civil cases.[3] Second appeals should be rare, and under section 55 the Court of Appeal (CA) will only hear a case that has already been heard on appeal by a lower court if it considers that the appeal will raise an important point of principle or practice, or there is some other compelling reason for it to hear the case.

The magistrates' court has very limited civil jurisdiction relating to family and licensing matters.[4] Subject to satisfying leave requirements, appeals on family matters will be made to the Family Division of the High Court and appeals on licensing matters to the Crown Court.

The vast majority of civil cases will commence in either the County court or High Court depending upon the subject matter and monetary value of any claim. Where a case has been heard in the County court and either party is dissatisfied with its ruling, subject to receiving permission to appeal, that party may appeal to the CA on the basis of errors of fact or errors of law on the part of the County court. Likewise, where a case has commenced in the High Court, there is a route of appeal to the CA on the same grounds[5] subject to permission to appeal having been granted by either the High Court or the CA.

Appeals by the CA will ordinarily be heard by three judges although in some circumstances one judge may hear an appeal sitting alone. Appeals seldom take the form of a rehearing of the case by the CA. Instead the CA will usually review the ruling of the inferior court on the basis of the notes made by the judge in the original hearing and other relevant documentary evidence. The CA effectively has three options in terms of the decision which it is entitled to reach.[6] It may affirm the decision of the inferior court, essentially indicating its agreement with the validity of that decision. Where the CA agrees with part but not all of the decision of the inferior court, it may vary its decision, thus allowing the appeal in part. This may arise, for example, where the CA agrees with the inferior court's decision on liability but not the remedy which it imposed. In such an event, the CA may confirm the decision whilst perhaps reducing the damages awarded to a claimant. Where the inferior court's decision is felt to be incorrect, the CA may allow the appeal and reverse the earlier decision. An appeal may only be allowed because a decision is wrong, unjust or has been reached in circumstances where there have been procedural irregularities. The CA cannot allow an appeal simply because it is of the belief that it might have reached a different decision, in the absence of any of the aforementioned grounds for allowing an appeal.

There is some scope for further appeals to be made from decisions of the CA to the Supreme Court on questions of law.[7] However, leave to appeal must be obtained from either court. In reality, very few cases are heard annually by the Supreme Court and in the overwhelming majority of cases the CA will in practice be the final appellate court.

[7] Although this point does not need to be laboured, you should mention the fact that appeals can be made from the CA to the Supreme Court, as this is a higher court within the court hierarchy.

There is a special procedure, known as the 'leapfrog procedure', which enables certain cases to be appealed directly from the High Court to the Supreme Court, thus bypassing the CA.[8] The 'leapfrog procedure' is governed by sections 12–15 of the Administration of Justice Act 1969. To be able to make use of the procedure and appeal directly to the Supreme Court from the High Court, all parties to the case must consent and under section 12(3) of the 1969 Act the High Court judge who heard the original case must certify that the appeal is either on a point of law which relates wholly or mainly to the construction of a provision of a statute or statutory instrument and has been fully argued and considered, or on a question of law where the High Court judge was bound by a CA or Supreme Court precedent and the matter had been fully considered in the relevant previous CA or Supreme Court judgments. The rationale for the 'leapfrog procedure' is to save on time and cost in court proceedings in those circumstances where, because of the effect of judicial precedent, the CA is unlikely to be able to satisfactorily resolve a case appealed from the High Court, which will probably require ultimate recourse to the Supreme Court anyway. No appeal can pass directly from the High Court to the Supreme Court without the aforementioned certification from the trial judge. The trial judge enjoys discretion over the granting of this certificate and there is no right to appeal

[8] The 'leapfrog procedure' is a very important mechanism for speeding up appeals and you should ensure that you demonstrate a clear understanding of the rationale for this procedure and the rules which govern its application. A clear explanation of this is likely to receive credit from the examiner.

against his decision in respect of this. It should also be noted that, even if the requirements imposed by the Administration of Justice Act 1969 are satisfied, leave to appeal will still need to be obtained from the Supreme Court.

✓ **Make your answer stand out**

- Make reference to the impact upon the civil appeals process of the Access to Justice Act 1999.
- Explain clearly the importance of the 'leapfrog procedure' for appeals against decisions of the High Court.
- Demonstrate that appeal is not usually available as of right, but is contingent upon permission being granted.
- Consider whether an appropriate balance is struck by the current rules on civil appeals between achieving civil justice and preventing the overburdening of the courts.

! **Don't be tempted to . . .**

- Simply provide an overview of the court hierarchy which details to which courts appeals can be made from lower courts.

# 🖎 Question 2

Discuss the range of circumstances in which verdicts in criminal cases may be appealed against.

## Answer plan

→ Consider the routes of appeal from decisions of the magistrates' court.

→ Consider the routes of appeal from decisions of the Crown Court.

→ Consider the circumstances in which the Court of Appeal will hear second appeals.

→ Consider the ability of the Court of Appeal to admit fresh evidence and the possible outcomes of appeals heard by the Court of Appeal.

→ Conclude upon the extent to which the English legal system provides a range of opportunities for appealing criminal convictions or sentences.

# Diagram plan

| Routes for appeal from Magistrates' Court | Routes for appeal from Crown Court | Second appeals to the Court of Appeal | Admission of fresh evidence in Court of Appeal | Conclusion: range of opportunities to appeal |

A printable version of this diagram plan is available from www.pearsoned.co.uk/lawexpressqa

# Answer

[1] It is worthwhile noting that it is rare for an appeal to be made against a decision of this court. However, you should begin your answer by considering the scope which exists for appealing against verdicts and sentences imposed by the magistrates' court, as all criminal cases commence here.

The overwhelming majority of criminal cases are concluded in the magistrates' court. Appeals are only made against the decisions of the court in 1% of cases and may take one of four forms.[1] Firstly, although not strictly speaking an appeal, a case may be retried by the magistrates' court itself to rectify any errors made by the court in the original hearing. Section 142 of the Magistrates' Courts Act 1980 permits such a retrial, before a different bench, where the interests of justice warrant this and the sentence imposed upon an offender can be varied. This procedure has been credited with leading to a reduction in the number of actual appeals to the higher courts. Secondly, a defendant may appeal as of right to the Crown Court on the grounds of having either been wrongfully convicted or handed a sentence that is unduly harsh, although a defendant who pleaded guilty may only appeal against his sentence. Appeals must be made within 28 days and the appeal will take the form of a rehearing of the facts by the Crown Court which enjoys the power to impose any sentence which could have been imposed by the magistrates' court. There is the potential for sentences to actually be increased by the Crown Court, although this is comparatively rare, with evidence pointing to a tendency for tougher sentences to be handed down by magistrates.[2]

[2] Where appropriate, you can draw upon your wider knowledge of appeals processes to make points such as this to illustrate your understanding of the impact of appeals processes in practice.

Thirdly, either prosecution or defence may appeal by way of case stated to the High Court on the grounds that the magistrates' court has made an error of law or exceeded its jurisdiction. Up to three judges from the Queen's Bench Division will sit to confirm, reverse or vary the magistrates' decision, or give their opinion on a point of law to the magistrates' court. They may also issue other orders, for example to require a rehearing of the case in the magistrates' court. This is effectively a means of appeal on limited grounds, but it was established in *R v Mildenhall Magistrates' Court,* ex parte *Forest Heath DC*

[1997] 161 JP 401 that a magistrates' court can refuse to state a case for the High Court where it feels it would be frivolous to do so. Finally, although not an appeal as such on the part of a convicted defendant, under the terms of the Criminal Appeals Act 1995, the Criminal Cases Review Commission (CCRC) can refer a case to the Crown Court if it feels a particular conviction or sentence is unsafe. This will then be regarded as an appeal, although it is very rare for the CCRC to refer cases heard in the magistrates' court.

Appeals against convictions or sentences handed down by the Crown Court can be made along similar grounds as they can from the magistrates' court.[3] Either party can appeal by way of case stated to the Queen's Bench Division of the High Court, just as they can from the magistrates' court. From there further appeal to the Supreme Court may be possible, but only where the Divisional Court certifies that the case raises a question of law of public importance and leave is obtained from the Supreme Court. A defendant can appeal to the Court of Appeal (CA) on grounds of an error of fact or law, or against the sentence imposed by the Crown Court. Leave to appeal must be obtained from either the Crown Court or the CA. According to Slapper and Kelly (2010), approximately 8,000 such appeals are launched annually. The overwhelming majority are against sentence as opposed to conviction, arguably encouraged by the fact that the CA may not increase a sentence imposed by the Crown Court. Although only a defendant can appeal to the CA, either party is entitled to appeal onwards to the Supreme Court on a point of law, although this is only possible if permission is given by either court and the CA certifies that the case involves a matter of general importance. The CCRC can also refer cases heard in the Crown Court to the CA where a conviction or sentence is regarded as unsafe. This has led to several notable cases being effectively revisited by the CA, among the most publicised of which was the case of Derek Bentley whose conviction for murder was set aside by the CA in 1998, more than 45 years after his execution.[4]

It was established in *Taylor v Lawrence* [2002] EWCA Civ 90 that in exceptional cases a second appeal may be brought to the CA even though a previous appeal has been rejected.[5] The case itself concerned new evidence which had come to light following an earlier appeal, casting doubt upon the validity of its outcome. However, to bring a second appeal it must be clearly established that a significant

[3] The routes of appeal from Crown Court decisions are similar to those that exist for appeals from the magistrates' court, so you should focus your discussion here on aspects of the appeals process more relevant to appeals from the Crown Court, such as appeals to the CA.

[4] Some discussion of the role played by the CCRC is worthwhile when you are considering appeals to the CA. You can illustrate its importance in relation to addressing miscarriages of justice by citing practical examples, and will receive credit for doing so.

[5] This is an important point to make and builds further upon the earlier discussion of ways in which the law on criminal appeals has developed in response to miscarriages of justice. It evidences an awareness of relatively recent changes in the law.

injustice has probably been done, the circumstances are exceptional and there is no alternative remedy. In reality, second appeals are likely to be extremely rare occurrences, but their availability provides an important additional safeguard against the perpetration of mis-carriages of justice.

Ordinarily, an appeal hearing by the CA will take the form of a review of the original case. However, section 23(1) of the Criminal Appeals Act 1968 allows it to admit fresh evidence 'if they think it necessary or expedient in the interests of justice'.[6] Essentially, this will be where the newly available evidence casts doubt upon the reliability of the original ruling. There is a series of factors which the CA is to have regard to in considering whether the admission of evidence will satisfy the requirements of section 23(1). Under section 2 of the Criminal Appeals Act 1968, an appeal should be allowed wherever the court thinks a conviction is 'unsafe'. The appeal ought to be dismissed if there is no reason to question the original ruling. Alternatively, the CA can order a new trial to be held and this is an option which it may choose where there are some reservations over the original decision, perhaps as a result of procedural factors, but the CA is not minded to simply overturn that decision.

There is clearly a range of opportunities for criminal convictions and sentences to be appealed against, leading Slapper and Kelly (2010) to comment that, when compared to other jurisdictions, it is 'unusual' to find 'as many opportunities for appeal and challenge as exist in the English system'.[7]

[6] As it is the main court responsible for hearing criminal appeals, you should comment upon some of the key features of appeal hearings before the CA. The ability of the CA to admit fresh evidence is particularly relevant to your answer and can be cited to reinforce the earlier points made in relation to the role which the appeals process plays in addressing miscarriages of justice.

[7] This brings your answer to an end nicely, evidencing awareness of the wider context of criminal appeals.

## ✓ Make your answer stand out

- Provide some discussion of the role of criminal appeals in addressing miscarriages of justices.
- Refer to the role played by the CCRC in bringing appeals against criminal convictions.
- Make reference to the human rights dimension of criminal appeals, particularly in relation to cases where irregularities compromised the right to a fair trial at first hearing.
- In a more critical extended essay you might consider in more detail the purposes of criminal appeals and whether the current system for appeals achieves these. A useful discussion of such issues is provided in Spencer (2006) 'Does Our Present Criminal Appeal System Make Sense?', *Crim LR*, 677.

> **!** **Don't be tempted to . . .**
>
> ■ Simply provide an overview of the court hierarchy which details to which courts appeals can be made from lower courts.
> ■ Describe individual miscarriages of justice in detail.

# ✍ Question 3

How does an action for judicial review differ from an appeal? Who is entitled to bring an action for judicial review and which bodies are susceptible to judicial review?

## Answer plan

→ Explain briefly what judicial review is.

→ Outline the main differences between an appeal and a judicial review action.

→ Explain the criteria which govern eligibility to bring an application for judicial review.

→ Explain the criteria which govern the susceptibility of bodies to judicial review actions.

## Diagram plan

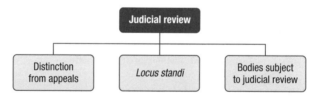

A printable version of this diagram plan is available from www.pearsoned.co.uk/lawexpressqa

## Answer

Judicial review refers to the process by which the decisions and actions of public bodies are subject to the oversight of the courts to ensure that they have been exercised in accordance with the law.[1] Applications for judicial review are made to the Queen's Bench Division of the High Court, which is responsible for exercising a supervisory jurisdiction over governmental and public bodies. Judicial review is essentially concerned with ensuring that public bodies do

[1] Before launching into an explanation of the differences between judicial review and appeals, you should briefly explain what judicial review is. This will set the scene for you to then go on to distinguish it from the appeals process. You should state what the main function of judicial review is and briefly refer to the grounds upon which an application for judicial review can be brought.

[2] The question asks you firstly how judicial review differs from an appeal. The main differences concern the grounds upon which an action may proceed and the basis for the courts' powers. You should clearly explain these. Although you have been asked about differences between the two, it is desirable to refer to the degree of overlap between the two concepts in order to illustrate the degree to which they differ.

[3] The second part of the question asks you who can bring an application for judicial review. It is crucial that you are able to explain the concept of *locus standi*. Depending upon the time that you have available, you should refer to relevant case law to illustrate how the 'sufficient interest' test has been applied in practice.

not act outside the powers with which they have been conferred by statute, and this consists of checking that they do not make decisions or take action which they are not permitted to (substantive *ultra vires*) and comply with all relevant procedures throughout their decision-making processes (procedural *ultra vires*). Judicial review plays an important function within the doctrine of separation of powers and in upholding the rule of law, being the primary means through which the executive branch of government is held to account for the legality of its decisions and actions by the judiciary. Applications for judicial review have increased considerably in recent years, Slapper and Kelly (2010) estimating the number of applications to have grown from in the region of 500 in 1980 to over 5,000 in 1998.

A judicial review action differs from an appeal in some very fundamental respects.[2] Unlike the appeals process, judicial review is not concerned with the merits of the decisions which the court is asked to review. The sole purpose of judicial review is to examine the legality of a decision. If it is lawfully made, the fact that its merits may be questionable is irrelevant. This differs from the appeals process, where the merits of a particular decision will often be the grounds for appeal against it. A second distinction relates to the legal basis for the powers exercised by the court in hearing applications for judicial review and appeals respectively. Where appeals procedures are grounded in statutory provisions, the origins of the courts' powers to subject public bodies to judicial review lie in the common law. Despite these fundamental differences, there is nonetheless a degree of overlap between judicial review and appeals. The same occurrence can potentially give rise to both an appeal and grounds for judicial review. For example, while there will ordinarily be a route of appeal from the decision of a statutory tribunal, its decisions may also be subject to judicial review if they exceed the tribunal's powers or do not comply with the appropriate procedural requirements.

An application for judicial review can only be brought by a party which enjoys *locus standi*, that is sufficient standing to bring the case to court. For purposes of judicial review, *locus standi* has been defined by the Supreme Court Act 1981, section 31(3) which defines this as 'a sufficient interest in the matter to which the application relates'.[3] The Supreme Court Act 1981 has now been renamed as the Senior Courts Act 1981 (see the Constitutional Reform Act 2005). The logic of this test is to prevent frivolous applications for judicial review being made, thus reserving the courts' time for hearing worthwhile cases. Whether a particular applicant or group of applicants will be able to establish a sufficient interest in a particular matter is essentially something to be decided on a case by case basis by the courts, although clear *locus standi* is likely to be satisfied when the private law rights of the party bringing the action are threatened. It was established in **R v Inland Revenue Commissioners, ex parte National Federation of Self-Employed and Small Businesses** [1982] AC 617 that the merits of the case can be taken into account when deciding whether the test for *locus standi* is satisfied.

The courts have taken a relatively flexible approach to the issue of *locus standi*, so, for example, pressure or interest groups may be able to demonstrate a sufficient interest in a matter with which they are principally concerned in order to be able to bring an application for judicial review. The Attorney-General will always have *locus standi* to bring an application for judicial review, and consequently he is able to permit 'relator' actions to be brought in his name where there may be doubts as to whether a party seeking to bring an application will be able to satisfy the *locus standi* test.[4] An example of a relator action can be found, for example, in the case of **R v Secretary of State for Employment, ex parte Equal Opportunities Commission** [1994] 1 WLR 910.

To be amenable to judicial review proceedings, a body must be responsible for performing a public function.[5] Government departments and agencies will clearly be amenable to judicial review, whereas bodies which are entirely of a private nature will not. However, it has been established for some time that where private bodies perform important public functions they will be amenable to judicial review. In the case of **R v Panel on Takeovers and Mergers, ex parte Datafin plc** [1987] QB 815, it was established that although the Panel on Takeovers and Mergers was essentially a privately con-stituted body, it performed an important public function and thus could be subject to judicial review. Similarly, the Advertising Standards Agency was deemed to be amenable to judicial review when the court in **R v Advertising Standards Agency Ltd, ex parte Insurance Services plc** [1990] 2 Admin LR 77 held that the ASA performed an important public function which if it did not exist would need to be performed by the Office of Fair Trading. This factor was central to its amenability to judicial review. In accordance with this

[4] Some credit should be given for mentioning the *locus standi* enjoyed by the Attorney-General, as his role can be very important in judicial review proceedings where would-be applicants may be unable to demonstrate *locus standi*.

[5] The final part of the question asks which bodies are susceptible to judicial review. The key concept to be discussed here is that of a 'public function' being performed on the part of the body concerned. You should refer to a range of appropriate cases to illustrate how this concept has been applied in practice, the *Datafin* case being especially significant in highlighting the susceptibility of private bodies to judicial review where they perform a public function.

approach, various self-regulatory bodies, such as the Bar Council, have been held to be subject to judicial review proceedings.

Despite its relatively broad approach to the question of which bodies can be subjected to judicial review, certain bodies have been clearly determined as being exempt. For example, religious bodies are generally not deemed to perform a public function, so entities such as the Chief Rabbi have been held exempt from judicial review, their functions being regarded as essentially religious in nature and not more broadly public. Domestic tribunals of a voluntary nature are also not regarded as performing a public function. Interestingly, in the case of *R v Parliamentary Commissioner for Standards,* ex parte *Al Fayed* [1997] EWCA Civ 2488, it was held that the Parliamentary Commissioner for Standards was not subject to judicial review as the office functioned as part of the proceedings of Parliament, which were immune from judicial review. Thus, judicial review can be seen as applicable to a relatively, but not too narrowly, restricted class of bodies.

## ✓ Make your answer stand out

- Demonstrate not only the differences between judicial review and appeals, but also the degree of overlap which they share.
- Make reference to the fact that the Attorney-General always enjoys *locus standi* for judicial review purposes.
- Consider the extent to which the test for standing in judicial review cases is broader or narrower than in some other forms of actions by reading and making reference to Ligere (2005) '*Locus Standi* and the Public Interest: A Hotchpotch of Legal Principles', *Journal of Planning and Environment Law*, 292.
- Consider the extent to which there is greater scope for policy considerations to enter into the courts' approach to questions of judicial review compared to appeals.

## ! Don't be tempted to . . .

- Embark upon an explanation of the procedure for judicial review.
- Confuse the differences and similarities between judicial review and appeals.
- Make the assumption that only public bodies can perform public functions, thus excluding all private bodies from susceptibility to judicial review.

#  Question 4

'A broad range of activity on the part of public bodies may potentially fall foul of the law.'
Discuss with reference to the grounds of judicial review.

## Answer plan

➜ Briefly explain the purpose of judicial review and that there are three broad grounds upon which a public body may be subjected to judicial review.

➜ Discuss the scope which exists for challenging actions of public bodies upon grounds of illegality.

➜ Discuss the scope which exists for challenging actions of public bodies upon grounds of irrationality.

➜ Discuss the scope which exists for challenging actions of public bodies upon grounds of procedural impropriety.

➜ Conclude by commenting upon the extent to which the judicial review process places broad checks upon the exercise of power by public bodies.

## Diagram plan

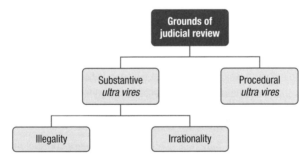

A printable version of this diagram plan is available from www.pearsoned.co.uk/lawexpressqa

## Answer

Judicial review is the ultimate mechanism used by the courts to hold public bodies to account for their actions and decisions. The purpose of judicial review is to ensure that public bodies act in conformity with the law. It is common to base the grounds of judicial review upon the concepts of substantive and procedural *ultra vires*. The

[1] It is worthwhile to make this distinction between the grounds of judicial review at the outset, these being the most common classifications utilised for the grounds of judicial review.

[2] Because substantive *ultra vires* covers both straightforward instances of bodies exceeding their jurisdiction and those cases where discretionary powers are exercised in a manner that cannot be taken to have been envisaged when the powers were conferred upon the respective bodies, in order to sustain a clear argument it may be helpful to adopt the terms set out by Lord Diplock to break down the grounds of judicial review.

[3] You need to explain that public bodies may not exceed the powers which they are given, and if they do so this will constitute a straightforward case of unlawful activity.

[4] Explaining the concept of irrationality or unreasonableness should constitute a significant part of your answer as there are several ways in which it is possible to demonstrate its presence in a decision or action of a public body.

[5] You should make reference to the landmark *Wednesbury* case as providing the origins of the concept of reasonableness/rationality as a ground upon which applications for judicial review could be grounded, in light of the fundamental importance of the case.

former arises where a body makes a decision or takes an action which it is not lawfully permitted to, thus acting outside its powers. The latter arises where a body fails to follow the appropriate procedures in its decision-making process.[1] Although the grounds of judicial review are often grouped under these two broad headings, they can also be ordered under the three headings outlined by Lord Diplock in *Council of Civil Service Unions* v *Minister for the Civil Service* [1985] AC 374, namely illegality, irrationality and procedural impropriety.[2] The first two headings both refer to forms of substantive *ultra vires*, whereas the last simply refers to procedural *ultra vires*.

The term 'illegality' encompasses those relatively clear-cut instances of substantive *ultra vires* in which a public body exercises a power which it does not have.[3] For example, in *R* v *Secretary of State for the Home Department,* ex parte *Leech (No. 2)* [1994] QB 198 it was held unlawful for a prison governor to censor a prisoner's correspondence with his solicitor, in the absence of any such power within the legislation governing such matters. However, not all cases of substantive *ultra vires* are so straightforward and the notion of 'irrationality' is applied to those scenarios where a public body is conferred with a broad discretionary power which it exercises in such a manner that it would be regarded as so irrational that no rational decision maker could have acted in such a manner.[4] Although not expressly prohibited by any statutory provision, it would not be a means of exercising the power reasonably contemplated by Parliament when conferring the power. The courts can use their powers of review to restrain such unreasonable exercises of broad discretionary power. This heading of judicial review has its origins in the case of *Associated Provincial Picture Houses* v *Wednesbury Corporation* [1948] 1 KB 223 from which the concept of unreasonableness derived.[5] The contribution of that case was to rule that any decision which was so unreasonable that no reasonable authority could make it would be regarded as *ultra vires*. There are several apparent instances where a body exercising discretionary powers is likely to fall foul of the test for unreasonableness or irrationality and thus to have acted *ultra vires*.

Exercising a discretionary power for improper purposes will constitute an unlawful action.[6] This occurred in *R* v *Derbyshire County Council,* ex parte *Times Supplements* (1990) COD 139, where

[6] You will improve your answer if you are able to highlight some of the specific cases in which an exercise of a discretionary power is likely to be deemed *ultra vires* due to its lack of reasonableness. Acting for improper purposes, taking into account irrelevant considerations and fettering discretion can all be highlighted with supporting examples from case law.

an authority's treatment of the publishers concerned was motivated by earlier criticism directed at it by the publisher's publication. Additionally, a body subject to judicial review may not take into account irrelevant considerations in exercising a discretionary power. Thus, in *R* v *Somerset County Council,* ex parte *Fewings* [1995] 3 All ER 20 the exercise of regulatory powers to ban deer hunting on Council-owned land was deemed to be unlawful, due to the Council having employed irrelevant considerations in the exercise of this power. A person or body conferred with a discretionary power is obliged to exercise that power and not to fetter that discretion by delegating this power to another. A decision that results from fettered discretion is likely to be unlawful, as *British Oxygen* v *Minister of Technology* [1971] AC 610 illustrates.

A failure to comply with required procedures will also render decisions or actions of public bodies *ultra vires*. Public bodies exercising discretionary powers must comply with the requirements of natural justice.[7] There are two notable rules, the rule against bias (*nemo judex in sua causa*, meaning that nobody should be a judge in his own cause) and the requirement of a fair hearing (*audi alteram partem*, meaning 'to hear the other side'). The rule against bias essentially requires that nobody should make a decision in respect of a matter in which he has a direct interest, which could give rise to charges of bias. For example, in *Dimes* v *Grand Junction Canal Proprietors* (1852) 3 HL Cas 759, the Lord Chancellor sat in judgment on a case concerning a company in which he owned a substantial number of shares and ruled in their favour. This was held to compromise his ability to exercise independent judgment on the case and he was declared disqualified from sitting on the bench in this case. More recently, in *R* v *Bow Street Metropolitan Stipendiary Magistrate,* ex parte *Pinochet Ugarte (No. 2)* [1999] COD 139, a court ruling in respect of the extradition of the former Chilean dictator Pinochet to face charges related to human rights abuses had to be set aside due to the fact that one of the judges hearing the case, Lord Hoffman, had close links to Amnesty International, a human rights pressure group which had been heavily involved in calls for Pinochet to face exportation and trial.

[7] In explaining the procedural grounds for judicial review, you must ensure that you evidence an understanding of the rules of natural justice. Use case law examples to show these being enforced in practice.

The requirements of a fair hearing will vary with the circumstances of each case, but a failure to satisfy what is reasonable in the circumstances will give rise to the charge that the public body concerned has acted procedurally *ultra vires*. Many statutory procedural requirements are now imposed in respect of public decision-making processes. These sometimes include the imposition of a requirement to enter into consultation with those to be affected by particular decisions, the provision of notice of pending decisions, the provision of an opportunity for affected persons to make representations to a decision-making authority, and the provision of reasons for decisions that have been taken. Although these procedural requirements vary from one situation to another, a failure to comply where obliged would posit strong grounds upon which an application for judicial review could be lodged.

[8] Your conclusion should flow naturally from your explanation of the different grounds of judicial review. By showing the broad grounds which exist you are able to conclude upon its importance in strengthening the accountability owed by public bodies for their actions.

Judicial review is undoubtedly an important mechanism through which the courts are able to hold public bodies to account for their actions and ensure that they act within the law.[8] The grounds of judicial review are broad enough to support the courts' ability to perform this function. Not only are the courts able to nullify the decisions or actions of public bodies that are clearly taken in excess of their powers, but they are also able to remedy situations where broad discretionary powers are exercised in a manner so unreasonable or irrational that they cannot be taken to have been envisaged upon the part of the discretion-conferring authority. Furthermore, the procedural grounds of judicial review reinforce the importance of standards of fairness within decision-making processes.

## ✓ Make your answer stand out

- Explain the different kinds of actions which may give rise to the unlawful exercise of a discretionary power.
- Use a good breadth of case law examples to illustrate the different grounds of judicial review in action.
- Make reference to the doctrine of separation of powers in illustrating the importance of judicial review as a mechanism for holding the executive to account.
- Consider the extent to which the courts are prepared to call into question the exercise of discretionary powers by public bodies, with reference to the arguments of Robertson (1993) *Freedom, the Individual and the Law*, London: Penguin.

> ! **Don't be tempted to . . .**
>
> ■ Confuse judicial review actions with appeals.
> ■ Explain the grounds of judicial review narrowly, without elaborating upon the various kinds of actions which may give rise to their invocation.

# 🖎 Question 5

Assess the case that exists for the maintenance of two appellate courts (the Court of Appeal and Supreme Court) within the English legal system.

## Answer plan

→ Explain the roles of the Court of Appeal and Supreme Court within the English legal system.

→ Consider the arguments in favour of the retention of a second appellate court.

→ Consider the arguments against the retention of a second appellate court.

→ Conclude by stating whether the status quo should be maintained or not.

## Diagram plan

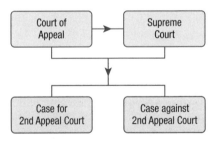

A printable version of this diagram plan is available from www.pearsoned.co.uk/lawexpressqa

## Answer

Within the English legal system the Court of Appeal and Supreme Court both have an entirely appellate jurisdiction. The Court of Appeal (CA) is the principal appellate court and has both criminal and civil divisions. Most cases which reach the CA end there, although a

[1] The introduction provides useful context for the arguments which will follow on the merits of two appellate courts. It points out that most cases end in the CA, and that virtually all cases must pass through there before they can be considered by the Supreme Court. Both these facts will be relevant to some of the later arguments. In an extended essay you might provide a little further context by saying something about the different structures of the two courts.

[2] Here you can effectively dismiss a weak argument for the retention of two appellate courts by referring back to the introductory points, alluded to in the previous comment.

[3] This is true. The stronger arguments tend to focus upon features of the Supreme Court and so you should give these some attention. This paragraph effectively touches upon a number of related features of the Supreme Court in illustrating the need for it to sit above the CA.

small number will be appealed further to the highest court, the Supreme Court. Ordinarily, a case can only proceed to the Supreme Court after being heard by the CA. However, in exceptional circumstances governed by section 12(3) of the Administration of Justice Act 1969, the 'leapfrog' procedure allows a case to be appealed directly from the High Court to the Supreme Court.[1]

Whether it is necessary to retain two appellate courts has been the subject of some debate. A number of arguments can be advanced in favour of the preservation of the status quo, leaving the current position of the Supreme Court and CA untouched. It has been argued that the combination of the two courts permits for the quicker handling of appeals than would be the case if there were to be just one appellate court. This is rather a peculiar argument, as it is not simply a case of dividing work between two courts.[2] With the exception of a tiny number of cases which are able to make use of the 'leapfrog' procedure, all appeals must be heard by the CA before reaching the Supreme Court. In this sense, the maintenance of two courts actually slows down the conclusion of those cases which currently end in the Supreme Court through the duplication of work across the courts.

A more convincing case can be made for the retention of a second appellate court by reference to some of the perceived strengths of the Supreme Court.[3] It has been argued that it is better placed to guide the harmonious development of the law through consistent leadership than is the CA as a consequence of its smaller membership. Since the Practice Direction of 1966 the House of Lords, and now the Supreme Court, has been able to depart from its own precedents when it is felt right to do so. This flexibility allows the court to reform the law in a way which the CA is unable to as it does not enjoy the same power. Furthermore, the fact that the CA is organised into divisions and considerably bigger in size than the Supreme Court means that there is a greater likelihood of it applying different interpretations of the law. The structure of the CA is not in itself a criticism, especially given that it bears the burden of hearing many more cases than the Supreme Court, but is arguably a reason for a smaller, more unified body to sit above it in hearing the most important of cases which come to court.

The special role of the Supreme Court is borne out by the important contributions which the House of Lords has made in some key areas

[4] You could, however, consider here whether such contributions might not be made by the CA in the absence of a higher appellate court.

[5] You can effectively cite statistical evidence to support your arguments, such as on this point.

[6] The weaker arguments for a single appellate court should be grouped together and tackled as quickly as possible in an examination setting, leaving you more time to probe the more compelling arguments.

[7] This is one of the stronger arguments against the retention of two appellate courts which should be mentioned. In an extended essay you may be able to draw upon further empirical evidence in exploring this argument.

[8] This is a good counterargument to the one just considered. Again, in an extended essay you may be able to draw upon some statistical evidence to demonstrate how few cases are actually affected by this.

[9] This challenges a key argument with a very good proposition which undermines it effectively.

of law,[4] for example in ruling that a man could be guilty of the rape of his wife in *R v R* [1991] 4 All ER 481. Statistical evidence would also appear to suggest that the existence of a second appellate court is necessary. Elliott and Quinn (2012) noted that in 2007 40% of appeals from the CA to the House of Lords were allowed, suggesting an important function in correcting wrong decisions.[5]

Notwithstanding the above, a number of arguments have been advanced in favour of a single appellate court. Some of these are not very convincing.[6] For example, it has been claimed that a litigant can ultimately win a case with only a minority of judges having heard the case ruling in his/her favour. This would be so where a case had been lost at first instance and in the CA, but successfully appealed to the Supreme Court. However, the system of judicial precedent attaches the utmost significance to decisions of the highest court and the outcome of litigation ought not to depend upon the numbers of judges persuaded by a legal argument across all courts, but the authoritative proclamation of the highest court to have considered it. It has also been suggested, most prominently by Griffith (1997), that the former House of Lords tended to side with the 'establishment'. However, much of his argument rested on the composition of the membership of that court and there is no reason to believe that if the CA were the final appeal court the nature of its membership would differ greatly. The Supreme Court has also been attacked for its lack of any specialist divisions, leading some commentators to criticise its limited contribution to the development of certain areas of law. However, the nature of the court as a small body hearing only the very most important appeals mean that its structure cannot fairly be compared to that of the CA.

The stronger arguments against the retention of two appellate courts are practical in nature. One consequence of the status quo is the resulting extra cost and delay which is brought to some cases as litigants seek to exhaust appeal opportunities in both courts,[7] often leading to the recruitment of expensive highly qualified teams of lawyers. Research by Jackson (1989) suggested that most cases were only appealed to the then House of Lords as it represented the final route of appeal. However, issues of time and cost should not perhaps be of great concern given that these affect very few cases, with most ending in the CA.[8] It has been suggested that, given the eminence of its judges, the CA ought to be a sufficient appeal

[10] Your conclusion accurately reflects the tone of the answer. You have clearly detected merit in some arguments for the retention of two appellate courts, albeit these have not been particularly powerful. However, at the same time you have been able to undermine much of the case for having just one appellate court. Therefore your ultimate conclusion makes much sense.

mechanism and that it is rather strange to give litigants two opportunities to achieve the outcome which they desire. There is some merit in this argument from a practical standpoint, but on grounds of principle it might be argued that there should be no price on justice and the greater the number of checks which exist within the appeal system, the more likely this is to be achieved.[9]

In conclusion, while there are some clear merits in maintaining two appellate courts, these are not as compelling as might have been expected. However, at the same time, the case for the abolition of a second appeal court is arguably even harder to make.[10] Therefore, given that the present system appears to function relatively satisfactorily, it should be left to do so.

## ✓ Make your answer stand out

- Refer to statistical evidence on the number of cases appealed to the Supreme Court and their success rate.
- Demonstrate that there are both practical and principled arguments in the debate over the retention of two appellate courts.
- Refer to academic commentary on the limited contribution of the House of Lords to some areas of law, for example that provided by Ormerod (2011) *Smith and Hogan's Criminal Law* (13th edn) Oxford: OUP. and Williams, G. (1983) *Textbook of Criminal Law*, London: Stevens & Sons in relation to its allegedly poor contribution to the development of the criminal law.
- Refer to the research into the cases appealed to the House of Lords conducted by Jackson (1989) *The Machinery of Justice in England*. Cambridge: Cambridge University Press.

## ! Don't be tempted to . . .

- Provide a detailed account of appeals processes.
- Enter into lengthy comparisons of the structures and compositions of the Supreme Court and the CA.

**www.pearsoned.co.uk/lawexpressqa**

Go online to access more revision support including additional essay and problem questions with diagram plans, You be the marker questions, and download all diagrams from the book.

# The criminal law process

7

## How this topic may come up in exams

Examination questions on this topic may relate to police powers to stop, search and arrest suspects, the rules applicable to the detention and questioning of suspects, and the taking of evidence. Your understanding of police powers may be assessed through the use of the essay or problem questions. Your understanding of the criminal trial procedure may also be assessed, and you should be particularly prepared to answer questions relating to the rules applicable to the grant or refusal of bail, plea bargaining, the admission and exclusion of evidence and the factors which inform the sentencing of offenders following conviction.

## Attack the question

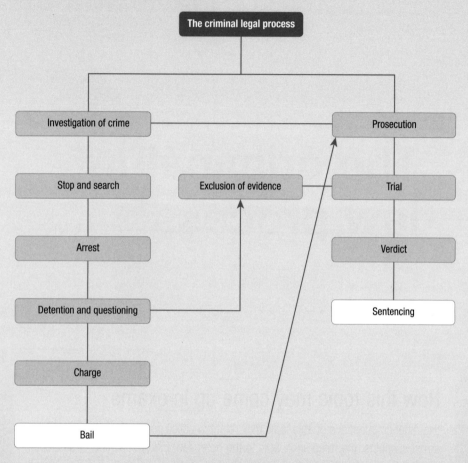

A printable version of this diagram plan is available from www.pearsoned.co.uk/lawexpressqa

#  Question 1

Discuss the safeguards which protect suspects against inappropriate police behaviour during questioning at the police station following arrest.

## Answer plan

→ Briefly explain the need for suspects to be protected against inappropriate police interrogation techniques.

→ Explain the importance of time limits upon the detention of suspects.

→ Briefly explain the importance of the requirements which apply to the treatment of detainees in police custody.

→ Consider the importance of the tape-recording of police interviews with suspects.

→ Consider the importance of suspects' entitlement to consult a legal adviser.

→ Comment upon the abolition of the so-called 'right to silence' and the extent to which this decreases the protection afforded to suspects against self-incrimination.

→ Briefly explain the ability of the courts to exclude evidence which is of dubious reliability.

## Diagram plan

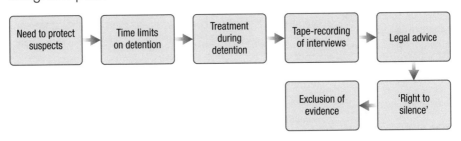

A printable version of this diagram plan is available from www.pearsoned.co.uk/lawexpressqa

[1] You can provide some useful context to your answer by making reference to the importance of safeguards in protecting against miscarriages of justice. If you have time you might cite some specific examples of miscarriages of justice that have arisen from improper police conduct during questioning.

## Answer

Police questioning of suspects detained at the police station is a key means of obtaining evidence as part of the criminal investigation process, yet without appropriate regulation there is a danger that in some instances police may adopt unscrupulous methods when questioning suspects, as a result of their urge to secure confessions or irrefutable evidence. The use of such practices have come to light through a number of miscarriages of justice which have emerged in which confessions have been secured from suspects through the application of oppressive interrogatory methods.[1] The Police and Criminal Evidence Act 1984 (PACE) provides a series of provisions which prima facie affords important safeguards to protect suspects from inappropriate police conduct.

Sections 40–43 of PACE limit the period for which a suspect may be detained for questioning,[2] requiring that regular reviews take place after six hours, then at nine-hour intervals when further authorisation for detention must be granted. Detention beyond 24 hours requires the authorisation of a superintendent, and beyond 36 hours of the magistrates' court, although after 96 hours a suspect must be charged or released. The requirement of regular reviews ensures that a case must be made for continuing to detain a suspect for questioning, especially beyond 36 hours where a magistrate must be satisfied that continued detention is necessary.

[2] Although the question asks about safeguards to protect suspects during police questioning, time limits upon the detention of suspects nonetheless serve to prevent the indefinite questioning of suspects and ensure that a case must be made for questioning to continue beyond specified periods of time.

The detainment of suspects for questioning is regulated by Code of Practice C[3] which specifies standards of accommodation which detainees are to be kept in, requires the provision of regular meals and regular breaks from questioning including adequate sleep. These requirements are important in order to ensure that suspects are able to remain fit and alert for questioning, minimising the danger of their unwittingly incriminating themselves during questioning.

[3] There is scope to outline these requirements in greater detail. Again, these requirements are relevant to the protection of suspects during questioning as they safeguard against the mistreatment of detainees resulting in their being more susceptible to incriminating themselves when under interrogation from the police.

Section 60 of PACE requires that all police interviews be tape-recorded. Theoretically, this provides a safeguard against oppressive interrogation techniques of suspects, although there has been some debate over the extent to which this has proven the case in practice.[4] Videotaping of interviews has been piloted which has the potential to improve the safeguards afforded to detainees when being questioned, interviews being clearly visible. However, it is costly and is unlikely to become a standard practice in the foreseeable future. In general, the courts appear to have attached much significance to compliance with recording requirements on the part of the police. For example, in *R v Canale* [1990] 2 All ER 187, where the evidence of an interview had not been contemporaneously written up, the court declined to admit it.

[4] This point could be explored further if you have time. There is certainly some evidence to suggest that tape-recording of interviews has not led to an end to heavy-handed interrogation tactics by police. By making reference to possible videorecording of interviews, you show awareness of recent developments and debates in this area.

Section 58 of PACE entitles any detained person to consult with a legal adviser privately and free of charge. The right to legal advice is widely recognised within most legal systems, and forms part of the right to a fair trial guaranteed by Article 6 of the European Convention on Human Rights. Appropriate legal advice can provide suspects with important protection against police tactics during interrogation which might otherwise lead them to unwittingly incriminate themselves. All detainees are entitled at a minimum to speak to a member of the Criminal Defence Service over the telephone, although any detainee who is to be interviewed by the police can have a legal adviser present during questioning even if the offence which he is being questioned in relation to is relatively minor. Although the right to consult a legal adviser can be denied where there is reasonable cause to suspect this will lead to other suspects being alerted, this should only apply in exceptional circumstances. The courts have shown that they are wary of admitting evidence obtained from suspects where legal representation has been denied. For example, in *R v Samuel* [1988] QB 615, evidence of a suspect's confession was held inadmissible where he had been denied access to legal advice. However, in cases such as *R v Alladice* (1988) 87 Cr App R 380, the courts have admitted evidence notwithstanding the denial of access to a legal adviser on the ground that it would not have affected the suspect's evidence in the circumstances.[5]

[5] It is essential that you discuss the right to legal advice and the possible impact of a suspect being denied legal advice, in light of some conflicting case law on this matter.

Historically, suspects could claim the benefit of the so-called 'right to silence', that is to say, their failure to answer police questions could not entitle juries to draw any adverse inferences against them during trial. However, section 34 of the Criminal Justice and Public Order Act 1994 now permits a jury to draw inferences as they deem appropriate from a suspect's refusal to answer police questions. This has been the subject of much controversy, although it was held in *Murray v UK* (1996) 22 EHRR 29 that this provision does not breach Article 6 of the ECHR. While the abolition of the so-called 'right to silence' has been regarded by some as a weakening of the protection afforded to detainees against self-incrimination during questioning, in practice, very few detainees avail themselves of it and commentators such as Zander (1979) have suggested that its value was overstated.[6] Furthermore, adverse inferences may not be drawn where a suspect has been denied legal advice (s. 34(2A)), and the courts have identified a number of cases in which adverse inferences should not be drawn.

[6] Much can be made of the abolition of the so-called 'right to silence' and the consequences of this for the protection which it affords to a suspect during questioning. There has been much academic debate upon the issue, which you could usefully make reference to.

A final safeguard against inappropriate police treatment of suspects during questioning can be found in section 76(2) of PACE, which

[7] Ensure that you don't overlook the provisions which enable the courts to refuse to admit police evidence where its reliability is in question. This is a 'final' safeguard as even where the police fail to comply with the other provisions which attempt to protect suspects, the courts are still able to decline to admit evidence which emerges from inappropriately conducted police interrogations.

enables the courts to refuse to admit evidence of confessions which have been extracted by oppression.[7] This ought to deter the police from using unscrupulous methods as part of the interrogation process. For example, shouting at a suspect who had denied involvement in an offence over 300 times will constitute oppression (*R v Paris, Abdullahi and Miller* [1993] 97 Cr App R 99). Furthermore, section 78(1) enables the courts generally to exclude any prosecution evidence where it appears that in the circumstances it would have an adverse effect on proceedings and that it ought not to be admitted. This provision can be invoked to prevent the admission of evidence which has been obtained by the police where serious breaches of safeguards have taken place, for example, the denial of legal advice to a suspect, mistreatment in custody or a failure to comply with other procedural safeguards.

In conclusion, there is a series of useful safeguards which go some way towards ensuring that suspects are protected against inappropriate police behaviour. The prescription of time limits for detention, minimum conditions which detainees are entitled to be kept within, recording of interviews, and the right to legal advice all theoretically minimise the risk of the police mistreating suspects in order to extract confessions or other evidence. The courts' power to exclude unreliable evidence is particularly important as a means of responding to situations in which the police have not complied with the relevant provisions designed to protect suspects being questioned in custody.

✓ Make your answer stand out

- Make reference to relevant research findings upon the relative value of safeguards such as the 'right to silence', the tape-recording of interviews and access to legal advice.
- Refer to McConville (1992) 'Videotaping Interrogations: Police Behaviour On and Off Camera', *Crim LR*, 52, to demonstrate the ability of the police to exert influence over suspects outside formal interviews.
- Consider any gap between the protection given to suspects by PACE provisions in theory and in practice.
- Place the issues into context by making reference to miscarriages of justice and the need for safeguards to be adequate to protect against these occurring.

- Focus narrowly upon the process of questioning suspects, without paying attention to broader issues, such as the exclusion of improperly obtained evidence.

# Question 2

Discuss the general powers enjoyed by the police to stop and search suspects in public and the safeguards which apply to these powers.

## Answer plan

→ Explain the balance that needs to be struck between competing interests in relation to stop and search powers.

→ Make reference to the common law position in relation to stop and search by the police.

→ Explain the power conferred upon the police by section 1 of PACE.

→ Explain the requirements imposed on the police by section 2 of PACE.

→ Explain the restrictions placed upon the police's ability to search suspects in public and the requirements imposed upon them in relation to recording stops and searches.

→ Make reference to the increased powers of stop and search conferred upon the police by various recent legislative provisions.

## Diagram plan

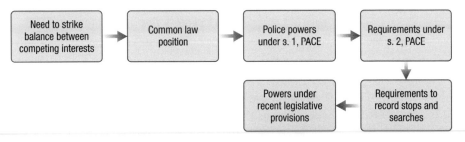

A printable version of this diagram plan is available from www.pearsoned.co.uk/lawexpressqa

# Answer

The ability of the police to stop and search individuals whom they may suspect of criminal activity gives rise to a series of competing tensions in respect of which the law needs to strike an appropriate balance. On the one hand, the police must be given powers that are sufficient to enable them to undertake legitimate investigations to perform their primary function to prevent and detect crime, yet there is also a need to protect against unnecessary interferences with individual liberty arising from abuse of police powers. In specific relation to the exercise of stop and search powers by the police, there has been ongoing concern for some time that ethnic minorities are discriminated against, [1] with statistical evidence pointing to disproportionately higher use of these powers against Black and Asian people, especially in London.

At common law it has long been established that the police have no power to detain suspects short of arresting them.[2] This was demonstrated in the case of **Kenlin v Gardiner** [1967] 2 QB 510 where it was held that the police had no power to detain a group of boys for questioning prior to arrest. However, where a police officer merely pursues a suspect in an attempt to ask questions as opposed to physically detaining them, this has been held to amount to a trivial interference with liberty as opposed to an instance of unlawful detention (**Donnelly v Jackman** [1970] 1 WLR 562). Although the police are entitled at common law to ask questions of members of the public, there is no corresponding obligation on the part of the public to answer as the case of **Rice v Connolly** [1966] 2 QB 414 established, although failure to answer questions when accompanied by abusive behaviour on the part of the person questioned may be held to constitute obstruction of a police officer (**Ricketts v Cox** (1982) 74 Cr App R 298).

Police powers to stop and search suspects were placed upon a statutory footing by the Police and Criminal Evidence Act 1984 (PACE), which seeks to provide the police with the powers necessary to effectively perform their functions whilst ensuring that adequate safeguards are placed upon the exercise of these powers to protect against abuse. Under section 1, a police officer may search a person or vehicle in a public place for stolen or prohibited articles, [3] which as a consequence of changes made by the Criminal Justice Act 2003 now extends to articles intended for use to cause criminal damage. A person may be detained for the purpose of conducting such a search. A search may

[1] You can provide useful context to your answer by citing evidence of discriminate use of stop and search powers, which underlines the importance of having effective safeguards against abuse of these powers.

[2] It is worthwhile briefly outlining the common law position in relation to stopping suspects. This serves to reinforce the significance of PACE provisions.

[3] You need to explain clearly the power conferred upon the police by section 1 and the safeguards attached to it.

only be undertaken if the police officer has reasonable grounds for suspecting that he will find one of the articles referred to. Guidance on what constitute 'reasonable grounds' for suspicion is to be found in code of practice A.[4] Paragraph 2.2 of the Code states that 'reasonable grounds' will be dependent upon the circumstances of the individual case. However, it goes on to add that there must be an objective basis for a police officer's suspicion which is based upon facts, information or intelligence relevant to the likelihood of finding an article of the kind covered by section 1 of PACE. The need for an objective basis for a search prevents police officers from acting out of irrelevant considerations or carrying out stop and searches on a mere whim. Ordinarily, a reasonable suspicion cannot be based purely on personal factors such as race, age or the fact that the individual concerned is known to have previous criminal convictions. This should minimise the risk of particular groups being discriminately singled out for stop and searches, although statistical data unfortunately suggests that discrimination on the part of the police continues in this respect. There is, however, some scope for a reasonable suspicion to exist in the absence of specific information, paragraph 2.3 of the Code providing the example of a police officer encountering someone on the street at night who is obviously attempting to hide something.

[4] You can only effectively illustrate the safeguards which accompany section 1 by referring to the guidance offered by Code A, in particular in relation to 'reasonable grounds' for suspicion.

As a further safeguard, section 2 of PACE sets out a series of minimum standards that must be satisfied by a police officer before a search takes place of a person or vehicle.[5] The police officer must identify himself, provide the name of the station at which he is based and explain the grounds upon which he is going to undertake the search. If the officer is not in uniform, he must provide documentary evidence of his identity. These standards serve as important safeguards against police abuse of stop and search powers by providing a degree of accountability on the part of police officers for their actions. Significantly, the Court of Appeal ruled in *R v Bristol* [2007] EWCA Crim 3214 that the failure of a police officer to provide the necessary information under section 2 when undertaking a stop and search will render it unlawful.

[5] Section 2 provides several safeguards which apply to stop and search powers and should be outlined.

Under section 117 of PACE, a police officer may use 'reasonable force' where necessary in order to exercise his powers.[6] Thus, while it may be necessary to employ some force to facilitate a search where a suspect refuses to cooperate with police, the requirement that force be 'reasonable' protects against the excessive use of

[6] You should refer to the fact that force may be used in order to perform a stop and search, but that this is qualified by the need for it to be 'reasonable', this providing a further example of PACE attempting to strike a balance between empowering the police and protecting the rights of suspects.

[7] Ensure that you do not overlook the recording requirements imposed by PACE. These provide a further safeguard against abuse of power.

[8] If you have time you could make more of this point, by providing examples of some of the areas in which police powers of stop and search have been increased, for example in relation to stopping vehicles en route to festivals, and terrorist suspects. You might offer further comment upon the extent to which such powers undermine the balanced framework for stop and search contained in PACE.

force, some degree of proportionality being required on the part of the police. Furthermore, where a person is subject to a search in public, section 2(9) of PACE provides that the only clothing which can be removed is outer clothing including coats, jackets or gloves, thus affording some protection to the dignity of the searched individual.

Wherever the police stop and search a person in public, that person's name, address and ethnicity must be recorded together with the reason for the stop and search and its outcome. A copy of the record must be provided to the suspect. If not searched, the person's ethnicity must be noted and a receipt given. The police are empowered under section 1(6) to seize any stolen or prohibited articles discovered as a result of a search, and must make a written record at the time detailing these unless exceptional circumstances exist which make this wholly impracticable. These recording requirements are an important means of ensuring police actions are justified and accounted for.[7]

While PACE provisions appear to attempt to strike a reasonable balance between empowering the police to perform their essential functions and providing necessary safeguards against abuse of these powers, a number of recent legislative provisions have introduced new powers to stop and search in relation to particular offences which arguably enhance police powers in this area further,[8] for example, under the Criminal Justice and Public Order Act 1994 and the Terrorism Act 2000.

✓ Make your answer stand out

- Provide context to your answer by referring to the disproportionate use of stop and search powers against certain groups in society, making reference to the findings detailed in Miller (2010) 'Stop and Search in England: A Reformed Tactic or Business as Usual?', *British Journal of Criminology*, v. 50, n. 5, 954.
- Make reference to the growth of stop and search powers under various recent pieces of legislation, and the extent to which this may undermine the balanced framework provided by PACE for the exercise of stop and search powers.
- Distinguish clearly between the general stop and search powers enjoyed by the police on a routine basis and those applicable only in more serious contexts, for example those conferred by anti-terrorism legislation.
- Draw firm conclusions on the merits of the current legal framework governing stop and search powers.

# 🖋 Question 3

Discuss the extent to which the rules on the granting of bail strike a balance between protecting the rights of defendants and the wider interests of society.

## Answer plan

→ Briefly explain what bail is.

→ Explain the various tensions which arise in the bail process and the need to have regard to competing objectives.

→ Explain which bodies are empowered to grant bail.

→ Discuss the statutory presumption in favour of bail and the circumstances in which bail may be refused.

→ Discuss the scope which exists for a grant of bail to be made subject to conditions.

→ Conclude upon the extent to which the current law strikes an appropriate balance between protecting the rights of defendants and wider interests of society.

## Diagram plan

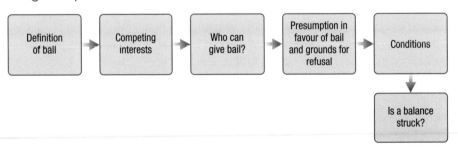

A printable version of this diagram plan is available from www.pearsoned.co.uk/lawexpressqa

# Answer

'Bail' refers to the release from custody of a person charged with a criminal offence pending and during trial.[1] Bail may be subject to conditions and may be dependent upon the willingness of another person to act as a surety whereby a sum of money is put down which will be forfeited if the defendant absconds or breaks bail conditions.

[1] You should begin your answer by briefly demonstrating that you understand what bail is.

Decisions over the grant or refusal of bail need to balance some very important competing interests.[2] On the one hand, a fundamental principle of English law is the presumption of the innocence of the accused until proven otherwise in a court of law. The increasing influence of human rights standards also requires that individual liberty, guaranteed by Article 5 of the European Convention on Human Rights, be protected unless there are compelling reasons for it to be compromised. Remanding defendants in custody puts a burden on the already overcrowded prison population, approximately 16% of which consists of those held on remand awaiting trial and yet to be convicted of an offence. This is arguably of special concern given that during the 1990s, of those remanded in custody awaiting trial for summary offences, 50% ultimately received non-custodial sentences and 25% were acquitted. However, granting bail comes with its own series of problems: 12% of those bailed fail to appear for their trial, a factor which led then Attorney-General in 2005, Lord Goldsmith, to call for a crackdown on those who 'skip bail', at a time when 60,000 warrants were outstanding for failure to appear in court. Those on bail may also commit further offences or possibly interfere with prosecution witnesses or obstruct the course of justice. Approximately 50,000 offences are committed annually by those on bail, which have included some high-profile instances of rape and serious assault offences. In light of these considerations, the law on bail has a difficult balance to strike.

[2] You should provide some contextual background to your answer by illustrating the competing interests which come into play when decisions are made to grant or refuse bail. It will be helpful to refer to statistical evidence relating to such matters as the number of offences committed by those on bail or instances of defendants failing to attend court. This goes to the very heart of the question and reinforces the need for the law on bail to strike a balance between various competing interests.

Bail can be granted by the police or the courts. Where a person has been arrested on a warrant, the warrant will indicate if bail is to be given. Where a person is arrested without a warrant, the decision to grant or deny bail following charge resides with the police.[3] Section 38(1)(a) of the Police and Criminal Evidence Act 1984 provides that a person must be released on police bail unless there are reasonable grounds for doubting the name and address given by the person, for believing detention to be necessary to prevent the accused harming

[3] Before considering the specific rules governing the grant or denial of bail, you should firstly explain who has the power to grant bail. The role of the police in this respect should be explained first as they are responsible for considering bail in the first instance. It is helpful to cite figures on the granting of bail to demonstrate the extent to which it is readily given or otherwise.

himself, others or property, or for believing that he will fail to appear in court or that his detention is necessary to prevent interference with the course of justice. Although broad, these considerations can only be used to deny bail where the custody officer has reasonable grounds for believing in their applicability. In practice, bail is over-whelmingly granted, with 83% of those charged with indictable offences and 88% of those charged with summary offences being bailed in 1990. If the police deny bail, the accused should be brought before the magistrates' court as soon as possible. The granting of bail by the courts is primarily governed by the Bail Act 1976,[4] and a duty is imposed on the courts to consider bail at each subsequent hearing, underlying the importance of the defendant's liberty pending any conviction. This is reinforced by the existence of rights of appeal against decisions to refuse bail.

[4] You should explain the continuing role of the courts in the bail process in order to illustrate the clear importance attached to bail.

Section 4 of the Bail Act 1976 contains a statutory presumption in favour of bail. Bail should be generally granted unless serious con-siderations militate against it. These are outlined in Schedule 1 to the Act[5] and are that the court is satisfied that there are substantial grounds for believing that the defendant will abscond, offend while on bail, interfere with witnesses or obstruct the course of justice. These reflect the main problems associated with the granting of bail and are arguably therefore very logical. Bail may also be denied where it is felt custody is warranted for the defendant's own protec-tion, where he has previously failed to answer bail, or the court requires further information in order to make a reasoned decision. The court must take all relevant factors into account when making its decision. Further grounds for the denial of bail were added by the Criminal Justice Act 2003, sections 14–15, these being where the defendant committed the present offence while on bail or has absconded previously in the same proceedings.

[5] It is essential that you explain the presumption which exists in favour of bail and outline the grounds upon which bail can be denied. This goes to the heart of the question and involves considering the extent to which an appropriate balance is struck by the law. You should point out that the grounds for the denial of bail relate directly to the main undesirable consequences which bail tends to give rise to.

[6] The impact of section 25 of the Criminal Justice and Public Order Act was controversial. By discussing the outcome of this attempt to restrict bail you are able to illustrate in action a key tension between competing values and the extent to which the law has struck a balance in respect of defendants charged with serious offences.

Arguably, the law appears to strike a reasonable balance by making a presumption in favour of bail, while enabling its denial where there is reason to believe that its grant may have one of the undesirable effects most closely associated with bail. That the overwhelming majority of defendants are granted bail would seem to reinforce this point. The law's relative flexibility is evidenced by the outcome of the attempt of section 25 of the Criminal Justice and Public Order Act 1994 to deny bail to those charged with serious offences who have previous convictions for other serious offences.[6] The provision was challenged in **Caballero v UK** (2000) 30 EHRR 1 by a defendant denied bail when charged with rape in 1996 due to his having a manslaughter conviction from 1987. This was deemed to breach Article 5(3) of the European Convention on Human Rights and was amended by the Crime and Disorder Act 1998, so that bail could be granted in such cases where the court is satisfied that 'exceptional circumstances' justify this. Thus, even where a very serious offence is committed by a defendant with a serious previous conviction, bail is no longer automatically excluded as a possibility.

[7] You should explain the scope which exists for conditions to be imposed on bail grants and how these may help to resolve some of the tensions which arise when deciding whether to award bail or not.

Conditions may be imposed upon bail.[7] There are no statutory limitations upon what conditions may be imposed, but they commonly include curfews or residency requirements, regular attendance at a police station, or the surrender of a passport. The objective of conditions is to minimise the risk of re-offending, absconding or interfering with witnesses or the course of justice without having to remand the defendant in custody.

[8] This conclusion flows logically from the discussion contained in the essay which has portrayed the law as essentially balanced between the competing objectives.

In conclusion, the law on bail appears to generally balance well the competing interests at stake.[8] There is a presumption in favour of bail, but the problems associated with bail are recognised in the provisions which enable bail to be denied where there are solid grounds to do so. Ultimately bail is awarded to the vast majority of defendants and the scope which exists for conditions to be placed upon grants of bail make it easier to strike an appropriate balance between protecting the individual liberty of those yet to be convicted of an offence and having regard to other legitimate concerns.

 Make your answer stand out

- Provide some context to your answer by illustrating the tensions which arise in the bail process with reference to relevant statistical evidence.
- Make reference to attempts to reduce the availability of bail.
- Consider the human rights dimension of the bail application process, with reference to Article 5 of the European Convention on Human Rights.
- Consider the extent to which the imposition of conditions on bail may strengthen the balance between guaranteeing the liberty of those yet to be convicted of an offence with protecting the public.

# 🖎 Question 4

Discuss the factors which inform a judge's approach to sentencing a convicted defendant.

## Answer plan

→ Briefly outline the main categories of sentence open to a judge to impose upon a convicted defendant and the factors which constrain a judge's discretion.

→ Explain the purposes of sentencing which judges are to be guided by.

→ Consider the use of sentencing guidelines to assist judges when sentencing.

→ Consider the increased control placed upon sentencing by legislation, such as the imposition of fixed or minimum sentences for certain offences, or requirements which must be satisfied for certain sentences to be imposed.

→ Explain the role formerly played by the Home Secretary in the imposition of life sentences, and how this has now been reformed.

→ Conclude upon the extent to which the law affords judges sufficient flexibility to impose sentences suited to the offence.

## Diagram plan

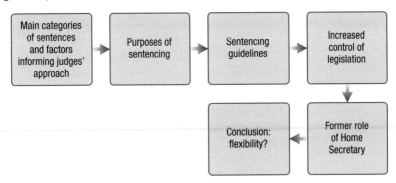

A printable version of this diagram plan is available from www.pearsoned.co.uk/lawexpressqa

# Answer

[1] While it is useful to refer to the main types of sentence which a court can impose in your introduction, the question does not ask for a detailed explanation of these and so is not necessary.

[2] It is helpful in the introduction to briefly outline the main factors which impact upon a judge's approach to sentencing as this enables you to highlight the key issues to be covered in the remainder of the answer.

[3] The question is not concerned specifically with the purposes of sentencing, but these are a factor which judges must have regard to and should thus be mentioned.

Following the conviction of a defendant, there are four main categories of sentence which a judge may choose to impose.[1] The ultimate sanction is that of the imposition of a custodial sentence, but sentences may also take the form of fines, various community sentences and other miscellaneous sentences. A judge's approach towards sentencing in any given case is constrained by a variety of factors.[2] Legislation prescribes certain sentences for particular offences, taking the form of minimum or maximum sentences. There are also sentencing guidelines which judges ought to have regard to when deciding upon the appropriate sentence in any given case, and reference is also to be made to the purposes of sentencing which are to be found in statute. Over time, judicial discretion upon sentencing matters has become increasingly regulated by legislation.

Section 142 of the Criminal Justice Act 2003 prescribes a number of recognised purposes of sentencing.[3] Firstly, sentencing should serve to punish offenders, that is to say there should be a degree of retributive effect in sentences, the idea being that any sentence should fit the crime committed. Secondly, sentencing should be designed to reduce crime. This applies both to individual offenders, deterring them from re-offending, and the general public, who may be deterred from committing similar crimes through the imposition of exemplary sentences upon offenders. Thirdly, sentencing should give consideration to the reform and rehabilitation of offenders, an objective which has been of increased interest recently. The fourth objective of sentencing is the protection of the public, hence dangerous offenders would ordinarily be expected to receive a custodial sentence. Finally, courts must have regard to the making of reparation by offenders to those affected by their offences, a relatively fresh approach to sentencing.

[4] Sentencing guidelines are a paramount consideration for judges sentencing offenders. If you have time, you might provide more detailed discussion of the background to the creation of the SC to replace the Sentencing Guidelines Council and the Sentencing Advisory Panel.

Until relatively recently sentencing guidelines were provided by the Court of Appeal. However, they are now the responsibility of the Sentencing Council (SC), set up by the Coroners and Justice Act 2009, which produces guidelines for judges.[4] Courts are obliged to have regard to these guidelines when sentencing an offender. While these guidelines provide a degree of discretion for judges to operate within, they suggest appropriate starting points for sentence levels for particular offences and direct the courts to consider relevant aggravating or mitigating factors which may warrant the imposition of a higher or lower sentence than the ordinary suggested starting point.

Judicial discretion is significantly curbed in those areas where legislation has been used to carefully control sentencing by the courts.[5] Magistrates' courts are restricted to imposing custodial sentences of 12 months in respect of any offence (s. 154, Criminal Justice Act 2003), although under section 3 of the Powers of Criminal Courts (Sentencing) Act 2000 it may send a defendant to be sentenced in the Crown Court if it deems that a tougher sentence than it has the jurisdiction to impose is warranted. Subject to any specific restrictions imposed in respect of certain offences, the Crown Court is able to make use of the full range of available sentences. There are no limits to its ability to impose fines, although in so doing it must take account of the seriousness of the offence committed and the means of the defendant to pay (s. 167, Criminal Justice Act 2003). Minimum sentences have been created for a number of offences, one example being that applicable to certain firearms offences under section 287 of the Criminal Justice Act 2003. Although maximum sentences exist for many offences, they are rarely imposed in practice. Mandatory sentences are carried by some offences, the most notable example being that of murder, for which nothing less than a life sentence will suffice.

Despite evidence of increased regulation of sentencing policy by legislation, there are several legislative provisions designed to guard against a hasty resort to sentences which may be harsher than are warranted by the offence committed.[6] For example, under section 152 of the Criminal Justice Act 2003 a court should not pass a custodial sentence unless it considers the offence is so serious that only this sentence can be justified. Section 153 of the same Act provides that custodial sentences should be for the shortest term commensurate with the seriousness of the offence. In determining the seriousness of an offence, section 143 directs the court to have regard to the culpability of the offender, harm caused by the offence and the offender's previous criminal record. Thus, while legislation has been increasingly used to control the imposition of sentences by judges, it has been used to discourage the rash imposition of harsh sentences in some circumstances as well as ensuring that minimum or specified sentences are imposed in others.

[5] A major point to be made is the extent to which judicial discretion has been curbed as a result of legislative provisions which pertain to the sentencing process. You can illustrate this effectively through the use of the examples cited.

[6] This is a useful point to make in order to provide a balanced account of the impact of legislation on the sentencing process.

A major area of controversy in sentencing policy has arisen from attempts to politicise the process. Crime is a significant area of political concern and successive governments have sought to portray themselves as tough on criminal offenders.[7] One example can be found with the Crime (Sentences) Act 1997, section 2 of which prescribed mandatory life sentences for those convicted of a second serious offence, such as manslaughter, rape or certain offences against the person. Criticism of the provision followed cases such as *R v Turner* [2000] Crim LR 492, where a life sentence was imposed following a conviction for grievous bodily harm with intent because the defendant had been convicted of manslaughter thirty years earlier. Although section 2 allowed courts to decline to impose a life sentence where of the opinion that there were exceptional circumstances to justify this, this was interpreted rigidly until the case of *R v Offen and others* [2001] 1 WLR 253 where the Court of Appeal ruled that mandatory life sentences were not intended to apply to defendants not posing a future risk to the public.

[7] If you have the time, there is scope for more detailed discussion of the extent to which the sentencing of offenders has given rise to some fierce political debates and the ensuing implications for the doctrine of separation of powers.

Another example of the danger of politicisation of the sentencing process is found in the role formerly played in the setting of tariffs for life sentences of those convicted of murder by the Home Secretary. This was found to breach Article 5(1) and 5(4) of the European Convention on Human Rights in *Stafford v UK* (2002) 35 EHRR 1121, and was subsequently removed. Section 269 of the Criminal Justice Act 2003 created instead a three-tier system of life sentences within which after considering specified starting points judges are able to apply aggravating and mitigating factors.

[8] This conclusion flows logically from the discussion contained within the answer which alludes to several factors which influence the approach taken towards the sentencing of offenders by judges in individual cases.

In conclusion, the sentencing of those convicted of an offence is not an automated process.[8] Whereas legislation has increasingly sought to control the process, judges retain a degree of flexibility within which they can operate in light of guidance which they are given and must have regard to.

Make your answer stand out

- Provide some discussion of attempts to politicise sentencing and the importance of the separation of powers within the context of sentencing by the courts.
- Emphasise the increased control over judicial approaches to sentencing exerted by legislation with reference to examples from specific statutory provisions.
- Consider the value of sentencing guidelines in achieving policy objectives by reading and referring to Wasik (2008) 'Sentencing Guidelines in England and Wales – State of the Art?', *Crim LR*, 253.
- Make reference to the Legal Aid, Sentencing and Punishment of Offenders Act 2012 and consider what impact it is likely to have upon the courts' approach towards sentencing.

! Don't be tempted to . . .

- Spend a lot of time explaining the purposes of sentencing.
- Spend a lot of time outlining the various types of sentences which the courts may impose.

#  Question 5

'The removal of the "right to silence" by the Criminal Justice and Public Order Act 1994 has had relatively little impact upon the protection afforded to defendants when being questioned.' Discuss.

## Answer plan

→ Briefly explain what is meant by the 'right to silence' and the pre-1994 legal position on its protection.

→ Explain the impact of sections 34–37 of the Criminal Justice and Public Order Act 1994.

→ Consider the rationale for the changes introduced by the 1994 Act.

→ Consider how the 1994 changes have been built upon by subsequent legal developments.

→ Conclude upon the extent to which the abolition of the 'right to silence' has had an impact upon the protection afforded to defendants when being questioned.

# Diagram plan

| 'Right to silence': pre-1994 | → | Impact of ss. 34–37, CJAPOA | → | Rationale for 1994 Act changes | → | Subsequent developments | → | Conclusion |

A printable version of this diagram plan is available from www.pearsoned.co.uk/lawexpressqa

# Answer

[1] At the outset of your answer you should explain what the 'right to silence' entailed, thus setting the scene nicely for you to move on to consider the impact upon this of the provisions of the 1994 Act.

[2] You should briefly explain the main provisions of the 1994 Act which permitted courts to draw adverse inferences from a suspect's silence.

[3] In considering the real impact of the abolition of the 'right to silence', it is important to engage with the debate over the merits of the right. This will enable you to consider whether the effect of the 1994 Act was to remove a hugely significant right, or was relatively inconsequential.

The 'right to silence' refers to the ability of suspects to refuse to answer questions during police questioning or when on trial without a jury being entitled to draw any adverse inferences from this silence.[1] Prior to provisions introduced by the Criminal Justice and Public Order Act 1994, although juries in practice might draw adverse inferences from a defendant's failure to answer any questions, judges were obliged to tell them that they should not do so. It is slightly misleading to say that the 1994 Act abolished the right to silence as no defendant can be compelled to answer any questions if he does not want to; however, the effect of the change to the law was that a defendant's silence could have adverse consequences for his defence which previously the law did not permit.

Sections 34–37 of the 1994 Act provide four circumstances in which a suspect's silence will entitle a court to draw any inferences they deem appropriate from this silence.[2] These are where a suspect fails to mention something during police questioning later relied on as part of his defence and which he could reasonably have been expected to mention, where a suspect fails to give evidence or answer questions during trial, where a suspect fails to account after arrest for objects, substances or marks on his clothing, and where a suspect fails to account for his presence at a place after arrest. The 1994 Act clearly introduces a wide range of circumstances in which a jury can draw adverse inferences from a defendant's silence.

Prior to the introduction of the 1994 Act there was much debate over the merits of the traditional 'right to silence' enjoyed by suspects.[3] Defenders of the right claimed that it was an important safeguard for suspects to protect themselves against self-incrimination during police questioning, particularly where interrogation involves oppressive techniques. While critics of the right to silence argued that the innocent had nothing to fear from its abolition if they simply answered police questions truthfully, the Criminal Law Revision Committee in 1972 identified a number of legitimate reasons why an innocent suspect may prefer to remain silent, such as confusion, fear of implicating oneself in embarrassing conduct, or to protect others. The Runciman Royal Commission recommended in 1993 that adverse inferences should not be permitted to be drawn from silence under police questioning. The main rationale behind the abolition of the right to silence would appear to have been the concern with suspects frustrating criminal investigations through non-cooperation with the police when being questioned. The Home Secretary at the time of the Act, Michael Howard, argued that hardened criminals disproportionately availed themselves of the right to frustrate the criminal justice process, wasting police time and making it more difficult to convict offenders. A particular concern was the use of 'ambush' defences by defendants, whereby they would launch last-minute defences not mentioned during questioning, which the prosecution would then have insufficient time to investigate in order to rebut in court.

[4] This is an important point to emphasise. It can be used to support either side of the debate on the merits of the right to silence, as on one hand it suggests that the right was not subject to heavy abuse and in no real need of reform, yet on the other hand by showing the limited extent to which the right was exercised, it can be argued that its abolition will have little impact upon the safeguards currently enjoyed by most suspects in practice.

[5] You can consider further the impact of the 1994 provisions by exploring case law upon the Act in order to assess the manner in which these have been applied by the courts. The cases cited here all evidence a reluctance on the part of the courts to allow adverse inferences to be drawn too easily.

However, while these appear prima facie logical grounds for wanting to remove the right to silence, the fact is that various studies – such as those conducted by Zander (1979) and Sanders et al. (1989) – have demonstrated that very few suspects remain silent during questioning, as few as 2% in the Sanders study.[4] This undermines any argument that there are huge gains to be made from abolishing the right to silence, especially where this may weaken the protection which the right can potentially afford to innocent suspects. However, it also suggests that any protection afforded to defendants by the right to silence was minimal given the relatively little use made of it. In this sense, it could be argued that the impact of the provisions of the 1994 Act, in practice, ought to be minimal.

The extent to which adverse inferences may be drawn from a defendant's silence has been the subject of debate in a number of post-1994 cases.[5] Although it was held in *Murray v UK* [1996] 22 EHRR 29 that the abolition of the right to silence did not breach the European Convention on Human Rights, the courts will not always permit adverse inferences to be drawn from a defendant's silence. For example, a defendant's failure to answer questions cannot lead to adverse inferences being drawn when he explained his conduct and defence at the time in a written statement to the police (*R v McGarry* [1998] 3 All ER 805). It was also held in *R v N* [1998] *The Times* 13 February, that adverse inferences could only be drawn from a defendant's failure to answer questions on a matter, not from his failure to mention something that he had not been asked about. Such cases show the courts adopting some caution when interpreting the 1994 provisions in order to ensure that suspects retain some reasonable safeguards.

The question of whether adverse inferences can be drawn where a defendant fails to answer questions as a result of a solicitor's advice has also been considered by the courts.[6] In *Condron v UK* [2000] Crim LR 679, it was held that remaining silent upon a solicitor's advice in itself does not prevent adverse inferences being drawn by a jury, but that good reasons must be provided as to why this legal advice was given. Subsequently, the Court of Appeal has ruled that a defendant remaining silent on a solicitor's advice must have both a genuine and reasonable reliance upon that advice (*R v Beckles* [2004] All ER (D) 226 (Nov)). There is, thus, a certain threshold for a defendant to satisfy in order to prevent any adverse inferences being drawn. However, where a suspect is denied the opportunity to consult a solicitor at the police station, the 1994 Act was amended by section 58 of the Youth Justice and Criminal Evidence Act 1999 to the effect that no adverse inferences may be drawn from the suspect's silence. This is arguably an important safeguard for suspects who may be especially vulnerable as a consequence of the absence of any legal advice of which they can avail themselves.

In conclusion, there is arguably difference between the theoretical and practical impact of sections 34–37 of the 1994 Act.[7] While theoretically a long-established safeguard is removed from suspects, the reality is that very few of them ever actually availed themselves of it. Furthermore, in some of the case law on the application of the statutory provisions the courts have shown a willingness to ensure that certain safeguards remain for defendants where adverse inferences cannot be drawn from their silence in certain circumstances.

[6] This is an issue worth exploring as the case law evidences the extent to which a court's ability to draw adverse inferences is based upon a number of factors, as the cases in this area demonstrate.

[7] This conclusion flows logically from the discussion contained in the answer. A strong case can be made from the outset for distinguishing between the theoretical and practical impact of the 1994 Act upon the right to silence, and this is reinforced to some extent by consideration of some of the case law.

### ✓ Make your answer stand out

- Consider both the merits of the abolition of the so-called 'right to silence' and the extent to which any negative consequences have been increased or ameliorated by subsequent legal developments.

- Draw upon relevant case law to illustrate the application of the 1994 Act provisions in practice, upon which you can refer to Jackson (2009) 'Re-conceptualizing the Right to Silence as an Effective Fair Trial Standard', *International and Comparative Law Quarterly*, v. 58, n. 4, 835.

- Demonstrate clearly any human rights implications of the abolition of the 'right to silence' by referring to decisions of the European Court of Human Rights.

- Draw upon statistical evidence on the invocation of the right to silence by suspects questioned by the police in drawing conclusions upon the significance of the 1994 reforms.

### ! Don't be tempted to . . .

- Simply outline the arguments for and against the removal of the 'right to silence'.

## 🖎 Question 6

Discuss the ability of the courts to exclude evidence in a criminal trial, with particular reference to evidence obtained by the police.

## Answer plan

→ Briefly explain the importance of relevance and reliability as key criteria governing the admissibility of evidence, and the central role of the police in the collection of evidence.

→ Briefly refer to some of the general rules which govern the admissibility of evidence, such as the rule against hearsay evidence and restrictions upon the admission of character evidence.

→ Explain the scope of section 76 of the Police and Criminal Evidence Act 1984 and discuss the extent to which it has been utilised by the courts to exclude evidence of confessions.

→ Explain the scope of section 78 of the Police and Criminal Evidence Act 1984 and discuss the extent to which it has been utilised by the courts to exclude evidence on grounds of its unreliability.

→ Conclude by commenting upon the extent to which the courts appear to be willing to exclude evidence obtained by the police.

# Diagram plan

Importance of relevance and reliability → General rules of evidence → s. 76, PACE → s. 78, PACE → Conclusions

A printable version of this diagram plan is available from www.pearsoned.co.uk/lawexpressqa

## Answer

A significant body of law governs the admission of evidence in criminal trials. The oral tradition of the English criminal trial places great emphasis upon the provision of testimony by witnesses present in court, and the suspicion attached to other forms of evidence is reflected in the law's careful regulation of its admissibility. The core principles upon which the law of evidence is based are, arguably, both the relevance and reliability of evidence that is admitted in court.[1] It must be relevant to the case being proven or rebutted, and its reliability should not be in question because it is tainted in some way. These principles are central to the guarantee of a fair trial, enshrined in Article 6 of the European Convention on Human Rights, now incorporated into domestic law by the Human Rights Act 1998. In the overwhelming majority of criminal trials, the primary body responsible for collecting evidence against the accused will be the police. In order to balance their need to conduct their legitimate investigations effectively with the protection of the rights of suspects, a statutory framework – found primarily in the provisions of the Police and Criminal Evidence Act 1984 – applies to the police's exercise of its powers of investigation which extend to the admissibility of police obtained evidence. Ultimately, whether a particular piece of evidence is admissible in a trial will be a matter for the judge who is the ultimate arbiter on such matters.

The law of evidence contains certain general rules applicable to the admission of evidence.[2] For example, as a general principle hearsay evidence may not be produced in court, to safeguard against the admission of unreliable evidence, subject to a number of well established exceptions. Similarly, to avoid juries being influenced by irrelevant considerations, it is not ordinarily permissible to adduce evidence of the accused's bad character, such as any previous

[1] You can provide some useful context to your answer by explaining the centrality of the criteria of relevance and reliability to the rules which govern the admission of evidence. The importance of reliability in particular will be built upon later when you explore the law's regulation of police obtained evidence.

[2] Although the focus of your answer should be upon evidence obtained by the police, you can demonstrate wider knowledge by making brief reference to some of the key planks of the law of evidence and relate these back to the point made about the importance of reliability and relevance.

criminal convictions, although the effect of section 101 of the Criminal Justice Act 2003 was to make it easier to refer to previous convictions as part of the prosecution case.

Restrictions upon the admissibility of evidence obtained during police investigations are to be found in sections 76 and 78 of the Police and Criminal Evidence Act. Section 76(2) applies to confession evidence and provides that evidence of a confession will be inadmissible where that confession has been obtained by oppression or in circumstances likely to render it unreliable.[3] Oppression is defined in section 76(8) as including 'torture, inhuman or degrading treatment, and the use or threat of violence'. In practice the courts have taken a relatively narrow approach to the question of what will amount to oppression. In *R v Fulling* [1987] QB 426, that the police extracted a confession from a woman after informing her that her partner had been unfaithful to her was held not to amount to an instance of oppression, the court ruling that the term should be given its ordinary dictionary meaning which entailed unjust treatment, cruelty or the wrongful use of power. In practice, the courts have seldom found oppression present in police interrogation procedures. For example, in *R v Miller* [1986] 1 WLR 1191, the existence of medical evidence that questioning of the suspect, a paranoid schizophrenic, produced voluntary insanity on his part was deemed by the Court of Appeal not to amount to evidence of oppression. By contrast, in *R v Paris, Abdullahi and Miller* [1993] 97 Cr App R 99, shouting at a suspect what the police wanted him to say after he had denied his involvement in the crime 300 times was held to amount to oppression. The value of section 76(2) is diluted by section 76(4) which states that, even where confession evidence is excluded, any facts discovered from it may still be admissible. This effectively condones oppressive police questioning adopted for the purpose of soliciting further evidence.[4] The ability of the courts to exclude confession evidence unreliable for other reasons is limited by the fact that its unreliability must arise from anything said or done by a person other than the defendant, a point confirmed in *R v Goldenberg* [1988] 152 JP 557. This means that circumstances pertaining solely to the suspect's mindset will not be grounds for contesting the reliability of his confession.

Section 78(1) applies to evidence generally and provides that a court may refuse to admit evidence if it appears that, having regard to all

[3] You should illustrate the extent to which the courts have made use of section 76(2) to exclude confession evidence by reference to a range of examples from the case law.

[4] It is important that you explain the limited nature of section 76 as a safeguard against the use of oppressive police techniques to obtain evidence.

[5] You are best able to illustrate the use of section 78(1) by the courts to exclude unreliable evidence by drawing upon case law examples to show the broad range of instances to which the provision can potentially be applied.

[6] You must demonstrate also that whereas section 78(1) has a potentially broad scope, the courts are not adverse to the admission of evidence obtained by deception on the part of the police *per se*. Again, you can make use of relevant case law examples to illustrate this point.

[7] Your conclusion reflects the balance of the case law considered. It is certainly not an overstatement to say that a stricter approach, whether desirable or not, could have been taken by the courts to the admission of evidence.

the circumstances, it would have such an adverse effect on the fairness of the proceedings that it ought not to be admitted.[5] Section 78(1) particularly comes into play where there have been breaches of PACE provisions. For example, in *R v Samuel* [1988] QB 615, the denial of access to a solicitor, and in *R v Absalom* [1988] Crim LR 748, the failure to advise a suspect of his right to legal representation, were sufficient grounds for making use of section 78(1). Similarly, a failure to maintain a proper record of an interview with the suspect has been used as sufficient reason for excluding police evidence (*R v Keenan* [1990] 2 QB 54). There is no detailed list of the circumstances in which section 78(1) will be relevant, it having been applied in a wide range of situations. For example, in *R v Mason* [1988] 1 WLR 139, the police's lie to the suspect and his solicitor in an arson case that his fingerprints had been found on a bottle of inflammable liquid led to the exclusion of the resulting confession. The House of Lords has also ruled that evidence obtained by torture abroad should be excluded (*A v Secretary of State for the Home Department* [2004] UKHL 56).

Notwithstanding the broad ambit of section 78(1), the courts appear prepared to tolerate a certain amount of deception on the part of the police as part of their investigative procedures.[6] For example, they refused to exclude evidence in *R v Latif and Shahzad* [1996] 1 WLR 104 where the defendant was tricked into entering the UK so that he could be prosecuted. Similarly, where police officers ran a 'mock' jewellers shop in order to intercept persons involved in handling stolen goods, this was regarded as a legitimate enterprise (*R v Christou and Wright* [1992] QB 979).

While it is possible to point to clear examples of the courts using sections 76 and 78 to exclude evidence where its reliability might be called into question, an examination of the case law demonstrates that the courts have set a relatively high threshold which must be satisfied if evidence is to be excluded,[7] with the admission of evidence being permitted in some instances where the police have either engaged in deceptive practices or otherwise failed to adhere to the standards ordinarily expected of them.

**Make your answer stand out**

- Use a wide range of case law to illustrate the courts' approach to the exclusion of evidence under sections 76(2) and 78(1) of the Police and Criminal Evidence Act 1984.
- Make connections between the courts' powers to exclude evidence and provisions designed to protect suspects against inappropriate police behaviour.
- Make reference to the role of improperly obtained evidence in producing miscarriages of justice.
- In an extended essay you might consider the courts' exclusion of evidence obtained from actions amounting to breaches of individuals' rights under the ECHR, for example, where the police adopt covert tactics which may infringe the Article 8 guarantee of the right to privacy. A good discussion of such issues is provided in Ormerod (2002) 'ECHR and the Exclusion of Evidence: Trial Remedies for Article 8 Breaches?', *Crim LR*, 61.

**! Don't be tempted to . . .**

- Provide a detailed account of the many rules of evidence which the law contains as the question does not ask for this.
- Provide discussion of only one of the two main provisions of the Police and Criminal Evidence Act 1984 that are relevant to the exclusion of evidence.

# ❓ Question 7

PC Pea and PC Bean are patrolling an area which has a high incidence of burglaries. They encounter Lentil, known to them as he has previously been convicted of several burglaries in the area during the last four years. Lentil is wearing a large rucksack, out of which appears to be sticking two silver candlesticks. PC Pea stops Lentil, saying, 'been up to your old tricks, have we?' PC Bean adds that, 'there have been a lot of break-ins around here recently and candlesticks aren't something you normally carry around. Let's take a look in there please.' Lentil opens his bag and allows the two police officers to search it. All they find are two plastic candlesticks, evidently designed for children to play with. They are labelled 'KID'S TOY KITCHENWARE' and a price label reading £1.99 is attached to them. Lentil claims that they are a gift for his nieces and produces a receipt for them. 'We don't care', responds PC Pea, 'you're trouble anyway. You're nicked.' Lentil is then taken to the nearest police station without further explanation.

Advise Lentil as to the legality of the stop and search and his subsequent arrest.

# Answer plan

➡ Explain the police power to stop and search suspects contained in Article 1 PACE and whether it justified stopping and searching Lentil.

➡ Explain the safeguards contained in section 1, PACE and whether they were satisfied in this situation.

➡ Briefly explain the requirement to inform a person of his arrest and the grounds for it, and whether the police complied with this requirement.

➡ Explain the need for an arrest to be based upon reasonable suspicion of involvement in an offence and whether this requirement was satisfied in respect of Lentil's arrest.

➡ Briefly explain the grounds upon which an arrest may be reasonably felt necessary and the ease with which they can be applied if reasonable suspicion of involvement in an offence can be demonstrated.

# Diagram plan

Section 1, PACE: stop and search of Lentil ▶ Section 2, PACE safeguards satisfied? ▶ Appropriate notification of arrest? ▶ Reasonable suspicion for arrest? ▶ Grounds upon which arrest may be necessary

A printable version of this diagram plan is available from www.pearsoned.co.uk/lawexpressqa

# Answer

Police powers of stop and search are governed primarily by sections 1 and 2 of the Police and Criminal Evidence Act 1984 (PACE). Section 1 empowers the police to search persons in public places for stolen or prohibited articles, and to detain them for this purpose. In this case, PC Pea and PC Bean clearly search Lentil's bag for stolen articles. PC Bean's comments to Lentil that there have been 'a lot of break-ins around here recently' and that candlesticks are not an item normally carried around serves to reinforce this. Lentil should be made aware, however, that the police may only carry out a search if they have reasonable grounds for suspecting that they may find stolen or prohibited articles.[1] Guidance to assist in considering whether PC Pea and PC Bean could legitimately claim to have held reasonable grounds for suspecting that they would find stolen articles in Lentil's bag can be found in code of practice A. Paragraph 2.2

[1] The first issue to address is whether the police officers had reasonable grounds for suspecting they would find stolen or prohibited articles in searching Lentil. You must relate the requirements imposed by section 1 of PACE directly to the scenario which you are presented with.

states that there must be an objective basis for a police officer's suspicion which is based upon facts, information or intelligence relevant to the likelihood of him finding the articles being searched for. However, reasonable grounds cannot be based upon purely personal factors, such as a suspect's age, race or the fact that he has previous criminal convictions. Thus, the fact that Lentil is known to the police as a former offender in itself would not be likely to constitute a reasonable ground to search him in the absence of any other objectively relevant information available to the police. However, in this situation, what appear to be candlesticks are sticking out of Lentil's bag – an unusual item to see being carried around – and he is apprehended in an area which has experienced a high incidence of burglaries. These facts may give an objective basis for the suspicion shown towards Lentil by the police officers concerned, something which may be reinforced by the fact that Lentil has a track record of having committed a number of burglaries. We do not have any further information upon the circumstances in which Lentil was apprehended,[2] but the existence of certain factors – for example, if it was late at night – may strengthen further the prospects of establishing reasonable grounds for the police officers' suspicion.

[2] It is common in a problem question to find that further information is required to adequately advise on a particular issue and you should not feel uncomfortable in saying so wherever this is the case.

Further requirements are imposed upon police officers by section 2 of PACE, which requires that before conducting a search, a police officer must identify himself, the police station at which he is based and the grounds for the search. A police officer not in uniform must provide documentary evidence of his identity. In this scenario, we are not provided with enough information to know whether section 2 has been satisfactorily complied with.[3] PC Bean does, possibly, allude to the grounds for the search when commenting to Lentil that there have been a lot of break-ins in the area and that candlesticks are not an item normally carried around. However, we do not know whether the two police officers have identified themselves and their stations appropriately. Furthermore, police are required to make a written record of any search. Again, we do not know if this has taken place. Lentil should be advised that if the requirements imposed by section 2 have not been satisfied, then this omission on the part of the police officers may render the stop and search unlawful, as was established in the Court of Appeal's decision in *R v Bristol* [2007] EWCA Crim 3214.

[3] Even where you lack enough information to definitively advise on a particular issue you should refer to the relevant legal provisions in order to establish what information is required and how this would affect the advice given.

When arresting Lentil, the police are obliged under section 28 of PACE to inform him of his arrest and the reasons for it.[4] There is no

[4] This is not a point which requires much detail, but it is important that you mention it for the sake of providing a thorough answer to the question.

set form of words for arresting a person, so PC Pea's telling Lentil that he is 'nicked' is sufficient to inform Lentil of his arrest if this is clearly understood by him to be PC Pea's meaning. However, it is questionable whether the reasons for his arrest have been adequately explained.

A police officer may arrest any person where there exists a warrant for that person's arrest under section 1 of the Magistrates' Courts Act 1980. It is highly unlikely that there exists a warrant for Lentil's arrest as he has merely been encountered by police in a chance meeting in public. Police powers to arrest without warrant are contained in section 24 of PACE. These have been widened as a result of changes made to PACE by section 110 of the Serious Organised Crime and Police Act 2005. A police officer may arrest a person wherever he has reasonable grounds for suspecting that person to have committed any offence, or be about to, or in the process of committing an offence. It is doubtful whether PC Pea and PC Bean would be able to argue that there were reasonable grounds for suspecting Lentil to have committed an offence, given that the only items found during the search of his bag were two inexpensive toy items for which he possessed a receipt.[5] A two-stage test for reasonable suspicion was established in *O'Hara* v *Chief Constable of the RUC* [1996] UKHL 6: there must be actual suspicion on the part of the arresting police officer (the subjective part of the test) and there must exist reasonable grounds for that suspicion (the objective part of the test). Even if the police officers personally suspected Lentil of an offence, it is highly questionable whether there can be said to have existed reasonable grounds for this suspicion given their failure to find any incriminating articles during their search of Lentil's bag. This may render Lentil's arrest unlawful.

If reasonable grounds for suspicion of Lentil's guilt of an offence were established, the police officers would still need to demonstrate that they reasonably believed his arrest to be necessary for one or more of several specified reasons.[6] These are very broadly phrased, however, and are likely to mean that wherever a police officer can demonstrate reasonable grounds for suspecting that a person has committed an offence, they can be invoked to justify arrest. For example, a police officer can arrest a suspect where he believes it necessary to ascertain or confirm that person's name and address, prevent physical injury to any person or damage to property, to

[5] This is a critical point as there are strong grounds for doubting that Lentil's arrest is compatible with the relevant legal provisions.

[6] While arguably not a major issue in relation to Lentil given the above point, this ought to be considered for the sake of comprehensivity.

protect a child or vulnerable person, to allow the prompt and effective investigation of the offence, or to prevent the disappearance of the suspect. Of these, the need for prompt and effective investigation of the offence will justify arrest in most instances. Thus, Lentil's best prospect of challenging the legality of his arrest is to demonstrate that there were no reasonable grounds for suspecting that he had committed any offence.

## ✓ Make your answer stand out

- Explain what further information you may require in order to be able to properly advise Lentil in respect of this incident.
- Make comparisons, if relevant, to any cases displaying similar facts.
- Explain clearly the need for police officers to demonstrate reasonable grounds for suspicion of an offence having been committed.
- Detail the various requirements of a lawful arrest and consider their satisfaction here.

## ! Don't be tempted to . . .

- Simply explain the applicable legal provisions without directly relating them to the scenario which you have been presented with.

# ? Question 8

Tommy is seen by PC Plum running away from the scene of an armed robbery carrying what he believes to be a weapon used in association with the crime. PC Plum chases Tommy and manages to overpower him. He then tells Tommy he is under arrest on suspicion of having committed armed robbery and cautions him. Tommy is taken to the police station once back-up has arrived. At the police station, Sergeant Strawberry decides that as part of the investigation into Tommy's involvement in the armed robbery he would like to take Tommy's fingerprints as well as a sample of his saliva, which he feels will be useful for DNA purposes. Tommy is adamant that Sergeant Strawberry is not entitled to take these samples.

Advise (a) PC Plum as to whether his arrest of Tommy was lawful, and (b) Sergeant Strawberry as to whether Tommy's fingerprints and a sample of his saliva may be taken, indicating what further information, if any, you would need to advise on these issues.

# Answer plan

→ Explain when a police officer may lawfully arrest a suspect and whether PC Plum has complied with the relevant provisions when arresting Tommy.

→ Explain that PC Plum may use reasonable force in order to arrest Tommy and inform him of the fact of, and reasons for, his arrest and consider whether these requirements have been complied with.

→ Briefly raise the question of the status of Sergeant Strawberry in the investigative process and explain why this is important.

→ Explain the provisions applicable to the taking of samples without consent and whether these permit the taking of a sample of Tommy's saliva.

→ Explain the provisions applicable to the taking of fingerprints without consent and whether these permit the taking of Tommy's fingerprints.

# Diagram plan

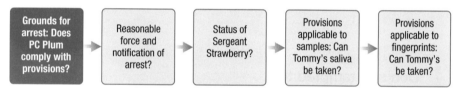

A printable version of this diagram plan is available from www.pearsoned.co.uk/lawexpressqa

# Answer

Beginning with PC Plum's arrest of Tommy, a police officer may arrest any person for whom an arrest warrant has been issued under section 1 of the Magistrates' Courts Act 1980, or without a warrant if the requirements of section 24 of the Police and Criminal Evidence Act 1984 can be satisfied. Given that Tommy is apprehended immediately following an armed robbery, there is not going to exist a warrant for this arrest. Section 24 of PACE permits a police officer to arrest a person who has, or he has reasonable grounds for suspecting has, committed any offence, is in the process of committing or about to commit an offence.[1] In this situation, the offence which Tommy would be suspected of having committed is armed robbery. As there is no evidence that PC Plum has actually witnessed Tommy committing this offence, it is important that PC Plum can

[1] It is important to explain the grounds upon which a police officer can make an arrest and consider whether these can be applied to the scenario under discussion. The key point is that the arresting officer has reasonable grounds for suspecting involvement in an offence.

demonstrate that he had reasonable grounds for suspecting Tommy's involvement in the commission of this offence. A two-stage test for reasonable suspicion is applied following the decision in *O'Hara* v *Chief Constable of the RUC* [1996] UKHL 6. There must be actual suspicion on the part of the arresting police officer, and there must exist reasonable grounds for this suspicion. PC Plum sees Tommy running away from the scene of an armed robbery, carrying what he believes to be a weapon used in association with the offence. It would be helpful to know what weapon PC Plum believes he has seen in Tommy's possession,[2] but assuming that it is an article of the kind ordinarily associated with armed robberies, then it would arguably seem reasonable for PC Plum to suspect Tommy's involvement in the offence.

Even where a police officer reasonably suspects a person has committed an offence, for an arrest to be legitimate under section 24(4) of PACE he must also have reasonable grounds for believing the arrest to be necessary for any one or more of a series of specified reasons outlined in section 24(5). However, these are very broad and it should not prove difficult for PC Plum to show that he reasonably believed Tommy's arrest was necessary for one of them.[3] For example, an arrest will be regarded as necessary to ascertain or confirm the name and address of the suspect, to allow the prompt and effective investigation of the offence, or to prevent the disappearance of the suspect. Any of these could, arguably, be applicable in this case.

Although we know that PC Plum 'overpowered' Tommy in order to facilitate his arrest, we do not know how much force was used.[4] Section 117 of PACE permits a police officer to use 'reasonable' force in order to perform his functions, including the power of arrest. As Tommy was running away from a crime scene, it can be envisaged that some force may have been necessary to prevent his escape and this will be lawful so long as reasonable in the circumstances. There is no evidence that PC Plum used excessive force, but the availability of more information could clarify this point. PC Plum must also comply with section 28 of PACE when arresting Tommy,[5] which requires that he inform Tommy that he is under arrest and the grounds upon which he is being arrested. It would appear that PC Plum has complied with these requirements, as the available information tells us that he tells Tommy he is under arrest on suspicion of armed robbery. Thus, based upon the available information, it

[2] You are not provided with this information and it is legitimate to raise this issue as it could be highly relevant to the likelihood of Tommy having been involved in the relevant offence.

[3] It is not necessary to list all of the reasons given in section 24(5) as it is lengthy. The key point is to emphasise its breadth and that it will nearly always be possible for an arresting officer to justify an arrest by reference to one of these reasons, the examples referred to being good cases in point.

[4] Again, it is legitimate to indicate that further information would have been useful in order to give fuller consideration to this issue.

[5] This point does not require a great amount of detail but should be covered for the sake of comprehensively considering the relevant issues.

would appear that PC Plum has acted in accordance with the law in arresting Tommy.

Before considering Sergeant Strawberry's wish to take samples from Tommy, it is worthwhile noting that we are not informed of the role being played by Sergeant Strawberry in the investigation of offences committed by Tommy.[6] For example, we do not know if he is the custody officer assigned to Tommy upon his arrival at the station. This could be relevant as the custody officer is responsible for maintaining a record of the treatment of the suspect while in police custody which will include details of any searches made and items seized or samples taken from his person.

In relation to the taking of samples from suspects in custody, a distinction must be made between intimate and non-intimate samples[7] as different rules apply to each of these. Sergeant Strawberry wishes to take a sample of Tommy's saliva. Intimate samples are defined by section 65 of PACE, as amended by section 119 of the Serious Organised Crime and Police Act 2005, as swabs 'taken from any part of a person's genitals or from a person's body orifice other than the mouth'. As saliva is taken from the mouth, it is only regarded as a non-intimate sample. Non-intimate samples can be taken from suspects notwithstanding their failure to consent. Under section 63 of PACE, the taking of non-intimate samples can be authorised in writing by someone of the rank of inspector or above where he has reasonable grounds for suspecting the person concerned to have been involved in a recordable offence and believes that the sample will prove or disprove this. Sergeant Strawberry would thus need the appropriate authorisation from an inspector in order to take a saliva sample from Tommy. However, an inspector would arguably be able to demonstrate that he had reasonable grounds for suspecting Tommy's involvement in a recordable offence given the circumstances of his arrest. We do not have any further information from which we can assess the likelihood of such a sample serving to prove or disprove Tommy's involvement in the offence, but if likely to do so there would be strong grounds to justify the taking of a saliva sample.

Section 61 of PACE governs the fingerprinting of suspects without their consent.[8] These are rather broad, having been extended by section 9 of the Criminal Justice Act 2003. They include where a

[6] Credit should be given for raising this issue. You are not told who Sergeant Strawberry is and his status may be relevant, for example if he is the custody officer who will have a series of specific obligations in respect of Tommy's detention and treatment. By raising the issue you evidence a wider understanding of the area of police powers.

[7] You must not make the mistake of assuming all samples taken from suspects are subject to the same rules. You need to identify the rules applicable to non-intimate samples and apply them to the scenario.

[8] The issue of taking fingerprints is fairly straightforward and it is likely to require only brief discussion in relation to the scenario.

person has been arrested and detained for a recordable offence, as indeed Tommy has. There is no requirement for authorisation to be obtained from a senior officer. Thus, there should be no difficulty in Sergeant Strawberry deciding to take fingerprints from Tommy.

## ✓ Make your answer stand out

- Indicate where the provision of further information would better enable you to advise on the issues raised by this situation.
- Raise the issue of the unknown status of Sergeant Strawberry and the possible implications of this.
- Make comparisons with any cases bearing similar facts.
- Distinguish clearly the provisions applicable to intimate and non-intimate samples taken by the police.

## ! Don't be tempted to . . .

- Simply explain the applicable legal provisions without directly relating them to the scenario which you have been presented with.
- Confuse intimate and non-intimate samples.
- Overlook changes made to PACE by more recent legislative provisions.

# ❓ Question 9

DC Lock and DS Key are questioning Poppy, who has been arrested on suspicion of drug-dealing. They have been questioning her for three hours consecutively, during which time she has not been provided with an opportunity to inform anyone of her arrest or to receive any legal advice, and they have been unable to extract from her the information they feel is necessary to secure a conviction against her. In frustration at their 'lack of progress', DS Key whispers in Poppy's ear that unless she confesses to the offence with which she is being charged he will ask DC Lock to go and 'see that your children spend a night in casualty'. In fear for her children's safety, Poppy confesses to the offence.

Advise Poppy as to whether DC Lock and DS Key acted lawfully when interrogating her, and how her treatment might be used as part of her case at her trial.

# Answer plan

→ Explain the provisions applicable to the detention of suspects for questioning and the time limitations applicable.

→ Explain the standards required for the treatment of detainees by code of practice C and that interviews must be tape-recorded.

→ Explain that Poppy is entitled to have someone informed of her arrest, and when the police would be entitled to deny her this right.

→ Explain that Poppy is entitled to consult with a legal adviser and the possible consequences of the denial of this right upon proceedings under section 78(1) of PACE.

→ Explain that DS Key's threat to Poppy is likely to constitute oppression which will make her confession inadmissible evidence under section 76(2).

# Diagram plan

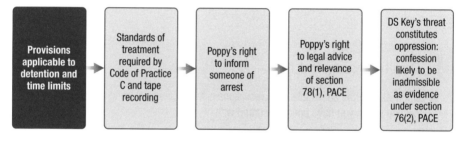

A printable version of this diagram plan is available from www.pearsoned.co.uk/lawexpressqa

# Answer

Several issues arise from Poppy's detention and questioning. Under section 37(2) of the Police and Criminal Evidence Act 1984 (PACE), an arrested person may be detained where the custody officer has reasonable grounds for believing it necessary 'to secure or preserve evidence relating to an offence for which he is under arrest or to obtain such evidence by questioning him'.[1] We do not know what information has been used in this instance as the basis for Poppy's detention, but given that she has been arrested upon suspicion of drug-dealing, it would not be unreasonable for the police to want to question her in order to solicit further evidence. Although time limitations apply to the detention of suspects, these are not in issue

[1] Although this may appear obvious, it is appropriate to begin your consideration of the situation involving Poppy as this is the first legal requirement which the police would need to be able to satisfy before Poppy could be detained for questioning in the first place.

[2] Although there is no problem in relation to the time for which Poppy has been detained, by mentioning it you show that you are aware of the application of time limitations to the detention of suspects.

here.[2] Poppy has only been questioned for three hours. Following arrest, a suspect may be detained for six hours before a review needs to take place and further authorisation for detention be granted (s. 40(3) PACE).

Although it may appear that Poppy's detention for questioning is prima facie lawful, it must be noted that further safeguards are applicable to her treatment while in custody. PACE code of practice C sets out a series of standards which must be complied with in relation to the detention of suspects, which include the provision of regular meals, rest and breaks from questioning. We are not provided with enough information to ascertain whether such standards have been satisfied,[3] although that Poppy has been interrogated for three hours without a break may be considered a breach of these guidelines. We are not told whether Poppy's interview with the police has been tape-recorded, but under section 60 of PACE this is a legal requirement. Any failure to comply with these procedural requirements could be used by Poppy as part of her case at trial, a point which will be addressed in detail later.

[3] It is common within problem questions to be given insufficient information to provide definitive answers to all points raised. Where you would benefit from the provision of further information you should indicate this.

Section 56 of PACE entitles someone who has been arrested to have someone informed of their arrest. This has prima facie been breached here by the denial of Poppy with the opportunity to inform anyone of her arrest.[4] However, this entitlement may be suspended for up to 36 hours where a suspect is being detained on suspicion of involvement in an indictable offence, and the relevant police officer reasonably believes that to permit the suspect to inform someone of his or her arrest would lead to interference with, or harm to, evidence connected to the offence or other persons, or will lead to the alerting of other suspects, or hinder the recovery of any property obtained as a result of the offence. Again, we are not party to the information upon which Poppy has been denied the opportunity to inform someone of her arrest although it is conceivable that given the nature of the offence being investigated there may exist reasonable grounds to believe that allowing Poppy to inform someone of her arrest may alert other potential suspects involved in the same offence and lead to the removal or destruction of evidence. Drugs offences are often of an ongoing kind involving a chain of several offenders, so there may be legitimate grounds for denying Poppy the right to have someone informed of her arrest.

[4] This is an important issue clearly raised by the details you have been given. You are not able to assess whether the denial of Poppy's right under section 56 is likely to be deemed unlawful unless you are given further information upon which you can base your assessment and must say so.

Access to legal advice is guaranteed by section 58 of PACE and is widely regarded as a key requirement of a fair trial. Although section 58 does permit the police to deny access to legal advice for up to 36 hours for the same reasons for which suspects may be prevented from informing a person of their arrest, the right to consult with a legal adviser can only be denied in very exceptional circumstances and a higher threshold must be satisfied for it to be justified. We do not have sufficient information to judge whether the police could legitimately deny Poppy the opportunity to consult with a legal adviser. However, at her trial the court could conclude that her non-access to legal advice constitutes sufficient reason to exclude any evidence obtained through DC Lock's and DS Key's interrogation of her.[5]

[5] This is an important point as it could be highly relevant to Poppy's case at trial, something which the question asks you to consider. You should refer to some of the relevant case law in order to show the likelihood of interview evidence being excluded where access to legal advice has been denied.

Section 78(1) of PACE allows a court to exclude any prosecution evidence where it appears, having regard to all circumstances, including those in which the evidence was obtained, that its admission would have such an adverse effect on the proceedings that it should not be admitted. This provision is essentially designed to enable the courts to exclude any evidence which has been obtained in such circumstances that its reliability can be called into question. In *R v Samuel* [1988] QB 615, the admission of evidence of a police interview was not permitted where the suspect had been denied the right to consult with a legal advisor under section 78(1). Notably the court stated that a belief on the part of a police officer that one of the grounds for denying access to legal advice contained in section 58 existed could only rarely be genuinely held. However, a court may decline to exclude evidence of an interview conducted in the absence of legal representation if it felt that this would have made no difference to the course and outcome of the interrogation, as occurred in *R v Alladice* (1988) 87 Crim App R 380. Section 78(1) could potentially be used by the court at Poppy's trial to exclude any evidence obtained in circumstances where the police had not complied with PACE requirements in relation to her treatment during questioning.[6] As noted above, we have insufficient information to draw any firm conclusions upon whether the police acted unlawfully in relation to some of the issues raised.

[6] You should make this general point in relation to any failings to comply with relevant procedural requirements on the part of the police.

[7] You should enter into as full a discussion of section 76(2) and its utility to Poppy as time will allow you and draw upon any relevant case law to demonstrate its relevance. This is the strongest tool which Poppy will have as part of her case at trial, as it is likely to render evidence of her confession inadmissible.

DS Key's threat to Poppy, which results in her confession, is highly relevant to her defence. It undoubtedly constitutes an unlawful means of seeking to extract a confession from a suspect, involving a threat to use unlawful force against her children. Her confession is consequently made under a form of duress. Section 76(2) of PACE provides that evidence of a confession will be inadmissible in court where it has been obtained by oppression.[7] Although the case law has given rise to varying interpretations of 'oppression', DS Key's threat will almost certainly constitute an instance of oppression. Section 76(8) provides a definition of oppression which includes the use or threat of violence, which is clearly what has emanated from DS Key, and has been a common theme in several cases of miscarriages of justice. Evidence of Poppy's confession is highly unlikely to be admissible at her trial, irrespective of whether other evidence obtained during her interrogation is excluded due to the failure of the police to conform to procedural requirements imposed by PACE.[8]

[8] This is a logical conclusion, as you show that the manner in which Poppy was coerced into making a confession is likely to be used to exclude this as evidence, while indicating still that other procedural failings may also have an impact upon the admissibility of evidence at trial.

## ✓ Make your answer stand out

- Make comparisons where appropriate with the police's treatment of Poppy and that of suspects in similar relevant cases, particularly where miscarriages of justice have resulted from police oppression to induce confessions.
- Indicate where appropriate what further information you may need in order to be able to provide a more definitive answer to certain questions.
- Be prepared to raise issues which are not expressly mentioned by the scenario, but may nonetheless be relevant, for example in this case the issue of tape-recording of Poppy's interview or the standards applicable to her detention under code of practice C.
- Consider the potential ability of the police to evade accountability under the PACE requirements by speaking to Poppy 'off the record'.

## ! Don't be tempted to . . .

- Omit to discuss any issue which you consider to be so straightforward as to not merit any attention, as you still have an opportunity to demonstrate your understanding of the applicable law.
- Make assumptions on factual matters where you are not provided with the relevant information.

**Question 10**

Following arrest on suspicion of involvement in drug smuggling, Tom, Dick and Harry were interrogated at the police station. However, they are now concerned that they have not been treated in accordance with applicable legal standards and seek your advice. Advise them in respect of the following issues:

(A) Tom was advised that he was entitled to be accompanied by a solicitor while being questioned. Although reminded of this on three occasions he declined to avail himself of any legal advice. Tom was interviewed for three hours with a short break halfway through this time, before being told he was free to leave.

(B) Dick was interviewed for several hours without any break, after which he was formally charged with offences related to the supply of illegal drugs. Dick declined to answer a substantial number of the questions put to him after he began feeling tired and frustrated by the lengthy questioning without a break.

(C) Harry confessed to an offence after a short period of questioning. However, he alleges that the officers questioning him made threatening gestures while questioning him.

## Answer plan

→ Advise Tom that there has been no breach of his right to legal advice under section 58 of PACE, as he failed to avail himself of this even though provided with the opportunity.

→ Advise Tom that his interrogation is likely to have taken place in accordance with conditions required by PACE code of practice C.

→ Advise Dick that his lengthy uninterrupted interrogation may have have breached PACE code of practice C.

→ Advise Dick that his failure to answer questions may entitle a court to draw adverse inferences under section 34 of the Criminal Justice and Public Order Act 1994.

→ Advise Harry that evidence of his confession may be rendered inadmissible under section 76 of PACE as having been procured by oppression.

# Diagram plan

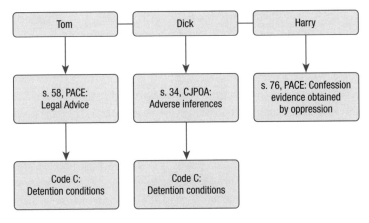

A printable version of this diagram plan is available from www.pearsoned.co.uk/lawexpressqa

## Answer

¹ Potentially this problem scenario could give rise to a number of issues. However, you must assume that you are only expected to discuss the issues expressly raised in relation to each of the parties whom you are asked to advise. However, by referring to the fact that the arrest and caution of suspects is governed by legislation you demonstrate some wider understanding of the area of law within which the problem is set.

² This issue is relatively straightforward and you can dispense with it quite quickly by simply citing the relevant legal provision and explaining why there has been no breach in this case.

A number of legal issues are raised by the scenarios involving Tom, Dick and Harry. As we are provided with no details concerning their arrest, we must assume that this took place in accordance with the applicable legal provisions and that they were cautioned in the manner prescribed by law.¹ It shall also be assumed that with the exception of those issues specifically raised by the scenario, the police have complied with the various requirements applicable to the detention and questioning of suspects contained in the Police and Criminal Evidence Act 1984 (PACE), its associated codes of practice, and other relevant legislation.

Two legal issues are potentially raised in relation to the questioning of Tom; the fact that he did not receive any legal advice/representation while being questioned, and the duration of questioning. Under section 58 of PACE, a suspect detained by the police is entitled to legal representation and this fact should be notified to the suspect. Only in exceptional circumstances can the right to legal representation be denied. In this scenario, Tom has been informed of his right to legal representation and he has declined to avail himself of this. There is therefore no breach of Article 58,² the police having done nothing to deprive Tom of his entitlement. PACE code of practice C governs the treatment of detainees at the police station and paragraph 12.8 requires that as a general rule there should be short refreshment breaks from questioning at approximately two-hour intervals.[3] Tom has only been questioned for three hours, with a short break in the middle of this period. This would appear to satisfy the requirements of code of practice C.

In relation to the questioning of Dick, issues arise from his failure to answer questions and the failure to provide him with any breaks from questioning. As noted above, code of practice C requires that suspects be afforded a break from questioning at least every two hours. We don't know how long Dick's questioning continued for, but as it is stated to have been for 'several hours without any break' it would appear that there has been a serious breach of the applicable code of practice.[4] Not only may this be a factor which would justify Dick's failure to answer some of the questions put to him, but it may render evidence obtained during interrogation unreliable and inadmissible in court. Section 78 of PACE allows a court to exclude evidence if it appears that it would have such an adverse effect on the fairness of the proceedings that it ought not to admit it.[5] Although we do not know what evidence the police have obtained against Dick, should any of it have been obtained while questioning him when he was tired and frustrated as a result of their failure to afford him regular breaks from questioning as they are obliged to, Dick may legitimately be able to assert that the admission of such evidence would adversely affect the fairness of the proceedings and ought to be excluded. In a number of cases evidence has been excluded where there has been a breach by the police of procedural safeguards set out by the PACE framework,[6] for example *R v Canale* [1990] 2 All ER 187 where interviews were not contemporaneously written up.

Dick should note that under section 34 of the Criminal Justice and Public Order Act 1994, his failure to answer questions during police interrogation may have adverse consequences for him when his case comes to trial. Section 34 provides that a defendant's failure to mention facts when questioned which s/he later relies upon as part of his/her defence, and which it was reasonable to expect to have been mentioned, will permit a court to draw such inferences from the defendant's failure as it considers appropriate. Effectively, the purpose of section 34 is to permit adverse inferences to be drawn where

[3] Again, this is a relatively simple issue to deal with. You strengthen the authority of your answer by citing the relevant provision of the applicable code of practice.

[4] Here you should correctly assert that on the basis of the available evidence there is likely to be a breach of Code C while noting that you do not have complete information upon the duration of his questioning, reinforcing the desirability of further information on some issues.

[5] This is an important point which you must not overlook.

[6] You can reinforce the importance of section 78 and its possible application to Dick's case by making reference to some of the case law on the application of section 78 in cases where procedural safeguards have not been complied with by the police.

a suspect refuses to answer questions asked by the police. However, this is not an absolute rule and the courts have proven themselves unwilling to allow adverse inferences to be drawn in some circumstances where procedural safeguards contained in PACE have not been complied with. Here there are serious failings on the part of the police in this respect and these may be relevant to the application of section 34 in any subsequent trial.[7]

Harry has confessed to the admission of an offence, but alleges that the police officers who questioned him made threatening gestures. This may enable him to argue that evidence of his confession ought not to be admitted in court on the grounds that it was obtained by oppression. Section 76 of PACE allows the courts to exclude evidence of a confession where this has been obtained by oppression. We are not provided with any details of the 'threatening gestures' made by the police officers to Harry. However, section 76(8) defines oppression as constituting torture, inhuman or degrading treatment or the use or threat of violence. While we would need more information concerning the behaviour of the police officers towards Harry, it would seem reasonable to assume that there is a strong likelihood that they broadly took the form of threats of violence.[8] In this case, Harry could appeal to the court for the evidence of his confession to be rendered inadmissible.

Although further information would be required in order to be able to provide definitive advice to Tom, Dick and Harry on the legal consequences of their treatment while questioned by the police, it appears that Tom has been treated in accordance with the applicable legal safeguards and can have no cause for complaint. There do appear, however, to have been serious failings in relation to the treatment of Dick and Harry.[9] Dick's lengthy questioning is likely to fall foul of code of practice C, possibly rendering evidence obtained through it inadmissible, and although his failure to answer questions may have adverse effects for him, the circumstances which led to this may prevent any adverse influences being drawn from his 'silence'. Harry's confession appears prima facie to have been obtained as a result of oppression and is unlikely to be admissible as evidence.

[7] It is important that you do not assume that section 34 will negatively affect Dick's case. You should make reference to the circumstances of his interrogation and draw upon some of the relevant case law to consider the prospects of the courts declining to permit adverse inferences to be drawn from his failure to answer questions.

[8] Again, you correctly highlight the benefit of being provided with further information on this matter while demonstrating understanding of the relevant provision. You can strengthen your answer here by considering some of the relevant case law under section 76 and how this may be of assistance to Harry's case.

[9] This is a balanced conclusion to your answer. You summarise the main points of the advice provided succinctly, while referring again to the fact that in order to provide a definitive answer to some of the legal questions raised you would need further information.

**Make your answer stand out**

- Indicate where appropriate what further information you may need in order to be able to provide more definitive advice on certain issues.
- Make direct reference to relevant provisions of PACE code of practice C where relevant.
- Consider the case law on section 34 of the Criminal Justice and Public Order Act 1994 in order to ascertain the likelihood of it being applicable to Dick.
- Consider the case law on section 76 of PACE and how this may be helpful to Harry's case.

**! Don't be tempted to . . .**

- Provide a discussion of the merits of some of the legal provisions raised, for example section 34 of the Criminal Justice and Public Order Act 1994.
- Assume that there is a definitive answer to the question.

**www.pearsoned.co.uk/lawexpressqa**

 Go online to access more revision support including additional essay and problem questions with diagram plans, You be the marker questions, and download all diagrams from the book.

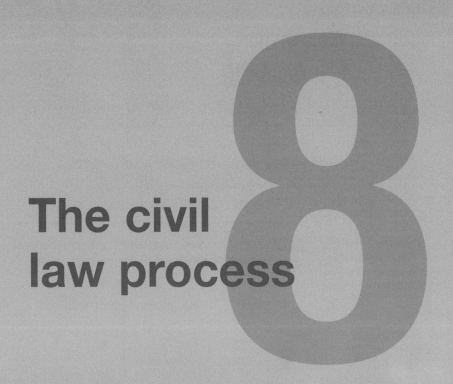

# The civil law process

## How this topic may come up in exams

Examination questions on the civil law process may require you to demonstrate an understanding of the civil jurisdiction possessed by different courts, particularly the County Court and High Court, as well as remedies available in civil law proceedings. You could be asked to explain and evaluate civil procedure rules, including awareness of the main reforms to the management of civil cases introduced in 1999. Questions which test your understanding of the funding of civil legal services are also possible within this topic, and you may specifically be asked to consider the merits of initiatives such as conditional fee agreements.

# Attack the question

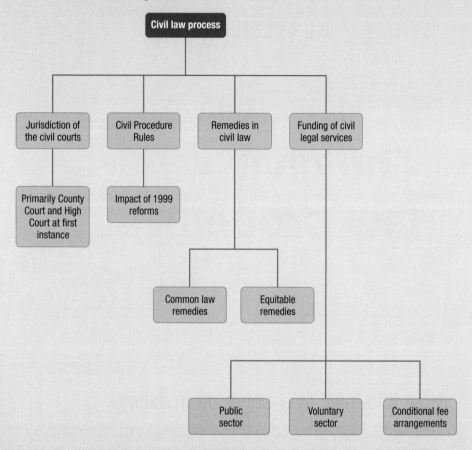

A printable version of this diagram plan is available from www.pearsoned.co.uk/lawexpressqa

#  Question 1

Evaluate the main differences and similarities in the civil jurisidiction of the County Court and High Court.

## Answer plan

➡ Provide some background by briefly explaining the origins and nature of the County Court and High Court.

➡ Explain the different tracks which civil cases are assigned to and how these determine which court will have jurisdiction to hear particular cases.

➡ Outline the areas of law where jurisdiction is restricted to the High Court.

➡ Comment upon the specialised jurisdiction exercised by divisions of the High Court.

➡ Explain the difference in the range of remedies which may be awarded by each court.

➡ Conclude upon the extent to which the civil jurisdiction of the two courts is radically different.

## Diagram plan

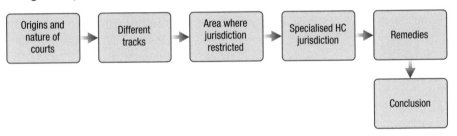

A printable version of this diagram plan is available from www.pearsoned.co.uk/lawexpressqa

## Answer

The significance of civil litigation is often overlooked, but the frequency with which individuals have resort to the civil courts is underlined by the fact that in the year 2008 over two million civil cases were initiated. The County Court and High Court serve as the two courts of first instance for civil cases.[1] County Courts were established by the County Courts Act 1846, with the intention of providing litigants with a forum within which small-scale litigation could be dispensed that was local and accessible to them. Today, according

[1] You can provide some context to your answer at the outset by briefly referring to the origins of the respective courts and the much greater geographic spread of the County Courts.

to Her Majesty's Courts Service, there are 216 County Courts spread throughout England and Wales, meaning that there will be a court located relatively conveniently for everyone. Cases in the County Court are ordinarily heard by a circuit or district judge, although High Court judges are competent to sit in the County Court. The High Court was established in 1873 under the Supreme Court of Judicature Act, and while centrally based in London it sits additionally in a number of regional centres and is presided over by High Court judges. Prior to 1999, separate procedural rules governed the workings of the High Court and County Court, although as a consequence of the Woolf reforms both courts are now subject to a unified set of civil procedure rules.

In comparing and contrasting the civil jurisdiction of the County Court and High Court, there are, arguably, four key considerations.[2] These are the financial limits upon the jurisdiction of the respective courts; the exclusion of certain categories of cases from the County Court's jurisdiction; the specialised jurisdiction possessed by the High Court; and the restrictions upon the remedies obtainable from the County Court.

[2] This is helpful to the marker as it identifies the key points to be addressed, providing a clear structure to the answer by breaking it down into four key parts.

In order to improve the efficiency with which the civil courts manage litigation, Part 26 of the Civil Procedure Rules introduced in 1999 established three different tracks to which cases could be allocated. These tracks are based largely upon the value of the civil action in question and will in turn determine which court is assigned jurisdiction to hear the case.[3] The three tracks are the small claims track, the fast track and the multi-track. Small claims cases are those where the value of the claim is under £5,000, or £1,000 where the action is one for personal injury. Small claims are to be handled by the County Court. Most civil actions are likely to fall within this bracket and small claims actions are well suited for relatively minor consumer disputes, accident claims and disputes between landlords and tenants. The high proportion of civil actions which these cases represent is probably evidenced by the fact that whereas 1.6 million proceedings were commenced in the County Court during 2002, only 54,500 were commenced in the Queen's Bench and Chancery divisions of the High Court combined. Claims for amounts exceeding £5,000 and below £15,000 (£50,000 where the action is for personal injury) are assigned to the fast track and also commence in the County Court. Actions for higher amounts will be assigned to the

[3] It is very important that you explain the different kinds of tracks to which cases can be assigned and the bearing which this has upon where jurisdiction is likely to lie, the value of claims being of the utmost importance in this respect.

multi-track and, while these are more likely to commence in the High Court they may begin in the County Court at the choice of the parties depending upon the nature of the claim.

The value of a claim is not the sole determinant of the court which will be assigned jurisdiction to hear it. Certain types of case may not be heard by the County Court. A Practice Direction [1991] provided that a number of specified actions were too important to be transferred to a County Court, underlining the higher status of the High Court within the court hierarchy.[4] These include actions for professional negligence, fatal accidents, allegations of fraud or undue influence, defamation, malicious prosecution or false imprisonment. However, such actions account for a relatively small proportion of litigation and the vast majority of civil actions are amenable to County Court jurisdiction.

[4] Although this is an important point to note, you should stress that these cases account for a small proportion of civil litigation, thus overstating the significance of the County Court's lack of jurisdiction to entertain them.

The superior status of the High Court is exemplified further by its division into three branches each having its own specialism in particular types of civil law,[5] and within these branches there are even narrower specialist courts for particular matters. The Queen's Bench Division has the highest workload of any of the branches, as a result of the fact that it deals predominantly with contractual and tortious actions. Of the actions begun in the Queen's Bench Division during 2008/9, 23% were for personal injury and 21% for debt. There are specialist commercial and admiralty courts within the division. The Chancery Division deals with a range of specific matters, including land, mortgages, trusts, bankruptcy, contentious probate, company and revenue law. It also has specialist courts, these dealing with patents and company matters respectively, and has appellate jurisdiction to hear some appeals from the County Court. Perhaps reflecting economic shifts, the Chancery Division saw a 14% increase in proceedings during 2008. The Family Division forms the final branch of the High Court. That the County Court deals with less serious actions for modest amounts of money is perhaps reflected in its lack of a specialist division of labour along the lines apparent in the High Court.

[5] This can be overlooked, but the various specialisms accommodated within the High Court structure does demonstrate that there is a somewhat different emphasis in its jurisdiction to that of the County Court.

[6] Don't overlook the issue of remedies. While the significance of this difference between the courts is unlikely to be of relevance in the majority of cases, it is nonetheless a difference in jurisdiction.

Whereas most remedies can be obtained equally from the High Court and the County Court, including the common law remedy of damages, there are some restrictions placed upon the range of remedies which the County Court is entitled to award.[6] It may not grant the prerogative remedies, which are reserved to the jurisdiction of the High Court, and freezing orders are also ordinarily outside of its jurisdiction.

In certain respects, the civil jurisdiction of the County Court does not differ radically from that of the High Court. Both abide by the same procedural rules and the most common types of civil action which form the subject of litigation can proceed in either court subject to the value of the claim. Theoretically, there are substantial differences between the jurisdiction of the two courts, but these can be over-stated.[7] While certain matters are reserved to the High Court, these only represent a relatively small proportion of civil actions. That the High Court consists of a number of specialised branches may reflect the more distinguished nature of the court, but it does not detract from the fact that the vast majority of cases will be amenable to the jurisdiction of the County Court and will be resolved within that forum. Although the High Court enjoys a broader range of remedies to award, in the vast majority of cases the ordinary remedies available in either court will be sufficient.

[7] The conclusion reflects the content of the answer. You show a number of differences in the jurisdiction of the two courts, yet throughout have demonstrated the extent to which these can be overstated.

 Make your answer stand out

- Provide context to your answer through the citation of evidence of the nature of modern civil legal action.
- Consider the accessibility of the County Court and High Court in the context of recent developments concerning civil legal aid assistance.
- Demonstrate that the jurisdictions of the two courts are not mutually exclusive.
- Make reference to any reform proposals in relation to the jurisdiction of the courts.

! Don't be tempted to . . .

- Provide a detailed point by point description of the jurisdiction enjoyed by the relevant courts.

#  Question 2

'Access to civil justice has been seriously weakened by a succession of reforms beginning with the Access to Justice Act 1999.' Discuss.

## Answer plan

➡ Make the point that access to civil justice depends upon some form of state assistance being available to those who lack the means to fund legal action.

➡ Discuss the main changes introduced to state funding for civil legal action by the Access to Justice Act 1999 and their consequences.

➡ Discuss the main changes introduced by the Legal Aid, Sentencing and Punishment of Offenders Act 2012 and their consequences.

➡ Conclude by saying whether you agree with the statement or not.

## Diagram plan

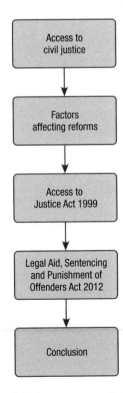

```
┌─────────────────┐
│   Access to     │
│  civil justice  │
└─────────────────┘
         │
         ▼
┌─────────────────┐
│    Factors      │
│ affecting reforms│
└─────────────────┘
         │
         ▼
┌─────────────────┐
│   Access to     │
│ Justice Act 1999│
└─────────────────┘
         │
         ▼
┌─────────────────────┐
│ Legal Aid, Sentencing│
│  and Punishment of   │
│  Offenders Act 2012  │
└─────────────────────┘
         │
         ▼
┌─────────────────┐
│   Conclusion    │
└─────────────────┘
```

A printable version of this diagram plan is available from www.pearsoned.co.uk/lawexpressqa

# Answer

Although greater emphasis has always been placed upon state funding for legal assistance in criminal cases, due to the fact that individual liberty is often at stake and the harmful implications of receiving criminal convictions, access to civil justice in many cases will be dependent upon the availability of legal assistance for those parties who lack the means to fund action themselves. Many civil cases, for example those concerning welfare, housing, education and employment disputes, involve parties of limited means. A 2004 survey by Pascoe Pleasance for the Legal Services Commission found that four-fifths of those living in temporary accommodation, two-thirds of single parents, and over half of unemployed persons experienced civil justice problems.[1] For vulnerable groups such as these to be able to adequately take or defend legal action will be contingent upon the provision of some form of state funded legal aid.

Prior to 1999 a number of schemes for civil legal aid existed, but these were swept away by the Access to Justice Act 1999 which introduced a new system for state funding of civil cases which curtailed considerably access to state funded assistance.[2] The administration of civil legal aid was tasked to the Legal Services Commission, which is conferred with a fixed budget for funding civil cases – the Community Legal Services fund – capped by section 5. Given the limited amount of funds available, section 7 prescribed that a financial eligibility test for applicants for funding to be set by the Lord Chancellor and a funding code to be drawn up by the Legal Services Commission and approved by the Lord Chancellor would govern the allocation of funds from the Community Legal Service.

The impact of the 1999 reforms was to significantly restrict access to state funded assistance in civil cases. The financial eligibility test introduced by 2007 regulations reduced considerably the numbers entitled to assistance. According to Elliott and Quinn (2012), whereas 52% of people would have been eligible in 1998, the proportion eligible had dwindled to just 29%. Furthermore, section 10 of the 1999 Act extended the range of financial conditions which could be imposed upon recipients of assistance, and a number of areas of law were excluded from eligibility for funding,[3] including personal injury, defamation, business disputes, and company and partnership law. Only providers of legal services who have been awarded a contract

[1] It is important to demonstrate at the outset the centrality of civil legal assistance for many people to be able to obtain justice in relation to legal problems which they are experiencing. Here you do this very well by referring to some of the examples of civil legal problems which may often affect those with limited means. Reference to statistical evidence reinforces this point even further.

[2] The Access to Justice Act is referred to in the question and should be your starting point for consideration of the attack on state funding in civil cases. You must detail the main features of the Act and their impact upon the availability of civil legal aid.

[3] These are very important points to make. By referring to not only provisions of the Act, but also statistical evidence, you are able to illustrate very clearly their impact in curtailing the availability of civil legal aid considerably.

with the Community Legal Service can dispense funded legal assistance. This has led to a large shortfall and disparity across regions in the availability of suitable providers of state funded civil legal aid. The introduction of the Act resulted in a drop of over 50% in the number of providers, from 11,000 to 5,000. Specialist areas such as housing and debt were particularly badly affected,[4] with the number of providers of services in these areas declining from 743 to 489, and from 462 to 206 respectively in the period 2000–2003 alone.

[4] Again, you should add to the strength of your arguments by introducing further statistical evidence which reinforces even more the points you have been making.

As the preceding discussion illustrates, the effect of the Access to Justice Act 1999 was to launch a serious attack on access to civil justice as the number of areas of law eligible for funding, persons who could satisfy the financial eligibility test, and providers of funded services all decreased markedly. However, there have since been further attacks upon state funding for civil legal assistance. In no small part influenced by attempts to slash public spending as part of their package of austerity measures, the coalition government introduced a consultation paper in 2010 with the aim of reducing expenditure on legal aid by £350 million a year.[5]

[5] You can provide useful context by briefly explaining the political background to recent reforms to the provision of civil legal aid.

The main recommendations of the consultation paper were implemented in the Legal Aid, Sentencing and Punishment of Offenders Act 2012. The changes introduced by the Act take effect from April 2013 and are likely to impact considerably further upon the availability of state funding in civil cases. A wide range of legal matters are no longer eligible for legal assistance at all.[6] These include welfare benefits, issues of employment law, consumer and contractual issues, and educational matters apart from those involving special educational needs. Most immigration, asylum and housing matters will also be ineligible for assistance. Private family law cases also become ineligible for funding unless they involve issues of domestic violence, child abduction, or forced marriage, although some funding is available for mediation as an alternative form of dispute resolution. The categories of cases removed from access to civil legal assistance are so wide-ranging that it stands to affect the ability of many potential litigants to pursue legitimate civil actions. Many of the excluded categories affect vulnerable classes of people who would otherwise be unable to pursue action or properly represent themselves.[7]

[6] By highlighting the areas that have been excluded a clear picture of the current availability of state funded assistance in civil cases emerges.

[7] It is important that you emphasise this point. The cuts to civil legal aid have not been concerned with the removal of assistance from well-resourced people pursuing lucrative commercial actions, but impact upon the ability of many vulnerable groups to pursue actions of a social welfare nature.

In addition to reducing the scope of areas which qualify for assistance, the 2012 reforms have also seen the means test to be satisfied by potential recipients of funds tightened further, thus reducing

[8] By again citing statistical evidence you add authority to the arguments which you have advanced.

the number of applicants who will be eligible by approximately half.[8] Another barrier to assistance has been introduced by the requirement that applicants must seek funding directly from the Community Legal Service itself. In another cost-cutting exercise, it is intended that there will be much greater use of telephone advice, as opposed to face to face interactions with legal service providers.

In conclusion, it is difficult to disagree with the assertion that reforms beginning with the Access to Justice Act 1999 have brought about a serious weakening of access to civil justice. Access to justice depends upon everyone, regardless of their means, being able to take legal action to pursue legitimate claims, and the story of the reforms introduced by the Access to Justice Act and more recently the Legal Aid, Sentencing and Punishment of Offenders Act 2012, is one attempt to curtail considerably the circumstances in which the state will provide legal assistance in civil cases. Although some of the gaps in provision that have been created will be plugged by other providers, such as law centres, Citizens' Advice Bureaux and charities, this will not by any means address the resulting shortfall in affordable, accessible legal assistance, and access to civil justice is likely to be unobtainable for more people than previously was the case.[9]

[9] In an extended essay you might wish to give greater consideration to the issue of the role which other providers have played in filling some of the gaps created by cuts to state funded civil legal assistance, although the conclusion correctly notes that all of these gaps will not be plugged through such means.

 **Make your answer stand out**

- Demonstrate a clear understanding of the impact of the Legal Aid, Sentencing and Punishment of Offenders Act 2012.

- Assess current shortfalls in the availability of civil legal aid by reading and referring to Hynes and Robins (2012) *The Justice Gap: Whatever Happened to Legal Aid?* London: Legal Action Group.

- Consider the extent to which the current shortfall in state funded civil legal assistance can be supplemented through alternative sources of legal assistance.

- Refer to statistical evidence to illustrate the impact of the reforms to civil legal aid.

**! Don't be tempted to . . .**

- Provide a detailed overview of the individual provisions of either the 1999 or 2012 Acts.
- Discuss issues pertaining to legal aid in criminal cases.

#  Question 3

'Greater use of conditional fee agreements should be encouraged.' Critically assess this statement.

## Answer plan

→ Explain what conditional fee agreements are and the circumstances which have led to their greater use in recent years.

→ Discuss the main benefits of the use of conditional fee agreements.

→ Discuss the main problems which are associated with conditional fee agreements.

→ Conclude by explaining whether you agree with the statement or not.

## Diagram plan

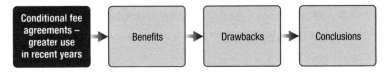

A printable version of this diagram plan is available from www.pearsoned.co.uk/lawexpressqa

## Answer

[1] You should begin your answer by briefly explaining what conditional fee agreements are and their recent emergence within the UK. This provides relevant context to your discussion to follow of their relative merits.

Conditional fee agreements have become an increasingly popular way of funding civil actions,[1] especially personal injury litigation. Under the terms of a conditional fee agreement, a solicitor takes on a client's case on the understanding that payment of the solicitor's fees will be conditional upon a successful outcome. Although common in the US, conditional fee agreements were not permitted in the UK until section 58 of the Courts and Legal Services Act 1990 provided for their use in a limited range of cases. The Access to Justice Act 1999 promoted greater use, making them available in all civil cases bar medical negligence. When entering into conditional fee agreements, solicitors are now entitled to raise their fees by up to double the normal fee, and courts can order losing parties to pay this 'success fee' in addition to ordinary legal costs. Although increasingly used by litigants, conditional fee agreements have generated some controversy, which warrants greater exploration of their merits.

Arguably, the most compelling argument for the encouragement of conditional fee agreements is that they reduce the financial burden placed upon the state.[2] Money which might previously have been spent funding certain civil actions can now be spent elsewhere. There is little doubt that conditional fee agreements have been hugely popular. Within two years of their introduction, 30,000 had been entered into, and have been used for several hundred thousand personal injury actions since. It should be noted, however, that while perhaps a convenient method for financing personal injury litigation, conditional fee agreements are not as likely to constitute a practical option in other forms of legal action. It is arguable that there are performance incentives for lawyers where their payment is dependent upon success. As they will not be paid unless successful, they should have all the encouragement which they need to 'be at their best'. Although the logic of this argument cannot be dismissed, it is somewhat overstated given that under conditional fee agreements lawyers will only ordinarily take cases where they are reasonably confident of success anyway. That said, it could be said that a virtue of conditional fee agreements is that they reduce the number of weak claims, as solicitors are unlikely to take them on.

It has been argued that conditional fee agreements facilitate greater access to justice. They provide a means of taking legal action for individuals who might not have the financial means to enter litigation otherwise, and may be used for types of legal action ineligible for state funding, for example defamation. The sustainability of the 'greater access to justice' argument is questionable.[3] Firstly, conditional fee agreements are only going to be a viable option for litigants with a sufficient chance of success to encourage solicitors to take on their case. Secondly, as the discussion to follow of some of the problems associated with conditional fee agreements will reveal, the consequences of their greater use for insurance costs, hardship faced by losing parties and the general promotion of a 'compensation culture' may warrant the assertion that whereas conditional fee agreements promote 'individual justice' they produce unjust results within society more generally.

Although some merits of conditional fee agreements are evident, a number of their alleged advantages are open to challenge, suggesting that greater encouragement of their use may not be desirable.[4] The experience of conditional fee agreements to date has highlighted

[2] It makes sense to begin your discussion of the advantages of conditional fee agreements with consideration of the less controversial arguments, as these can be dealt with quickly and build up to the more debatable issues to follow.

[3] It is essential that you probe this argument as there are obvious flaws to it as alluded to here. You can relate the criticisms of this argument to some of the criticisms of conditional fee agreements to be considered later.

[4] This comment serves as both an accurate summary of the consideration of the perceived advantages of conditional fee agreements, and an introduction to an overview of the problems associated with their use.

a number of problems associated with their use. A major criticism of conditional fee agreements is that they have given rise to a 'compensation culture', encouraging speculative claims fuelled by solicitors advertising 'no win no fee' deals with such vigour that they have become commonly dubbed 'ambulance chasers'. This perception led the former Secretary of State for Justice, Jack Straw, to express concern over soaring legal costs arising from a significant increase in (particularly personal injury) litigation. There is evidence that the promotion of conditional fee agreements has proceeded to a stage where their aggressive marketing has led to many claimants being misled in relation to the nature of the undertakings which they thought they were entering into.[5] This problem was highlighted in a 2005 report by the Citizens' Advice Bureaux, which investigated the tactics adopted by claims management companies, organisations which effectively canvass business which can be passed on to solicitors for a fee. The report found that some claimants actually stood to lose more than they would gain from litigation as a result of being incorrectly advised by the claims management companies who sometimes artificially escalated costs. An example of such a case is **Bowne and ten others v Bridgend County Borough Council** (2004) Unreported 25 March, where the compensation awarded to a group of claimants was less than the legal costs sought by their solicitors.

Litigation proceeding on the basis of conditional fee agreements may give rise to unfair trials,[6] where the defendant is unrepresented. This is illustrated by the case of **Steel v UK** (2005) 41 EHRR 22, the well publicised case of the 'McLibel Two'. The defendants had distributed material which made a series of allegations against McDonalds. This resulted in McDonalds bringing a libel action. As legal aid is not available for defamation proceedings and they could not afford legal assistance, the defendants were not legally represented in court whilst McDonalds were represented by a prolific team of eminent lawyers. The unfairness of the case was pronounced upon by the European Court of Human Rights when determining that there had been a breach of both the right to fair trial and the right to freedom of expression, under Articles 6 and 10 of the European Convention on Human Rights.

Finally, it must be noted that the greater use of conditional fee agreements, and the increase in litigation which it has given rise to, has

[5] This is a very important issue upon which you might be able to cite practical examples from your studies to receive greater credit.

[6] More could be made of this point, perhaps, by relating it to the later point about the need for defendants to be adequately insured in anticipation of litigation.

[7] This point could be reinforced in a coursework essay by reference to statistical evidence illustrating the increased cost of insurance.

hugely escalated insurance costs.[7] This has consequences for all of society. Increased insurance costs for public-sector bodies drains public resources, diverting funds from other uses, whereas private-sector bodies must raise operating costs to finance higher and more comprehensive insurance premiums. Individual defendants facing litigation may need to take out 'after-the-event insurance' at the cost of great personal and financial hardship.

[8] The conclusion reflects the discussion provided in the answer, which emphasised a number of problems with conditional fee agreements without questioning their merits completely.

In conclusion, it is difficult to accept that a compelling case exists for the greater encouragement of conditional fee agreements. Whilst they have their benefits, the various concerns which have been highlighted in relation to their operation suggests that rather than promote their even more extensive use, a detailed review of the problems which they give rise to would be worthwhile.[8]

 Make your answer stand out

- Provide context to your answer by illustrating the extent to which the law has facilitated the greater use of conditional fee agreements since they became permitted.

- Cite statistical evidence to reinforce some of the problems associated with the use of conditional fee agreements, such as increased insurance costs and aggressive marketing by claims management companies.

- Refer to Citizens Advice Bureaux (2005) *No Win, No Fee, No Chance* in considering the argument that, contrary to their objectives, conditional fee agreements have resulted in reduced access to justice for many in the area of personal injury litigation.

- In a lengthy coursework essay, you could draw comparisons between the operation of conditional fee agreements in the UK with their use in other jurisdictions.

! Don't be tempted to . . .

- Simply summarise the main arguments for and against conditional fee agreements.

# 🖎 Question 4

Evaluate the major changes introduced to the management of civil cases by the 1998 Civil Procedure Rules.

## Answer plan

➜ Explain the perceived problems which led to the Woolf reforms.

➜ Briefly explain the major objectives of the reforms.

➜ Discuss the major changes to case management brought about by the reforms.

➜ Conclude by evaluating the consequences of the reforms.

## Diagram plan

A printable version of this diagram plan is available from www.pearsoned.co.uk/lawexpressqa

## Answer

Prior to 1999 there were separate rules of civil procedure for the County Court and the High Court, the former being governed by County Court rules and the latter the rules of the Supreme Court. Whereas High Court actions began with a writ, County Court actions were commenced by a summons. In addition, there was a series of specialised and complicated procedures applicable to certain actions. The pre-1999 civil justice system was perceived to suffer from a number of problems.[1] Firstly, the system was regarded as being too expensive for many parties to civil actions. For example, the Woolf Review found that, for claims lower than £12,500, in 40% of cases the amount at stake was exceeded by one side's costs alone. The old system was notorious for experiencing delays in conclusion of court proceedings, which could typically amount to three years in the County Court and five years in the High Court. The adversarial process, which effectively emphasises a 'contest' between two sides, was felt to discourage co-operation between the parties, and the emphasis on oral evidence which is a key feature of

[1] Before proceeding to discuss the changes introduced by the 1998 rules, you should explain what problems created the need for reform. This also provides standards against which you can later measure the success of the reforms.

the English trial also served to slow down progress in proceedings as well as often being unnecessary. Injustice was also threatened in the huge number of cases where settlement was reached out of court, as a result of the unequal bargaining powers of the parties.

To address these problems, the Lord Chancellor in the government of John Major, Lord Mackay, requested Lord Woolf to undertake a review of the civil justice system and make recommendations for reform, which he did in his 1996 report. Most of these recommendations were implemented in the new Civil Procedure Rules ('the Rules') issued in 1999. The Rules constituted a unified procedural code containing simplified procedures and documentary requirements which replaced the previous separate sets of rules used by the County Court and High Court. The Rules aimed to address the perceived problems of the old system. While there is much emphasis upon avoiding litigation and encouraging early settlement, the overriding objective of the reforms was to ensure that the civil courts deal 'justly' with the cases they receive.[2]

[2] This is a good summary of the driving objective of the reforms, against which you can assess their outcomes.

[3] This is a key feature of the reforms and will be further illustrated as you discuss some of the specific changes which they introduced.

In order to improve the efficiency of civil proceedings, the Rules place great emphasis upon the role to be played by the courts in case management.[3] Courts were required to become 'active' managers of litigation by taking on a much more direct role in handling the progression of actions. Case management is governed by Part 3 of the Rules, which make provision for the use of case management conferences and pre-trial reviews in facilitating more efficient progression of cases through the courts. Active case management by the courts theoretically makes it harder for litigants to delay proceedings and a 2000 poll found that 76% of solicitors felt that the new rules increased the prospects of early settlement.

Part 26 of the Rules concerns the allocation of cases to particular tracks and courts. Small claims cases will be heard in the County Court, as will fast-track cases ordinarily, whereas multi-track cases will usually be reserved for the High Court. This relatively smooth division of labour is another step designed to enhance the efficiency with which civil litigation progresses through the courts. Both time and cost efficiency are also theoretically enhanced by the duty imposed upon courts to restrict the admission of expert evidence to where this is absolutely necessary. To ensure that the Civil Procedure Rules (CPR) are strictly complied with, the courts now enjoy the ability to impose tough sanctions to enforce them, including an adverse award of costs against a defaulting party or striking out part or all of that party's claim.[4]

[4] In this paragraph you demonstrate effectively some of the potential benefits of the reforms in terms of enhancing efficiency.

In pursuit of the objective of avoiding litigation, a number of mechanisms are promoted by the 1999 Rules which should make early settlement of disputes easier to achieve.[5] A number of pre-action protocols have been introduced under the CPR for specific types of action. These establish timetables according to which proceedings should progress which are designed to encourage early settlement. Under Part 36 of the CPR, when deciding upon the award of costs, courts are required to take into account any pre-trial offers to settle which have been made, thus providing incentives to settle out of court and avoid litigation. Courts are also to encourage the use of alternative dispute resolution at various stages during proceedings, another initiative that is likely to lead some potential litigants to attempt to settle their disputes out of court.

[5] As this was a driving objective of the reforms, it is imperative that you consider ways in which the reforms have sought to achieve this.

The main changes introduced to civil procedure by the 1998 CPR have not met with universal satisfaction. That the main objective of the reforms was to discourage litigation and encourage early settlement of disputes becomes very apparent when consideration is given to some of the major features of the reforms discussed above. In this respect, it is arguable that the reforms have achieved their objective.[6] There has been a huge increase in the number of cases now being settled out of court; 70% of disputes are in fact settled much earlier than the trial stage. There is evidence that commercial proceedings within the High Court have more than halved since the introduction of the new CPR. This considerable reduction in litigation and increase in out of court settlements should theoretically yield benefits in time and cost savings for individual litigants and the civil justice system as a whole. However, there remain charges that despite the 1998 reforms, problems remain within the civil justice process which have yet to be adequately tackled.

[6] After having considered the main features of the reforms, you should evaluate their main benefits and cite evidence in support of these.

[7] Continuing problems associated with civil procedure should also be emphasised. In a longer coursework essay there may be scope for you to consider how continuing problems might be addressed through possible further reforms which you are able to suggest.

Notwithstanding the reduction in litigation, there is evidence that civil legal costs have continued to increase.[7] These have been complicated by the growth in conditional fee agreements under which losing parties are required to pay the other side's costs. Court fees have also increased significantly, and while this forms part of a drive to make courts self-funding, unaffordable costs undoubtedly have a disproportionate effect upon the ability of the less well off to attain successful resolution of legitimate civil problems. Enforcement of judgments has also given rise to some problems. For example, difficulty has been experienced by parties seeking to enforce small claims awards in 25% of cases. New provisions, however, have been introduced by the Tribunals, Courts and Enforcement Act 2007 to improve enforcement.

[8] This is a logical, balanced conclusion which reflects the discussion contained in the answer. As noted in the previous comment, you might elaborate here to consider further possible reforms if time constraints permit.

In conclusion, the 1998 reforms have clearly brought about some benefits. However, they have not been a panacea for rectifying all of the problems of the civil justice process which continues to evidence a number of shortcomings which may benefit from additional reforms.[8]

 Make your answer stand out

- Suggest further possible reforms to civil procedure rules and their potential benefits.
- Reinforce your arguments with documentary evidence where appropriate.
- Assess the long-term consequences of the reforms to civil procedure by considering the arguments made in the 2008 Hamlyn lectures by Hazel Genn (2009) *Judging Civil Justice*, Cambridge: Cambridge University Press.
- Draw out the tensions which exist between providing a mechanism for civil redress for as many people as possible and controlling spiralling court costs.

! Don't be tempted to . . .

- Provide a detailed account of the various provisions contained in the Civil Procedure Rules.
- Confuse the 1999 changes to civil procedure with reforms to civil legal aid contained in the Access to Justice Act 1999.

**www.pearsoned.co.uk/lawexpressqa**

 Go online to access more revision support including additional essay and problem questions with diagram plans, You be the marker questions, and download all diagrams from the book.

# Alternative dispute resolution

9

## How this topic may come up in exams

Questions on this topic are likely to assess your understanding of methods of dispute resolution other than the courts, and may require you to consider their relative strengths and weaknesses when contrasted to other forms of dispute resolution. You may specifically be asked to explain and evaluate the role performed by tribunals and ombudsmen as systems of dispute resolution, either individually or in comparison to one another or the courts. You could also be asked to explain and comment upon the increased prominence of mediation, conciliation and arbitration as forms of ADR.

## Attack the question

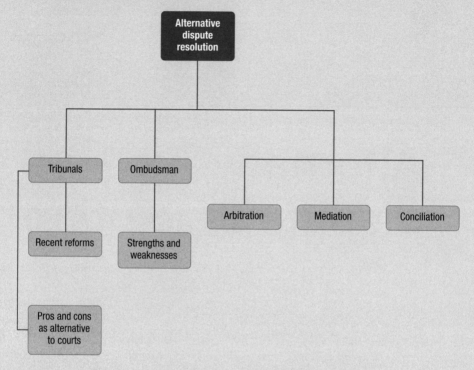

A printable version of this diagram plan is available from www.pearsoned.co.uk/lawexpressqa

#  Question 1

'The administrative tribunal system has been greatly improved by changes introduced by the Tribunals, Courts and Enforcement Act 2007.' Discuss, with reference to the requirement that tribunals be characterised by openness, fairness and impartiality.

## Answer plan

→ Briefly explain the nature and function of administrative tribunals.

→ Discuss the main criticisms of the tribunal system made by the Leggatt Review.

→ Discuss the main proposals of the Leggatt Review.

→ Explain the major changes introduced by the Tribunals, Courts and Enforcement Act 2007.

→ Evaluate the extent to which the changes have improved the tribunal system.

## Diagram plan

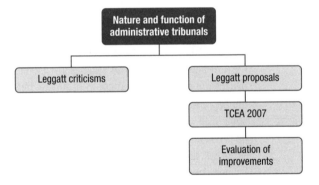

A printable version of this diagram plan is available from www.pearsoned.co.uk/lawexpressqa

## Answer

Although dating back over two centuries, modern tribunals are a product of the expansion of the welfare state. In response to the subsequent growth in the number of disputes between individuals and state bodies, a substantial number of tribunals have been created which now hear over one million cases annually. Unlike courts, tribunals enjoy specialist jurisdiction and traditionally operate on a more informal basis free of the procedural rules associated with court hearings. Other main strengths usually associated with tribunals

[1] You can provide useful context to your answer by briefly referring to the main features and perceived advantages of tribunals.

include the expertise they afford, the relative speed with which cases are heard and the low costs associated with their utilisation.[1] However, concerns over the operation of tribunals led the Lord Chancellor to task Sir Andrew Leggatt in 2000 with conducting a review of tribunals and making proposals for any necessary reforms, which he did the following year.

The Franks Committee which investigated the operation of tribunals back in 1957 recommended that tribunals should operate in accordance with principles of 'openness, fairness and impartiality'. Leggatt reiterated the importance of these standards, but felt that they were not adequately satisfied by tribunals as they currently functioned.[2]

[2] This focus is important as it relates back to the question's concern with 'openness, fairness and impartiality'. This paragraph effectively considers ways in which tribunals workings pre-2007 could be seen as falling short of adequately satisfying these requirements, usefully leading into the later consideration of the merits of the changes introduced in 2007.

He found that the quality of administrative tribunals varied 'from excellent to inadequate' and directed a number of specific criticisms at tribunals. These related to their openness or accessibility, relationship with government departments, and the incoherence of the tribunal system as a whole. Tribunals were not sufficiently open or accessible as in order to be so required that citizens knew of their existence and the circumstances in which they could make use of their procedures to resolve a dispute against a government department or agency. It is easy to assume that tribunals are accessible because of citizens' entitlement to use them, but of course unless the aggrieved citizen is aware of their relevance in any given situation, their theoretical accessibility becomes meaningless because he is not in a position to make practical use of their procedures. The perceived fairness and impartiality of tribunals was compromised by their dependence upon the government departments whom they would hear disputes concerning. Each tribunal's administrative support would be provided by the department whose decisions and actions it was concerned with, and that department's minister would also appoint the tribunal's members. Not only do such arrangements threaten to breach Article 6 of the European Convention on Human Rights' guarantee of a fair trial, they run counter to one of the core principles of natural justice, the rule against bias,[3] which has been invoked in judicial review proceedings to render decisions invalid where judgment has been given by a person with an interest at stake in the matter in contention. Leggatt also concluded that there was no coherent tribunal system. Individual tribunals were created in a haphazard manner, in response to needs in a particular area. As a result, they were all subject to their own different procedures and provided

[3] This is a good argument which not only highlights problems with the dependence of tribunals on government departments, but also evidences awareness of other areas of law which have relevant application to the operation of tribunals.

various routes of appeal. There was no uniformity across the tribunal system, and it could rightfully be asserted that the resulting confusion impacted negatively upon their user-friendliness and, thus, accessibility.

The main proposal of the Leggatt Review was to create a single unified tribunal to be responsible for administering all administrative tribunals.[4] Existing tribunals could be brought within one tribunal system, where they would operate by the same procedures. Citizens would submit cases to the tribunal service which would decide which tribunal to allocate them to. Although clearly aimed at improving the coherence of the tribunal system, and consequently its user-friendliness, it was intended also to address the other perceived problems of tribunals. The creation of a tribunal service responsible for the administration of tribunals which was independent of individual government departments would go a long way towards answering criticisms that tribunals were too reliant upon the departments against which they heard disputes. It would also be hoped that the creation of a specialist tribunal service would be able to generate greater public awareness of the existence of tribunal procedures, thus enhancing their accessibility to citizens who could benefit from their use.

[4] This leads into consideration of the 2007 reforms. You need to explain how this seemingly rather straightforward proposal, which was largely acted upon in the 2007 Act, could enhance the 'openness, fairness and impartiality' of tribunal proceedings.

The Leggatt Review's recommendations were largely endorsed in a 2004 white paper, the main proposals becoming part of the Tribunals, Courts and Enforcement Act 2007.[5] In accordance with the proposal that there be a single tribunal service, the Act created two generic tribunals to which the jurisdiction of most existing administrative tribunals would be transferred; the new generic tribunals are divided into a number of chambers each with their own specialist area of jurisdiction. Whereas previously tribunals were subject to their own individual procedures, the 2007 Act created a Tribunal Procedure Committee charged with establishing rules of procedure for the new tribunals, which it has now produced; the common procedural rules created for tribunals bear the influences of the rules of civil procedure established for the courts following the Woolf reforms in 1999. The 2007 Act also created a unified appeal structure for tribunals and legally qualified tribunal members are now conferred with the title of 'judge', meaning that their independence is guaranteed by the Constitutional Reform Act 2005.

[5] You do not need to attempt to outline in great detail the provisions of the 2007 Act. The question is concerned with the extent to which they improve the 'openness, fairness and impartiality' of tribunals. You only need to ensure that you mention the main changes introduced insofar as they impact upon these requirements.

Prima facie, the reforms made by the 2007 Act appear designed to enhance the 'openness, fairness and impartiality' of administrative

[6] This conclusion reinforces the arguments advanced earlier in respect of the merits of the reforms proposed by the Leggatt Review. At this stage you can briefly summarise the main likely benefits of the changes to build upon the earlier discussion.

tribunals.[6] It is to be hoped that the creation of a unified, coherent tribunal system will ultimately improve the publicity afforded to the workings of tribunals to the extent that citizens aggrieved by administrative decisions will be sufficiently well informed of their availability as a forum for airing their disputes. The accessibility or openness of tribunals will thus be improved. The creation of a tribunal service responsible for the administration of all tribunals should also enhance their perceived fairness and impartiality by severing their dependence upon the government departments against which they subsequently hear disputes brought to them. As noted, the independence of legally qualified members will be reinforced by their elevation to the status of 'judge'. However, while the 2007 changes are welcome for these reasons, a couple of caveats are necessary.[7] Firstly, it is too soon to know what impact the changes will have upon the functioning of tribunals in the longer term as the new tribunal system has only been in place since 2008. Secondly, it is possible that some of the changes will have negative effects upon some of the traditional features of tribunals. For example, the creation of unified procedural rules for all tribunals and the conferment of 'judge' status upon some tribunal members have been seen by some commentators as evidence of increasing formalisation of tribunals at the expense of their traditional perception as an informal alternative to the courts.

[7] These are useful points to make. In an extended essay on this question you could explore further the extent to which the 2007 reforms have, or may, affect some of the traditionally perceived virtues of tribunals.

## ✓ Make your answer stand out

- Refer to documentary evidence in order to reinforce your arguments.
- In considering the likely benefits of the recent reforms to the tribunal system read and make reference to Carnwath (2009) 'Tribunal Justice: A New Start', *Public Law*, 48.
- Suggest possible further reforms which may address any weaknesses of the tribunal system not adequately tackled by the 2007 changes.
- Consider the impact of reforms to the tribunal system on the perceived overburdening of the civil courts.

## ! Don't be tempted to . . .

- Provide a descriptive account of the content of the Leggatt Review and the 2007 Act.

#  Question 2

'Administrative tribunals are much better suited to the resolution of disputes between individuals and the state than ordinary law courts.' Discuss.

## Answer plan

→ Briefly explain the origins of the modern tribunal system, and comment upon their nature and function.

→ Discuss the main benefits of tribunals as an alternative to litigation in the courts.

→ Discuss the main shortcomings of tribunals as an alternative to litigation in the courts and briefly comment upon the extent to which any shortcomings have been addressed by changes introduced by the Tribunals, Courts and Enforcement Act 2007.

→ Conclude by directly addressing the statement contained in the question.

## Diagram plan

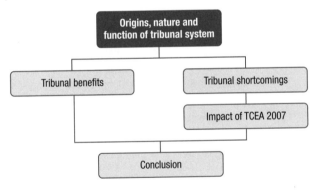

A printable version of this diagram plan is available from www.pearsoned.co.uk/lawexpressqa

## Answer

Tribunals are not a new phenomenon, having their origins over two centuries ago, although the modern system of administrative tribunals stems from the growth of the welfare state since 1945. As the state became engaged in a greater number of disputes with citizens, many specialist tribunals have been established over the past few decades to hear a wide range of disputes. Over a million cases are heard by tribunals annually. Tribunals differ from courts in a number

[1] As the question asks you to consider the benefits of tribunals vis-à-vis the courts, it is helpful if you briefly explain how they differ in nature from the courts.

of important respects.[1] They enjoy specialist jurisdiction and are not traditionally bound by all of the formal procedures applicable to court hearings. While chaired by a legally qualified person, lay members also sit upon tribunals. Until recently, each tribunal was subject to its own rules and procedures, but the Tribunals, Courts and Enforcement Act 2007 has created a new unified tribunal system.

[2] The main focus of the question is the purported benefits of tribunals over courts and this should form the bulk of your discussion. It is logical to begin with the strongest arguments for the use of tribunals.

Administrative tribunals are regarded as having a number of distinct advantages over ordinary courts.[2] For example, the specialisation they offer is often cited as one of their foremost virtues. As specialist bodies, they are able to develop expertise in the subject matter of their jurisdiction. For example, a tribunal handling social security disputes is likely to have a much greater appreciation of the issues involved where this is the sole focus of the tribunal's work in contrast to a court which will only deal with such matters as a small proportion of a larger, varied caseload. Furthermore, as a result of their specialisation tribunals should be able to draw upon a greater awareness of policy matters. Tribunal hearings are also held in private, which may be particularly appealing to parties who for various reasons may not want to air their business in public as would happen in court proceedings. This feature of the tribunal system may be particularly important for individuals with especially sensitive disputes, although the closed nature of tribunal proceedings does appear to fly in the face of the recommendation of the Franks Committee that tribunals exhibit the characteristics of 'openness, fairness and impartiality', a requirement more recently reiterated by the Leggatt Review of the tribunal system.

While a number of supposed strengths of the tribunal system can be highlighted, the extent to which these constitute undisputed benefits of taking cases to a tribunal rather than the courts in some cases is questionable.[3] It is commonly asserted that tribunals provide a much quicker resolution of disputes than the courts with many hearings being concluded within a day and tribunals being able to specify precise hearing times unfettered by the kinds of procedural backlog which can clog up the courts. This is good for individuals and more generally relieves the burden placed upon ordinary courts. However, while it is not unreasonable to expect a tribunal to resolve a dispute with greater speed than the courts, this strength can be overstated. As far back as 1993, the Vice-Chairman of the Employment Lawyers Association commented that hearings which had previously taken

[3] Having considered the stronger arguments in favour of the use of tribunals, you can move on to consider those arguments which are more questionable. These arguments are related and can be effectively considered in the same paragraph.

three to five months to be concluded by tribunals had come to take over 18 months. Furthermore, the greater formalisation of the tribunal system introduced by the 2007 Act may run the risk of eventually dragging out tribunal proceedings longer. Traditionally, the informality of tribunal proceedings has been held up as one of their key virtues. The inapplicability of strict rules of evidence employed by the courts and the absence of many of the hallmarks of an ordinary court case help to put individuals at ease, as well as speeding up proceedings. However, while tribunals remain less formal forums than the ordinary courts, the degree of this informality is certainly being challenged by the 2007 reforms.[4] For example, tribunals are now presided over by judges. Greater formalisation of the tribunal system may impact upon another of its commonly cited strengths, namely its relative inexpensive cost for users when compared to the far greater costs associated with litigation in the courts. Tribunals do not usually charge fees, the infrastructure used by tribunals being small scale. Parties usually pay their own costs and are often able to dispense with the need for legal representation. The 2007 reforms may come to have some bearing upon the costs associated with tribunal hearings if they do result in greater formalisation of procedures and, for example, increase the need for parties to be legally represented.

Although the advantages of using tribunals over courts will hold good in many circumstances, the point being made is that they should not be overstated, particularly in light of what may in the long term come to be the consequences of the reforms introduced to the tribunal system by the 2007 Act. There are, however, some drawbacks of the tribunal system which have received the attention of commentators. Traditionally, there was no uniformity to tribunals with each one enjoying its own procedures and routes of appeal. This was a source of confusion to some individuals. This has, however, been remedied as a result of the creation of one unified tribunal system by the 2007 reforms.[5] All tribunals now share a common procedural code and appeals mechanisms. One ongoing issue of concern is the unavailability of state funding for actions brought in tribunals in most instances. Although less costly than court proceedings, on some occasions the lack of funding will put individuals at a disadvantage when bringing a dispute against a government department which will have a wealth of resources to draw upon, as research by Hazel Genn (2009) has highlighted. Although specialist help will sometimes be

[4] In considering the relative merits of tribunals it is worthwhile considering any possible impact upon these by the reforms introduced by the Tribunals Courts and Enforcement Act 2007. This is very relevant to the question and evidences awareness of recent developments in the area.

[5] Again, you are showing the impact of the 2007 Act, in this case highlighting one of the ways in which it has addressed one of the perceived weaknesses of tribunals.

[6] This is a good point to make as you demonstrate that a weakness of this form of dispute resolution does not imply a strength of the alternative.

available from sources such as community law centres or the Citizens' Advice Bureaux, this cannot be guaranteed. The lack of state funding, however, should not be seen as a reason for pursuing litigation in court instead, as state funding for civil legal disputes is also heavily restricted.[6]

[7] Based upon the discussion provided in the answer, this is a reasonable conclusion. The answer has demonstrated a number of strengths of the tribunal system and, while you have shown that these have their limitations, you have not given any cause to presume the courts to be a better alternative for resolving individual–state disputes where this availability of recourse to a tribunal is present. At the same time, the conclusion acknowledges that tribunals are not always the preferable method of dispute resolution.

There are certainly various reasons why tribunals are likely to be better suited to resolving disputes between individuals and the state than ordinary law courts in many cases. However, the purported benefits of tribunals cannot be assumed to apply to every instance where an individual is in dispute with a government department. Although too early to draw any conclusions, the possible effects of the 2007 reforms upon the nature and functioning of tribunals also need to be borne in mind. The drawbacks of using tribunals are not numerous or overly exceptional, and so it would thus seem reasonable to accept the assertion that very often tribunals will provide a better forum for the resolution of disputes between individuals and the state than the courts.[7]

 Make your answer stand out

- Cite documentary evidence to reinforce your arguments where appropriate.
- Consider the impact of the 2007 Act on the relative benefits of the tribunal system.
- Demonstrate clearly that different kinds of cases will be better suited to courts and tribunals respectively.
- Contrast the merits of tribunals with other administrative law grievance redress mechanisms.

! Don't be tempted to . . .

- Present your answer as just a briefly explained series of pros and cons of the tribunal system.

#  Question 3

Discuss the extent to which the Parliamentary Commissioner for Administration provides a meaningful mechanism for the redress of citizens' grievances.

# Answer plan

→ Briefly explain the origins of the ombudsman system within the UK.

→ Comment upon the main features of the ombudsman's jurisdiction.

→ Discuss the vague concept of 'maladministration' and the extent to which it restricts the range of cases which the ombudsman may investigate.

→ Discuss the restrictions placed upon the utility of the ombudsman system by the MP filter and his lack of enforcement powers.

→ Conclude upon the extent to which the ombudsman system provides a meaningful mechanism for the redress of citizens' grievances.

# Diagram plan

A printable version of this diagram plan is available from www.pearsoned.co.uk/lawexpressqa

# Answer

The ombudsman concept is Scandinavian in origin and is intended to provide citizens with an additional mechanism through which grievances against state bodies can be investigated and remedied. The 1961 Wyatt Report noted a number of shortcomings in the existing mechanisms through which individuals could pursue grievances against state bodies and recommended that an ombudsman system be established within the UK.[1] This eventually happened with the passage of the Parliamentary Commissioner Act 1967, which created the post of Parliamentary Commissioner for Administration, commonly referred to as the ombudsman. The ombudsman was created to investigate complaints of maladministration made against central government departments, although the ombudsman concept has been extended with the creation of an ombudsman system for local government, the NHS and legal services. There are now also some ombudsmen systems within the private sector in such areas as banking and insurance.

[1] The first paragraph provides useful contextual background to your answer. In a longer coursework essay on this question you could devote more attention to the problems with other mechanisms for grievance redress identified by Wyatt and consider how the ombudsman system addresses these.

[2] Before considering the main problems associated with the ombudsman system, you should demonstrate an understanding of its main features, ensuring that you note any strengths – for example, robust powers of investigation – as well as flagging up problems for further scrutiny.

Section 5(1) of the 1967 Act summarises the ombudsman's principal function,[2] which is to investigate complaints emanating from members of the public who claim to have suffered injustice as a consequence of maladministration on the part of a government department or body arising from the performance of its functions. Importantly, the ombudsman is not concerned with the merits of decisions or actions of government bodies, but simply the process by which they are taken. This limits the range of grievances for which recourse to the ombudsman is likely to be appropriate. However, the ombudsman has determined maladministration to have occurred in some well-publicised cases. For example, in the Sachsenhausen case he found there had been defects in the administration of compensation payments to victims of Nazi persecution, and in the Barlow Clowes case found maladministration on the part of the Department of Trade and Industry to have contributed to huge losses on the Stock Exchange. An individual may not submit a complaint directly to the ombudsman. Instead it must be submitted to an MP, who can then forward it on to the ombudsman. The 'MP filter' system thus means that there is no guaranteed access to the ombudsman in any given situation. In order to investigate complaints of maladministration leading to injustice, the ombudsman does enjoy relatively robust powers. The powers conferred upon the ombudsman to collect evidence and call witnesses under section 8 are akin to those of a High Court judge, and obstruction of his investigations can amount to contempt of court (section 9). In this sense, the ombudsman is provided with the means to conduct his investigations thoroughly. However, upon conclusion of an investigation he is limited by section 10 to only being able to issue a report detailing his findings. He has no power to impose any sanctions in the case of an adverse finding against a government department.

[3] Here the essay is given clear focus as three main issues worth particular consideration are flagged up.

[4] Several attempts have been made to give greater clarity to this term and you should illustrate your awareness of these, while acknowledging the difficulty of providing a definitive definition.

The utility of the ombudsman as a grievance redress mechanism, arguably, is restricted in three main ways.[3] Firstly, the need to establish the presence of maladministration in the decision-making process of a government body means that the ombudsman cannot be used as a vehicle through which the merits of a decision itself can be challenged. Even accepting the restriction of the ombudsman to procedural matters, the term 'maladministration' gives rise to difficulties.[4] No statutory definition has been given to the term. The cabinet minister Richard Crossman provided an indicative list of examples of maladministration in the early years of the Ombudsman's operation. A detailed list of examples of maladministration was provided by then Ombudsman William Reid in his 1993 Annual Report to Parliament, which among a substantial number of varied instances of maladministration included rudeness, giving misleading advice, and showing bias. The courts have contributed to the definition of maladministration in some cases, such as **R v Commissioners for Local Administration, ex parte Bradford MBC** [1979] QB 287, where it was held to constitute 'faulty' or 'bad' administration. Nonetheless, there is still no definitive agreed definition of maladministration. That said, it is a difficult concept to define and in most cases it is arguably relatively straightforward to identify occurrences of maladministration.

A major criticism of the ombudsman system has been the retention of the MP filter, preventing individuals from being able to submit complaints directly to the ombudsman.[5] While the filter system can be used to weed out frivolous complaints, one danger is that whether complaints are referred to the ombudsman or not will depend upon the political views of the MP to whom it is initially submitted. The filter also slows down the progress of complaints through the addition of an extra layer of bureaucracy within the process and is not common within ombudsman systems in other jurisdictions. For reasons such as these there have been growing calls for the abolition of the MP filter. However, many MPs remain committed to the view that they serve an important constitutional role as the primary defenders of constituents' rights, and as an instrument of Parliament, it is their function to handle complaints en route to the ombudsman. In 2000, a bill to abolish the MP filter was rejected by Parliament.

[5] This is arguably the biggest criticism of the ombudsman system and must be addressed.

The final main restriction placed upon the utility of the ombudsman lies in his inability to enforce his findings. While he must produce a report detailing the findings of any investigation, which is provided to the body investigated and MP who referred the complaint, he cannot impose any sanctions.[6] Despite this, the power of the ombudsman should not be underestimated. He has the important power of publicity in issuing his reports and can make recommendations for compensation where appropriate, or changes to administrative procedures, which are often acted upon. For example, his reports upon the Sachsenhausen and Barlow Clowes cases discussed above led to compensation being paid to those affected by the maladministration found to have occurred.

[6] While an important point, you should also emphasise the extent to which the ombudsman's reports can produce positive outcomes in individual cases.

[7] This summarises well the balance of the arguments considered in the answer. While problems are identified within the ombudsman system, it is important to remember that it was created to supplement, not replace, existing mechanisms for the redress of grievances, and in light of this the perceived drawbacks of the ombudsman system can easily be overstated.

While there are clearly limits to the role which the ombudsman can play in redressing citizens' grievances, it is possible to overstate some of these.[7] Although restricted to considering claims of maladministration and lacking any real sanctions, it should be remembered that the ombudsman is one of several mechanisms for the redress of grievances, and is designed to serve as an additional mechanism to the courts and tribunals, not as a replacement. The removal of the MP filter would, arguably, improve access to the ombudsman, but generally speaking there is a high level of satisfaction with the function performed by means of the mechanism provided by the ombudsman system for the redress of grievances.

 Make your answer stand out

- Reinforce your arguments by referring to practical examples from the work of the ombudsman.
- Refer to academic and official commentary on the strengths of the ombudsman system, for example Ann Abraham's 2004 speech to the Council on Tribunals, available online at http://www.ombudsman.org.uk/about-us/media-centre/ombudsmans-speeches/archive/sp2004-02
- Make comparisons with other mechanisms for resolving disputes between citizens and the state, such as tribunals or the courts.
- Make suggestions for possible reform to the ombudsman system.

! Don't be tempted to . . .

- Provide a detailed account of each feature of the Ombudsman system as set out in the Parliamentary Commissioner Act 1967.
- Confuse the different ombudsmen systems in operation: your answer should relate primarily to the Parliamentary Commissioner for Administration.

# 🖎 Question 4

To what extent is the increasing popularity of alternative dispute resolution an indication of its effectiveness as an alternative to the courts?

## Answer plan

→ Explain what ADR is and briefly illustrate the main forms it takes.

→ Explain the factors behind efforts to encourage the greater use of ADR.

→ Discuss the circumstances in which ADR may be more effective than the courts.

→ Discuss the limitations of ADR as an alternative to the courts.

→ Conclude by making comment upon the extent to which ADR is an effective alternative to the courts as a mechanism for the redress of grievances.

## Diagram plan

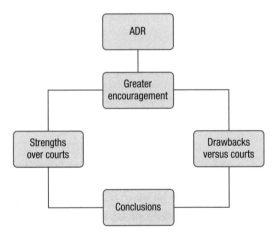

<sup>1</sup> While the question is specifically concerned with the merits of ADR as an alternative to pursuing litigation in the courts, you should begin your answer by briefly explaining what ADR is.

## Answer

Alternative dispute resolution (ADR) refers to the use of techniques for the resolution of disputes which do not involve recourse to the courts. There are three main forms of ADR.[1] Arbitration involves the appointment of a third party empowered to make a legally binding decision in relation to the issue in dispute. Arbitration is particularly relevant in the commercial context, where it is governed by the Arbitration Act 1996. Mediation involves the intervention of a third party to assist the parties to a dispute to resolve their differences, and is commonly used in divorce cases, while conciliation is a form of mediation which involves a more interventionist role being played by the third party mediator/conciliator. One of the best known examples of conciliation is found with its use in unfair dismissal cases under the auspices of ACAS.

Primarily driven by the objectives of relieving the caseload faced by the courts and to reduce the costs of legal action, efforts have been made in recent years to encourage the greater use of ADR by poten-tial litigants. Rule 1.4 of the Civil Procedure Rules requires courts to encourage the parties' use of ADR where appropriate.[2] While it was established in *Halsey* v *Milton Keynes General NHS Trust* [2004] EWCA 3006 Civ 576 that the courts have no power to force the use of ADR, the Court of Appeal has nonetheless demonstrated a willingness to punish parties who fail to make use of it when making decisions over the award of costs (*Dunnett* v *Railtrackplc* [2002] EWCA Civ 302). However, it is misleading to believe that ADR has grown enormously in popularity. Although a substantial rise in its use was seen following the adoption of the 1998 Civil Procedure Rules, its usage rate then levelled off.[3] That it remains used at lower than anticipated levels is perhaps reinforced by a 2011 Ministry of Justice consultation paper's consideration of making recourse to mediation compulsory in civil cases.

In certain circumstances the benefits of ADR over recourse to the civil courts is evident. The main advantages to be had in most cases concern time and money. Litigation can be a very expensive and time-consuming affair.[4] As ADR relies on more informal processes it is generally much quicker than litigation. Furthermore, as parties are not faced with the formal and prolonged legal procedures which accompany litigation, their need to avail themselves of legal assis-tance will often be reduced, thus producing sometimes considerable financial savings. Research by Genn (2009) reinforces these appar-ent benefits of ADR, finding that huge costs are saved where ADR is successful and that in 62% of the cases surveyed settlement was reached at the appointment stage. However, there is a note of caution as she also observed that, where ADR fails to resolve a dispute and requires litigation, the costs can actually be higher than they would ordinarily have been.[5]

[2] This is an important point and provides crucial context to your answer. The question refers to the increased popularity of ADR, so you should demonstrate that you understand the pressures for its greater use and why these have emerged.

[3] This is a very relevant point and challenges the assumption made by the question. By pointing this out you will receive credit for being sufficiently informed upon the current take-up rate of ADR to be able to challenge an erroneous assumption contained in the question.

[4] These are undeniably the most obvious and compelling benefits of ADR as an alternative to litigation and should be discussed in some detail. Reinforce your arguments by citing statistical evidence in support of your arguments here.

[5] This is an important point to make and it adds weight to the proposition that the merits of using ADR over having recourse to litigation will vary with the nature of each individual case.

In certain cases, parties to a dispute can avail themselves of greater expertise in helping them to reach a settlement through recourse to ADR. Unlike the courts, comprised of judges with a generalist legal training, many providers of ADR services are specialists in the kinds of issues with which they deal.[6] For example, ACAS enjoys a reputation for its conciliation of employment disputes, there are a number of specialist trade association arbitration schemes, and in the family law context there are mediators skilled at assisting with the resolution of disputes stemming from relationship breakdowns. ADR can also prove to be advantageous for parties in a sensitive relationship, or where confidential material is at stake. Litigation proceeds on an adversarial basis, which encourages confrontation between the parties, and ordinarily takes place in the public domain.[7] Where the long-term interests of the parties requires that they be conciliated – for example, in the case of a divorcing couple with children – there may be sound reasons to avoid attempting to resolve their disagreements in court. In commercial cases involving sensitive information, the parties may prefer to avoid any damaging publicity by submitting their dispute to resolution by arbitration which takes place in private.

[6] This point is well supported by reference to examples, as you provide here.

[7] This is a point which again can be reinforced well by reference to relevant examples, as provided here.

There are obviously certain kinds of cases which appear suited for ADR, but it is not always a preferable option to litigation. It has been claimed that ADR procedures can perpetuate imbalances of power between the parties. This claim has been made particularly in relation to employment disputes, where employers tend to be better represented than their employees. However, this argument cannot be applied as strongly to most commercial or family disputes.[8] It is also worth noting that any imbalance between parties is just as likely, if not more so, to arise in litigation that takes place before the courts. Recourse to ADR may also be seen to suffer from the lack of legal expertise which the parties are assured of when they resort to litigation. However, the extent to which this is necessarily to be regarded as a matter of concern will vary with the nature of the dispute that requires resolution.[9] While for some particularly complicated commercial disputes, legal expertise may be regarded as critical, this may not be the case in respect of many other disputes, for example divorce-related matters, where the key objective of the parties is to achieve conciliation through compromise.

[8] In an extended essay you may wish to probe this argument further by drawing upon relevant empirical evidence, perhaps contrasting further its application to different kinds of cases.

[9] This can equally be a strength and weakness of ADR depending upon the nature of the particular case in question and reinforces the point that runs throughout the answer, namely that whether ADR is preferable to litigation will vary with the circumstances of each case.

One drawback of making use of ADR procedures lies in the limited enforceability of settlement reached through their utilisation.[10] While

[10] This is a very important point which you should ensure that you mention. Again it illustrates the need to ensure that a particular dispute is suited to ADR.

arbitration is a legally binding process, mediation and conciliation are not. Should one party fail to fulfil their obligations under the term of any settlement, it may be necessary for the other party to go to court in order to enforce it, thus increasing the financial costs of having had recourse to ADR.

Although ADR has not increased in popularity at the levels which might have been expected, it is possible to see clear benefits which should make it appealing to many would-be litigants. However, the extent to which it will be suitable for any given situation will be dependent upon the nature of the dispute and the amenability of the parties to resolution. Where these factors are favourable, recourse to ADR can have considerable benefits in terms of time, cost and the avoidance of damaging confrontation encouraged by the adversarial process. However, it should not be assumed that ADR is always to be preferred to litigation. Where disputes are not best suited to its techniques and/or parties enter it reluctantly, there is a danger that the overall costs of action and/or enforcement will be increased.[11] It is thus important that cases are subject to proper assessment for suitability before being referred to ADR.

[11] This is a balanced and logical conclusion which follows naturally from the discussion provided of the key arguments concerning the merits of ADR as an alternative to litigation in the courts.

## ✔ Make your answer stand out

- Refer to the efforts of both government and the courts to promote the greater use of ADR, and the reasons for this
- Refer to academic commentary on the merits of ADR as an alternative to litigation, for example Partington (2004) 'Alternative Dispute Resolution: Recent Challenges, Future Developments', *Civil Justice Quarterly*, 99
- Illustrate clearly that the utility of ADR will vary from one kind of dispute to another
- Directly challenge the assumption contained in the question by citing statistical evidence on the low take-up rate of ADR

## ! Don't be tempted to . . .

- Simply describe the different forms of ADR.

# Bibliography

Abel, R.L. (1987) 'The Decline of Professionalism', *Arbitration*, v. 53, n. 3, 187.

Abrahams, A. (2004) Council on Tribunals Conference Speech, www.ombudsman.org.uk/about-us/media-centre/ombudsmans-speeches/archive/sp2004-02.

Allan, T.R.S. (1985) 'The Limits of Parliamentary Sovereignty', *Public Law*, 614.

Auld, R. (2001) *Review of the Criminal Courts in England and Wales*, webarchive.nationalarchives.gov.uk/+/http://www.criminal-courts-review.org.uk/.

Baldwin, J. and McConville, M. (1979) *Jury Trials*. Oxford: Clarendon.

Bennion, F.A.R. (1978) 'Statute Law: Obscurity and Drafting Parameters', *British Journal of Law and Society*, v. 5, n. 2, 235.

Bingham, T.H. (1993) 'The European Convention on Human Rights: Time to Incorporate', *Law Quarterly Review*, v. 109, 390.

Bradley, A. (2007) 'The Sovereignty of Parliament', in J. Jowell and D. Oliver (eds) *The Changing Constitution* (6th edn) Oxford: Oxford University Press.

Burns, S. (2006) 'Tipping in the Balance', *New Law Journal*, v. 156, 787.

Burrows, A. (2002) 'We Do This at Common Law but That in Equity', *Oxford Journal of Legal Studies*, v. 22, n. 1, 1–16.

Carnwath, R. (2009) 'Tribunal Justice: A New Start', *Public Law*, 48.

Citizens' Advice Bureaux (2005) *No Win, No Fee, No Chance*. www.citizensadvice.org.uk/microsoft_word_-_no_win-_no_fee-_no_chance_report_final.pdf.

Constitutional Affairs Select Committee (2007) *The Governance of Britain: A Consultation on the Role of the Attorney-General* (Cm 7192) Norwich: TSO, www.official-documents.gov.uk/document/cm71/7192/7192.pdf.

Craig, P. (2007) 'Britain in the European Union', in J. Jowell and D. Oliver (eds) *The Changing Constitution*, 6th edn. Oxford: Oxford University Press.

Darbyshire, P. (1991) 'The Lamp that Shows that Freedom Lives – Is It Worth the Candle?', *Crim LR*, 740.

Dicey, A.V. (1982) *Introduction to the Study of the Law of the Constitution*. Liberty Classics.

Duxbury, N. (2008) *The Nature and Authority of Precedent*. Cambridge: Cambridge University Press.

Elliott, C. and Quinn, F. (2010) *English Legal System*. (11th edn.). Harlow: Longman.
Elliott, C. and Quinn, F. (2012) *English Legal System* (13th edn). Harlow: Longman.

Genn, H. (2009) *Judging Civil Justice*. Cambridge: Cambridge University Press.
Griffith, J.A.G. (1997) *The Politics of the Judiciary*. London: Fontana.

Hale, B. (2002) 'Equality and the Judiciary: Why Should We Want More Women Judges?',
    *Public Law*, 489.
Hynes, S. and Robins, J. (2009) *The Justice Gap: Whatever Happened to Legal Aid?* London:
    Legal Action Group.

Jackson, J. (2009) 'Reconceptualizing the Right to Silence as an Effective Fair Trial
    Standard', *International and Comparative Law Quarterly*, v. 58, n. 4, 835.
Jackson, R.M. (1989) *The Machinery of Justice in England*. Cambridge: Cambridge
    University Press.

Kavanagh, A. (2009) 'Judging the Judges under the Human Rights Act: Defence
    Disillusionment and the 'War on Terror', *Public Law*, 287.

Leigh, I. and Lustgarten, L. (1999) 'Making Rights Real: the Courts, Remedies and the
    Human Rights Act', *Cambridge Law Journal*, v. 58, n. 3, 509.
Ligere, E. (2005) '*Locus Standi* and the Public Interest: a Hotchpotch of Legal Principles',
    *Journal of Planning and Environment Law*, 292.
Lloyd-Bostock, S. (2007) 'The Jubilee Line Jurors: Does Their Experience Strengthen the
    Case for Judge-only Trials in Long and Complex Fraud Cases?' *Crim LR*, 255.

McConville, M. (1992) 'Videotaping Interrogations: Police Behaviour On and Off Camera',
    *Crim LR*, 532.
McHarg, A. (2006) 'What Is Delegated Legislation?', *Public Law*, v. 50, 539.
Macklem, T. (2006) 'Entrenching Bills of Rights', *Oxford Journal of Legal Studies*, v. 26,
    n. 1, 107.
Miller, J. (2010) 'Stop and Search in England: a Reformed Tactic or Business as Usual?',
    *British Journal of Criminology*, v. 50, n. 5, 954.

Office of the Attorney General (2008) *The Governance of Britain: Constitutional Renewal*,
    (Cm 7355). Norwich: TSO http://www.official-documents.gov.uk/document/
    cm73/7355/7355.pdf.
Ormerod, D. (2002) 'ECHR and the Exclusion of Evidence: Trial Remedies for Article 8
    Breaches?', *Crim LR*, 61.
Ormerod, D. (2011) *Smith & Hogan's Criminal Law* (13th edn). Oxford: Oxford University
    Press.

Partington, M. (2004) 'Alternative Dispute Resolution: Recent Challenges, Future Developments', *Civil Justice Quarterly*, 99.

Robertson, G. (1993) *Freedom, the Individual and the Law*. London: Penguin, 1993.
Roskill Committee (1986) *Fraud Trials Committee Report*. London: HMSO.

Sanders, A., Bridges, L., Mulvaney, A. and Crozier, G. (1989) *Advice and Assistance at Police Stations and the 24-Hour Duty Solicitor Scheme*. London: Lord Chancellor's Department.
Slapper, G. and Kelly, D. (2010) *The English Legal System*, 11th edn. Oxford: Routledge.
Spencer, J.R. (2006) 'Does Our Present Criminal Appeal System Makes Sense?', *Crim LR*, 677.
Steyn, J. (2001) '*Pepper* v *Hart*: A Re-examination', *Oxford Journal of Legal Studies*, v. 21, n. 1, 59.

Vick, D.W. (2002) 'The Human Rights Act and the British Constitution', *Texas International Law Journal*, v. 37, n. 2, 329.

Wasik, M. (2008) 'Sentencing Guidelines in England and Wales – State of the Art?' *Crim LR*, 253.
Williams, G. (1983) *Textbook of Criminal Law*. London: Stevens & Sons.
Windlesham, Lord (2005) 'The Constitutional Reform Act 2005: Ministers, Judges and Constitutional Change', *Crim LR*, 211.

Zander, M. (1979) 'Investigation of Crime', *Crim LR*, 211.

# Index

1242

divisional courts, and precedent 45
DNA samples, as evidence 178

early settlement, and CPR 204, 205
education, judicial appointments 95, 96
*ejusdem generis*, and statutory interpretation 62
employment, magistrates 112
employment disputes, and ADR 223
equal pay, and EU law 25
equity
  and HRA/ECHR 80–1
  relationship with common law 4–6
ethnic background
  judges 95, 96
  magistrates 112
  and stop and search 153, 154, 173
European Commission, and EU law 27, 33, 34, 35
European Convention on Human Rights (ECHR)
  before HRA 83
  and family life 81
  and freedom of expression 201
  and individual liberty 156, 158, 162
  relationship with HRA 12, 41, 59–60, 76, 84, 85
  and retrospective application of law 49
  right to fair trial 60, 82, 86, 149, 168, 201, 210
  and right to silence 165
  and rights violations 80
European Council, and EU law 27, 32–3
European Court of Human Rights (ECtHR), CA to defer to 40, 45
European Court of Justice (ECJ)
  CA to defer to 40, 45
  and EU law 26–7, 29, 33, 34–5
European Parliament, and EU law 34, 35
European Union (EU)
  institutions 27, 32–6
  law 23–31
    binding nature 29–30
    and delegated legislation 16
    direct applicability/direct effect 24–5, 26
    directives 26–7
    regulations 25–6
    treaties 25
    and UK parliamentary sovereignty 8, 10, 28–31
  member states' courts' references to ECJ 35

evidence
  admissibility 149–50, 168
  and tribunals 215
executive
  and HRA 83–6
  and judicial review 133
*expressio unius exclusio alterus*, and statutory interpretation 62
expression, freedom of, and ECHR 201
external aids, and statutory interpretation 58

fair hearing, and judicial review 138–9
family disputes, and ADR 223
family life, and ECHR 81
fast-track cases, and CPR 204
fingerprinting, as evidence 178–9
force, and stop and search 153–4
Franks Committee, and tribunals 210, 214
fraud, and juries 116, 119

gender
  judicial appointments 95–6
  magistrates 112
golden rule, and statutory interpretation 54–5, 56
Goldsmith, Lord, as Attorney-General 107
government law officers 105–9
government lawyers, judicial appointments 94
green papers 11, 58

*Hansard*
  and statutory interpretation 58–9, 60, 65–9
    restrictions on 67–8
High Court
  appeals from 125–6
  appointments 89
  civil appeals
    from magistrates' court 126
    leapfrog procedure 127–8, 141
  civil cases
    contrasted with County Court 191–4
    and delegated legislation 18
    and judicial review 132
  and civil procedure rules 203, 204–5
  criminal appeals
    from Crown Court 130
    from magistrates' court 129–30
  and human rights 9
  and precedent 43, 44